Lee Van Cleef

Lee Van Cleef

A Biographical, Film and Television Reference

by MIKE MALLOY

McFarland & Company, Inc., Publishers
Jefferson, North Carolina, and London

The present work is a reprint of the library bound edition of Lee Van Cleef: A Biographical, Film and Television Reference, *first published in 1998 by McFarland.*

LIBRARY OF CONGRESS CATALOGUING-IN-PUBLICATION DATA

Malloy, Mike, 1976–
 Lee Van Cleef : a biographical, film and television reference / by Mike Malloy.
   p.   cm.
 Includes bibliographical references and index.

 ISBN 0-7864-2272-6 (softcover : 50# alkaline paper) ∞

 1. Van Cleef, Lee, 1925–   . I. Title.
PN2287.V32M36   2005
791.43'028'092 — dc21   98-13033

British Library cataloguing data are available

©1998 Mike Malloy. All rights reserved

No part of this book may be reproduced or transmitted in any form or by any means, electronic or mechanical, including photocopying or recording, or by any information storage and retrieval system, without permission in writing from the publisher.

On the cover: Lee Van Cleef in *Day of Anger*, 1967.

Manufactured in the United States of America

McFarland & Company, Inc., Publishers
 Box 611, Jefferson, North Carolina 28640
  www.mcfarlandpub.com

For my mother and father, Patrick, Reda,
and Lee Van Cleef

Contents

Introduction 1

1. The Life of Lee Van Cleef 3
2. The Films 33
3. Television Work 145

Appendix: Chronological Listing of Films 185
Bibliography 187
Index 191

Introduction

The moviegoing public got its first look at Lee Van Cleef in *High Noon*, the Academy Award–winning 1952 Western. Gary Cooper was the star, but Van Cleef's angular face, with its hawklike nose, high cheekbones and steely eyes, was the first to appear on screen, and he caught the attention of viewing audiences.

From that first appearance until his last film work in 1989, the actor played a wide variety of roles. Van Cleef worked most frequently in the Western genre, however, and for this work he is best remembered. In fact, his acting career serves as an excellent cross-section of Western films made during the fifties, sixties, and seventies.

Twice Van Cleef was an important player in a resurgence of the Western. His big-screen debut, *High Noon*, was one of the films that boosted the Western's popularity in the 1950s by bringing more complex psychological elements to the genre. Van Cleef had roles in many subsequent Westerns released during this era of renewed popularity. More than a decade later, Van Cleef starred in "Spaghetti Westerns" made in Europe that became internationally successful and revitalized the fading genre in the United States.

His entire acting career, including Westerns and non–Westerns, can be roughly divided into three categories. In the early period, following his appearance as the outlaw in *High Noon*, Van Cleef was generally cast in secondary roles as a heavy, or "bad guy." Next, his appearance in Spaghetti Westerns such as *The Good, The Bad, and the Ugly* (in which Van Cleef played "The Bad") began a new phase in his acting life, often supplying him with leading roles. He became an international Western star, especially popular in Europe. Finally, after the decline in the Western's popularity, Van Cleef acted in a variety of motion pictures outside the genre, none of which won any high acclaim. Many of these films, reviewers agreed, were downright bad.

With this three-part division of his acting career, it is a temptation to summarize his career as going from bad ... to bad ... to bad. But such a summary does not do justice to the professionalism and acting expertise that Lee Van Cleef displayed in his various roles.

And various they were. In addition to appearing in so many Westerns, Van Cleef performed in science fiction, gangster, paramilitary, martial arts, juvenile, detective and race car motion pictures.

His television career began with small parts in the *Range Rider* Western series. He made appearances in other TV Westerns, in dramas and in some situation comedies. He later starred in telefilms and in a short-lived weekly TV series.

To even the most absurd of scripts (and some of his later ones certainly fit that description), Van Cleef's presence added a dimension of legitimacy. Van Cleef looked at motion picture and television acting as a paying job. In exchange for his pay, he offered professionalism and a genuine effort to give a good performance, no matter how poor the script or the conditions. A minor cult following has grown up around Van Cleef's performances.

Many of Van Cleef's films won critical acclaim. Many others received — and deserved — poor reviews. Seldom, however, has the sincerity of his performances been criticized.

Most of the existing coverage of the actor's work concentrates on his Western roles. This is understandable, for the Western introduced him to the public, then later elevated him to star status. Van Cleef himself obviously felt comfortable in Western roles. Nevertheless, the full extent of his long and varied career should be better known.

This book attempts to make it so.

1.
The Life of Lee Van Cleef

Lee Van Cleef was born Clarence LeRoy Van Cleef, Jr., on January 9, 1925. He was the only child of Clarence LeRoy Van Cleef and Marion Levinia Van Fleet Van Cleef.

He was born in Somerville, New Jersey, a community founded by Dutch traders. Many of the residents, including the Van Cleefs, were of Dutch ancestry.

During Lee Van Cleef's childhood, his father — a World War I veteran who had served nearly two years in Europe — worked as an accountant and bank cashier in Somerville. His mother, by some reports, had once been a professional singer.

Somerville was a farming community (the seat of Somerset County and a trading center for a large agricultural area), and Lee was attracted to a life out of doors. He attended camps and retreats with the Boy Scouts and the YMCA. From his father, who when not on the job was apparently outdoor-oriented, he learned to shoot at the age of ten. His father also encouraged Lee's love of the outdoors by taking the family on a canoe trip.

Lee Van Cleef's early jobs were not the type to confine the young man to a stuffy office. One of his first jobs was as a delivery boy for a Somerville meat market and grocery, a position he held for over a year.

Soon after that, Lee became part of the agriculture industry that was so prevalent in the area. In June of 1942, after his junior year at the public Somerville High School, Lee began working a summer job as a farmer for Wilbur Everett in New Center, New Jersey. His duties on the farm included planting and harvesting grains and vegetables, caring for livestock, and operating a gasoline tractor. He quit the farming job in September of 1942, around the time that he began his senior year in high school.

That senior year did not turn out to be a lengthy one for him. The United States was involved in World War II, and on October 16, 1942, seventeen-year-old Clarence LeRoy Van Cleef, Jr., became the first of his senior class to join the war effort, enlisting in the navy.

In the World War II era, many high school seniors were given condensed courses so that they could complete school before going into the service. Conflicting reports cloud the issue of whether Van Cleef actually graduated from high school prior to his entry into military service, but navy documents show that he did receive a high school diploma.

Upon enlisting, Van Cleef was immediately sent to Recruit Training at Newport, Rhode Island. By January 1943 he had graduated from the Navy's Fleet Sound School in Key West, Florida, with a rating of Sound Man 3rd Class.

His navy photo of that time shows a fresh-faced young man with piercing eyes, a sharp nose and high cheekbones — the facial characteristics that would later make him known to audiences all over the world.

He received further training in naval installations in Brooklyn, New York, and St. Albans, New York. He was sent to the Mine Craft Training Center in Creek, Virginia, and was assigned to the USS *Incredible*.

On December 10, 1943, Van Cleef married his high school sweetheart, Patsy Ruth Kahle. Soon afterwards, he was sent to sea. He would serve in both the Atlantic and the Pacific.

By December 1944, he had been promoted to Sound Man 2nd Class and had been assigned to a minesweeper in the Mediterranean. A letter to his parents related an interesting story. By then, he had taken to smoking a pipe (an activity that would also be familiar to his later audiences). The ship's mascot, a spaniel named Rusty, was swept overboard by a wave. Van Cleef was given permission to dive in after the dog. "When I hit the water," Van Cleef wrote, "I heard something snap in my mouth

... my pipe stem. I had smoked my pipe while diving about 30 feet." The dog apparently considered Van Cleef a special friend after that. His narrative concluded, "I guess that swim was worth my favorite pipe."

Van Cleef was discharged from the navy on March 6, 1946. He had seen service in the Caribbean on board a subchaser, a small surface vessel equipped to destroy submarines. Then, he had seen minesweeper service in the Mediterranean, the Black Sea, and the China Sea. He had earned the Asiatic-Pacific Medal, the African-European-Middle East Medal with one star, the American Area Medal, the Good Conduct Medal, and the World War II Victory Medal.

After Van Cleef left the navy, he and his wife Patsy worked in a Maine hunting and fishing camp, helping to get it ready for the season. Van Cleef was assistant manager, and Patsy was secretary.

Before 1946 was over, he briefly returned to farming. For a short time he was a farmer on the estate of socialite Doris Duke.

Although he apparently enjoyed outdoor life, the birth of his first two children, Alan (1947) and Deborah (1948), forced him to look for better paying jobs, and he began work in a factory in the Somerville area. In a 1979 interview with William R. Horner, recorded in *Bad at the Bijou*, Van Cleef said, "I had to go working where more money was: ... I said I'd never work indoors in my life. I swore I *wouldn't*, but I *did*." His work at the plant included time and motion studies.

Like his father, Van Cleef was apparently good with numbers. In 1946, he had begun a private practice as an accountant for several local businesses. This practice lasted until 1950.

Van Cleef's professional life around the time of the war does not suggest an interest in the arts. His personal life was somewhat different; he had an interest in music and had been playing the trombone since before the war. But perhaps few people knew of the enormous creative potential that the factory worker and accountant possessed.

Encouraged by a co-worker at the factory, Lee Van Cleef tried out for an amateur theatrics group, the Clinton Music Hall Players, in nearby Clinton, New Jersey. He was given the part of George in *Our Town*. He did well in that role and was soon cast as boxer Joe Pendleton in an amateur production of *Heaven Can Wait*.

A number of people were impressed with his stage ability. He went to New York, where he was awarded his first professional acting job: a small role as a military policeman in Joshua Logan's popular play

In *Kansas City Confidential* (United Artists, 1952), Joe Rolfe (John Payne, *left*) and Tony Romano (Lee Van Cleef, *center*) board a boat to receive their share of the loot but instead discover they have been set up by former policeman Timothy Foster (Preston Foster).

Mister Roberts. Van Cleef was part of the 1950-1951 road company that presented *Mister Roberts* on a 15-month tour of United States cities. Any nervousness this fledgling actor might have had was possibly eased by his familiarity with the play's setting; the events of *Mister Roberts* took place on a navy vessel during World War II.

Although Van Cleef's part was small, he caught people's attention. One of those people was film producer Stanley Kramer, who was assembling personnel to begin the production of a Western film entitled *High Noon*. With his lean and angular face, Lee Van Cleef was a natural to play one of the film's villains.

But perhaps Van Cleef, in his small stage role, had made more of an impression with his acting talent than with his distinct facial features. The *High Noon* role initially offered to Van Cleef was not a villain, but a much more prominent character, a deputy (a part that eventually went to Lloyd Bridges). The deputy role was offered to Van Cleef only on the condition that he have his nose surgically altered to a less menacing shape. Van Cleef refused to change his face, and he took the villain role.

For his part in *High Noon*, Van Cleef earned $500 a week, but the actor had to learn to ride. His farming experience was with trucks and tractors and had not included horses. Rance Howard (father of actor and director Ron Howard), with whom Lee Van Cleef had appeared in the *Mister Roberts* road company, taught him what he needed to know. Van Cleef told Horner about Rance Howard's assistance: "He had me doin' every kind of mount, dismount, run, walk, or any other darn thing on a horse, so that I could finally do the job properly in *High Noon*."

Filming of *High Noon* began in September of 1951. Van Cleef, with a relatively small part in the film, was able to do other acting work before the year was over. By that time an accomplished horseman with credentials as a Western actor, he got his first television work. In 1951, he made two episodes of *Range Rider*, a television series starring Jock Mahoney.

High Noon was released in 1952 to box-office success, and it went on to win several Academy Awards. Filmgoers were getting their first look at the actor, who turned in a memorable performance (his is the first character seen on screen though without a word of dialogue) as one of the four villains who makes trouble for the film's hero, played by Gary Cooper. Perhaps it was because Van Cleef's big-screen debut was in such a popular film that he became instantly typecast as a heavy, or bad guy.

The year 1952 saw the release of two other films with Lee Van Cleef in the cast. These are *Untamed Frontier*, a Western starring Joseph Cotten, and *Kansas City Confidential*, a gangster film starring John Payne. In *Untamed Frontier*, Van Cleef is another Western miscreant, and in *Kansas City Confidential*, he is again one of four bad guys. (*Confiden-*

tial's title in Great Britain was *The Secret Four*, giving Van Cleef, within the first year of his movie career, a title role.)

By 1953, Lee Van Cleef had been accepted as a dependable actor, and his career as a supporting player was becoming more successful. His number of film roles increased, and he got chances to prove his acting talent more fully. He was given not only his usual heavies, but also some character parts. Variety in the types of his films increased. Van Cleef's 1953 credits include not only Westerns, but also a science-fiction movie (*The Beast from 20,000 Fathoms*), a costume drama (*The Bandits of Corsica*), a cop picture (*Vice Squad*), a sports film (*White Lightning*), and a comedy (*Private Eyes*).

Despite this variety, Van Cleef was still primarily a Western actor. He had been part of *High Noon*—a film that renewed the Western's popularity by ushering in the "thinking" or "adult" Western—and the revitalized genre thanked Van Cleef by giving him plenty of work. His 1953 credits include five Westerns: *Jack Slade*, *The Lawless Breed*, *The Nebraskan*, *Tumbleweed*, and *Arena*.

The up-and-coming film actor maintained contact with his home town of Somerville—where, reportedly, the billing for his first picture read "Lee Van Cleef in *High Noon* with Gary Cooper." In 1953, he offered to write a column for the *Somerville Gazette* about his observations of Hollywood.

(Van Cleef's desire to write remained through the years. In September 1955, he wrote a *Screen Stars* article titled "Should Married Couples Take Separate Vacations?" He opposed the idea, and he used his ostensibly happy marriage with Patsy Ruth as an example. Van Cleef could express himself well in print, as he proved in a late–1960s published defense of Italian Westerns, which had been criticized as too violent.)

The actor kept working steadily. His association with the Western film and his typecasting as a villain were still firmly in place. Five Westerns in which Van Cleef appears were released in 1954: *Rails into Laramie*, *The Desperado*, *Arrow in the Dust*, *The Yellow Tomahawk*, and *Dawn at Socorro*. Van Cleef's other two films of that year are *Princess of the Nile* (a costumer) and a children's film entitled *Gypsy Colt*.

In 1955, seven films were released with Lee Van Cleef in the cast. He put in work on five Westerns that were released that year: *Treasure of Ruby Hills*, *Ten Wanted Men*, *Road to Denver*, *A Man Alone*, and *The Vanishing American*. His other two films of the year are both crime dramas, *The Big Combo* and *I Cover the Underworld*. *The Big Combo* is probably the most noteworthy of his 1955 films. It includes sadistic torture scenes, and censors did some heavy cutting before it was released.

Van Cleef made a career choice that might have been dangerous to his health when he agreed to appear in *The Conqueror*, a 1956 costumer starring John Wayne. *The Conqueror*, which was set in a twelfth-century Asian desert, was made near Yucca Flats, Nevada, where 11 atomic test explosions had occurred a year before the film's production began. Later, 91 members of the film's cast and crew developed cancer, including John Wayne. Fortunately for Van Cleef, the filming apparently had little effect on his health.

The usual Western ties were there in 1956, providing Van Cleef with less hazardous work. Van Cleef played bit parts in two 1956 Westerns, *Tribute to a Bad Man* and *Pardners*. Footage of the actor turns up in another 1956 oater, *Red Sundown*, but only because clips of 1954's *Dawn at Socorro* had been spliced into the later film.

Lee Van Cleef was doing extensive film work and had proven himself a capable supporting actor, but he had not yet made the leap to starring film roles. In 1956 his toil paid off at last when he received his first lead, in cult director and producer Roger Corman's *It Conquered the World*. Van Cleef gave a fine performance — as a scientist who rids the Earth of an invading creature from Venus — and proved that he could handle the lead of a film.

Nevertheless, his starring role for Corman did not lead to anything bigger, and in 1957, filmgoers again saw Van Cleef only in character roles and "heavy" parts.

His career as a supporting player was still going strong, however. In 1957 the actor appeared in more films than in any previous year (or, indeed, in any year thereafter). He also began landing roles in more major releases. One such 1957 film is *Gunfight at the O.K. Corral*, a Western starring Kirk Douglas and Burt Lancaster. Most all of Van Cleef's other 1957 films were also Westerns: *The Quiet Gun, Badge of Marshal Brennan, The Lonely Man, The Last Stagecoach West, Joe Dakota, Gun Battle at Monterey, Raiders of Old California,* and *The Tin Star*. Of the others, *Accused of Murder* is a crime film. *China Gate*, in which he plays a significant role as an Asian military leader, is an early screen treatment of the conflict in Vietnam (then French Indo-China).

Only four 1958 feature films were released with Lee Van Cleef as a participant, but two of these appearances were in some of the year's biggest releases. *The Bravados*, a Western starring Gregory Peck, features Lee Van Cleef — again — as one of four bad guys. *The Young Lions*, a World War II picture with Marlon Brando, Dean Martin, and Montgomery Clift, includes Van Cleef as an army sergeant. In *The Young Lions* Van Cleef portrayed, for the first time on film, an American serviceman in World War II, the war in which he had actually served.

His other two 1958 appearances were in minor films. In *Day of the Badman*, a Western starring Fred MacMurray, Van Cleef is yet again one of four heavies. He also appears in *Machete*, a film set on a sugar plantation.

It was in the fall of 1958 — around two years since the hazardous *Conqueror* production — that Van Cleef's health was again jeopardized by a job-related incident. This time, Van Cleef did not fare well.

Van Cleef was driving to his home after doing location film work at Lone Pine, where a Western with Randolph Scott was being lensed. Van Cleef's wife and three children (by that time he had another son, David) were traveling in a car a short distance ahead. A motorist in the oncoming lane accidentally crossed the center line and struck Van Cleef's car head-on, demolishing the actor's vehicle.

Lee Van Cleef's left arm was fractured in two places, and his left kneecap was shattered. The actor was hospitalized for weeks. For a period of time after Van Cleef returned home from the hospital, a steel rod remained in his arm.

Van Cleef was told that he would probably never be able to ride a horse again and would not walk without a limp. For an actor whose principal parts had been in action Westerns, this was devastating news.

The accident and its aftermath were traumatic for Lee Van Cleef and his family. Although the reports cannot be substantiated, it was said that Van Cleef had a drinking problem, which may have begun or worsened at this time. By the end of the year, the 15-year marriage of the Van Cleefs had ended in divorce.

Two 1958 productions on which Van Cleef had finished working prior to the auto wreck were released in early 1959: the Randolph Scott Western, titled *Ride Lonesome*, and *Guns, Girls, and Gangsters*. These two films could very well have been Van Cleef's last, and perhaps a lesser man would have allowed them to be.

Lee Van Cleef, however, in an amazing struggle he later described

1. *The Life* 11

Van Cleef had an important role in *China Gate* (20th Century–Fox, 1957) as the leader of a Communist army. His first appearance in the film comes here, standing before a giant painting of Mao Tse-Tung.

as "mind over matter," disproved the theories that he would never again walk normally or ride a horse. Van Cleef seemed determined to again make himself valuable as a Western player, and he did whatever was necessary. The actor was back to mounting horses, even though he required a stepladder to do so.

There was a period of more than two years during which no Van Cleef films were released. He was apparently able to find some television work at this time, though.

Van Cleef did not let his stalling career ruin his life. In June of 1959, his spirits were high enough for a return to Somerville as the guest of honor for his hometown's fiftieth anniversary celebration. And in 1960, he married his second wife, Joan Miller. The new Mr. and Mrs. Van Cleef adopted a daughter, Denise.

In 1961, the hiatus in Van Cleef's film career ended when *Posse from Hell* was released. Van Cleef appears, once more, as one of four bad men.

Lee Van Cleef had small character roles in two 1962 Westerns: *The Man Who Shot Liberty Valance* and *How the West Was Won*. In *Liberty Valance*, he appears alongside Lee Marvin, who, with Van Cleef, was one of the best screen villains of the fifties. But whereas Van Cleef's career was experiencing a lean time, Lee Marvin was headed for bigger things. Van Cleef was cast as a secondary character to Marvin's chief villain.

Although Van Cleef's career was struggling, his status as a Western veteran could not be disputed. His inclusion in *How the West Was Won*, a motion picture with an all-star Western cast, seemed proof of his standing in the genre.

With the early 1960s came a decline in the popularity of the Western in America, which perpetuated the decline of Lee Van Cleef's film career. Meanwhile, however, Western films made in Europe by Europeans were achieving remarkable success on that continent. Although Westerns had been made in Europe before, the Eurowestern craze did not begin until shortly after 1963, when Italian filmmaker Sergio Leone imported an American television actor named Clint Eastwood to make a highly successful Western entitled *Per un pugno di dollari*. Other European filmmakers were inspired by Leone's success, and they imitated his style for their Western films.

These European-made Westerns, which would become better known as "Spaghetti Westerns" (for the heavy participation of Italian filmmakers), are markedly different from the traditional American

Westerns. Most are set in the border regions between the United States and Mexico, perhaps largely because those regions could be accurately represented by the locations in Spain where many Spaghetti Westerns were filmed. They present a dingy Old West, with the protagonists and their adversaries often looking equally grimy and bedraggled.

Morality is rarely relevant in these films, and killings seem to come more often than lines of dialogue. Most of the stories featured in Spaghetti Westerns deal with revenge, a power struggle, or a search for hidden loot.

Washed-up and minor American stars would often be cast as the leads. They would perform with actors of various nationalities, with all of them reading their parts in their native tongues. During post-production, voice dubbing would be used to make versions of the films in various languages.

Like the dialogue, the titles were translated for different language markets. For instance, *Per un pugno di dollari* was released in Germany as *Fur eine handvoll Dollar* and to the United States as *A Fistful of Dollars*.

Legal difficulties delayed the United States release of *A Fistful of Dollars* until 1967. Spaghetti Westerns that were made after the groundbreaking *Fistful* were delayed in similar fashion. Thus the Spaghetti Western and the actors involved did not become widely popular in America until years after their success in Europe.

One of the most memorable aspects of these films is their haunting, rousing musical scores. This unique music is usually very prominent in Spaghetti Westerns. Ennio Morricone, the most prolific composer of Spaghetti scores, contributed music that outlasted the popularity of the movies themselves.

In 1965, Sergio Leone began making a sequel to *A Fistful of Dollars*. He secured the return of Eastwood as the film's lead, but he also wanted another, older protagonist to complement Eastwood's character. Unable to get Henry Fonda, Lee Marvin, Jack Palance, or Charles Bronson, Leone then remembered Lee Van Cleef, whom he had seen in 1950s Westerns.

Discrepancies exist in the stories of Van Cleef's first encounter with Leone. However, by using mainly a story related by Spaghetti Western historian Christopher Frayling, as well as other sources, a composite tale can be created. The sequence of events apparently went something like this:

Unusual and exotic guns were featured in a number of Van Cleef's films. Here, as bounty hunter Douglas Mortimer, Van Cleef selects a rifle to down a fleeing fugitive in *For a Few Dollars More* (1965).

Leone, who was pressed for time to cast this part, contacted Van Cleef's agent, who had temporarily lost track of the actor. After some searching, Van Cleef — in bad financial shape — was found doing freelance house painting. (Just a few days prior, he had been unable to pay a twelve-dollar phone bill or to buy his wife a wedding anniversary present. The Van Cleef family was subsisting mainly on Lee's television royalties and Joan's salary as an IBM secretary.) A meeting was arranged — a meeting for which Sergio Leone made his first trip to America.

1. The Life

The meeting took place in Leone's hotel room with the aid of an interpreter. The interpreter was perhaps superfluous, though, as Leone apparently wanted to hire Van Cleef upon first sight. "I saw him from some way away," Leone later remarked (as quoted in Christopher Frayling's *Spaghetti Westerns*), "and was struck by his silhouette, his extraordinary attractiveness: he was perfect for my character."

Van Cleef and his agent were called back the next day—a Saturday—and Van Cleef was awarded the part and presented with an attaché case full of American cash, in 20- and 50-dollar denominations. According to Van Cleef, the pay was 30 percent higher than any of his previous film earnings. On the spot, Lee Van Cleef counted off 10 percent and handed it to his agent.

There remained only one hitch. Van Cleef had already made a commitment to do some house painting in the coming week. In order to keep his shooting schedule, Leone had to find a replacement painter. Once that was settled, he rushed Van Cleef off to Europe.

Van Cleef read the script to the sequel, which came to be called *For a Few Dollars More*, while on the plane. When he met with Clint Eastwood, Van Cleef seemed wary of the project. Eastwood warned that this was not a traditional Western and suggested that Van Cleef watch *A Fistful of Dollars*. Van Cleef did so, and then he understood what he later called Leone's "operatic Italian approach" to the Western.

The actor did not play his usual "heavy" role for the film. Instead, like Eastwood, he was a bounty-hunting protagonist.

Van Cleef had to adjust to a very different production environment, working with cast and crew who spoke little English. The giving and receiving of direction from Leone relied partly on gestures.

Despite the fact that Van Cleef was learning a different approach to the Western, a different type of character, and a different working environment, he fit very naturally in the part and turned in an excellent performance. The film was released in Europe in 1965 and was a hit, outgrossing *A Fistful of Dollars*. Leone retained Van Cleef's acting services for a second sequel, *The Good, the Bad, and the Ugly*.

Having a second American actor had worked so well in *For a Few Dollars More* that Leone added a third American, Eli Wallach, to the cast of *The Good, the Bad, and the Ugly*, a 1966 production. Van Cleef, although he had fared so well as a hero in *For a Few Dollars More*, played a more villainous role in this third installment of the "*Dollars*" trilogy.

After the completion of *The Good, the Bad, and the Ugly*, Van Cleef

Van Cleef questions a prostitute in **The Big Gundown** *(1966).*

stayed in Europe and went straight to work on his next Spaghetti Western, *The Big Gundown*. This was his first unshared lead. For this film, Van Cleef worked under the direction of a different Italian director, Sergio Sollima. But the work of composer Ennio Morricone, who had scored all three of Leone's "*Dollars*" films, was again present for this Van Cleef picture. *The Big Gundown* was Van Cleef's third straight success in Europe, and the hit film spawned a sequel, *Run Man, Run*, which saw the return of director Sollima and some of the cast, but not of Van Cleef.

After Eastwood and Van Cleef had become major stars on the continent, efforts were made to supply eager audiences with more material by these actors. Episodes of *Rawhide*, Eastwood's American television show, were patched together and released in Europe as a feature film. Similarly, audiences were able to see more of Van Cleef in 1966, when three episodes of the American television series *Branded* featuring Van Cleef as a guest villain were edited together and released outside the United States as a feature entitled *Call to Glory*.

Both American actors were tremendously popular in Europe, but Clint Eastwood had started in European film earlier than Van Cleef. Since the release of *A Fistful of Dollars*, Eastwood had been the most popular Spaghetti Western player. By 1967, however, Van Cleef had the popular *Big Gundown* under his belt, and Eastwood had returned to the States. Other American stars were arriving in Europe to make Western films, but it was Lee Van Cleef who succeeded Clint Eastwood as the most popular star of Spaghetti Westerns.

After *The Big Gundown*, though, Van Cleef's next two projects, both produced in 1967, were made with apparently lower production values and decidedly poorer scripts. Neither of these films has endured in the way that the Leone Westerns have. Both, however, are still considered classics of the Spaghetti Western genre.

Day of Anger, an Italian-German Western, provided Van Cleef with his first film work of 1967. For this film, he teamed with actor Giuliano Gemma, the first and one of the most popular non–American stars of European Westerns. The pairing proved successful, especially in Italy, where *Day of Anger* raked in millions of dollars and still ranks as one of the most successful Spaghettis. The film's excellent musical score was composed by Riz Ortolani, making *Day of Anger* the first of Van Cleef's Spaghetti Westerns to be scored by someone other than Ennio Morricone.

Death Rides a Horse, the other 1967 Van Cleef picture, is an Italian oater which also stars American character actor John Phillip Law. Ennio Morricone was once again part of the crew for a Van Cleef film, enhancing *Death Rides a Horse* with another fine musical score. This is Morricone's last work for a picture containing Lee Van Cleef.

Around this time, Van Cleef was offered a cameo appearance in director Sergio Leone's 1968 production, *Once Upon a Time in the West*. Leone wanted to say farewell to the era of his life that produced the "*Dollars*" trilogy. The director planned to have Van Cleef, Clint Eastwood,

In *Sabata* (1969), Van Cleef's dynamite-carrying title character confronts Stengel (Franco Ressel), the criminal he is blackmailing.

and Eli Wallach all make a brief joint appearance during the opening sequence, and to be gunned down by this new film's hero, played by Charles Bronson. Alas, fans were deprived of the chance to see Van Cleef again under Leone's direction, because, while Van Cleef and Wallach both accepted the offer, Eastwood refused. Leone apparently had wanted all three or none — so instead he employed veteran Western stars Jack Elam and Woody Strode, and Spaghetti Western actor Al Mulock.

A reunion with Leone would have put Van Cleef back in familiar territory. Instead, the 1968 Van Cleef roles that were realized provided the actor with a departure.

Van Cleef had been playing reserved, hardened characters since his breakthrough in 1965 with *For a Few Dollars More*. But in *Beyond the Law*, a 1968 Italian Western, Van Cleef took his first crack at playing a humorous lead. (It is worth noting that by the end of the film, Van Cleef's character transforms to the actor's familiar cool, collected persona.) His other 1968 entry was *Commandos*, an Italian-German picture set in World War II, featuring Van Cleef as a very irate American army sergeant. *Commandos* was a further departure for Van Cleef because of its setting, and the film is Van Cleef's only non–Western of the 1960s.

Neither *Commandos* nor *Beyond the Law* seems to have done much for Van Cleef's career, besides keeping him in the minds of European moviegoers. Van Cleef was riding on the momentum created by his earlier successes.

However, Van Cleef did not return, as audiences might have expected, to the dead-serious Western roles that made him famous. He instead tried a different type of Spaghetti Western. This time, a departure turned out to be a very successful move.

He chose to work under director Frank Kramer (a.k.a. Gianfranco Parolini), who had directed a 1968 Eurowestern entitled *Sartana*. The film's eponymous hero became so popular that the character was recreated by different studios and different actors for numerous unofficial sequels, which capitalized on the craze started by the original film. (Other Spaghetti Western characters, including "Django" and "Ringo," inspired similar film fads.)

Van Cleef had been involved with two films that spawned sequels, *For a Few Dollars More* and *The Big Gundown*, but had never played a character that became popular enough to prompt recreations. That changed when Van Cleef starred in Frank Kramer's stylish, over-the-top Italian Western, *Sabata* (1969). Upon its release, *Sabata* became an international success, and Van Cleef's character became the object of another Spaghetti Western craze.

Frank Kramer capitalized on *Sabata*'s success by changing the name of his next production, originally titled *Indio Black* (1971) to *Adios, Sabata*. Star Yul Brynner's title character was, of course, changed from Indio Black to Sabata. Other, more unofficial sequels were made, without the participation of either Van Cleef or director Kramer. These films, which use the Sabata character (or at least the Sabata name), include *Sabata the Killer* (1970), *Dig Your Grave Friend ... Sabata's Coming* (1970), *Wanted Sabata* (1970), and *Watch Out Gringo! Sabata Will Return* (1972). Sabata and Sartana, both characters that originated in Kramer productions, were combined in 1972 for *I Am Sartana, Trade Your Guns for a Coffin*.

After making *Sabata*, Lee Van Cleef returned to the United States, a star in his home country. As of 1967, when *For a Few Dollars More* was at last released in America to great success, Lee Van Cleef had become a popular star in the United States. The American releases of *The Good, the Bad and the Ugly* (1968), *The Big Gundown* (1968), and *Sabata* (1970) were also very successful and further strengthened the American cult following that Van Cleef's film work had generated.

Americans were at last getting to see the Van Cleef performances that had impressed European audiences. At the same time, American film buffs were becoming aware of how extensive Van Cleef's often unnoticed work in Hollywood had been. Film-magazine readers wrote in, trying to compile a definitive Lee Van Cleef filmography.

Not everyone in the United States paid such close attention to what Van Cleef had actually done. American advertisements for *The Big Gundown* read "Now! Mr. Ugly Is the One" and "Mr. Ugly Comes to Town," trying to cash in on Van Cleef's fame as a title character in *The Good, the Bad, and the Ugly*. A New York radio station even held a "Mr. Ugly Contest" in which the winner received a week's vacation at a Colorado Dude Ranch. Actually, this whole line of advertising was fundamentally flawed (making the entire promotion seem rather silly), since it was Eli Wallach who played "the ugly" and not Van Cleef, who was "the bad." Nevertheless, it was clear that Van Cleef had a growing American fan base, and the stage was set for him to begin starring in American motion pictures.

A 1970 American Van Cleef Western, *Barquero*, was lensed in Colorado, and another, *El Condor*, was filmed in Spain. Both films borrowed heavily from the Spaghetti Western style, but neither one was especially well received.

Apparently Van Cleef had waited too late to return to America and try to transfer his popularity. The resurrection of the Western in America, which had been sparked by the importing of Eurowesterns, was through. The genre's popularity was on the wane. Had *Barquero* and *El Condor* been successful, Van Cleef's career might have been something like that of Clint Eastwood, who successfully made the jump from Spaghetti Westerns to American Westerns and then on to blockbuster non-genre films. In the wake of their failure, however, Van Cleef returned to Europe, where the Western continued to be popular.

Even in Europe, however, the Western was showing signs of faltering. Many of the Eurowesterns were having to spoof the genre and include large doses of humor to achieve good audience reception. In 1971, Van Cleef made a tongue-in-cheek Spanish-British Western, *Captain Apache,* and a comedic Spanish Western, *Bad Man's River.* Also about this time, he reunited with director Frank Kramer to make *Return of Sabata,* the only true sequel to their 1969 hit, *Sabata.*

Despite the lower quality of these films and his others, Van Cleef was again able to ride on the momentum of his previous successes. By the early part of the 1970s, Lee Van Cleef was one of the five most popular box-office stars in Italy, and among the ten most popular throughout Europe. An indication of his popularity was the fact that he remained the top-billed star among other established actors. Stars such as Carroll Baker, Stuart Whitman, James Mason, and Gina Lollobrigida took lower billing in Lee Van Cleef films.

In 1972, Van Cleef tried another cinema homecoming, and despite his disappointments in 1970 with *El Condor* and *Barquero,* Van Cleef again chose to make a Western. Van Cleef played the lead for *The Magnificent Seven Ride,* the third sequel to the very popular 1960 Western, *The Magnificent Seven.* He starred as the leader of the seven, the role originally played by Yul Brynner, thus reversing the pattern set when Brynner had replaced Van Cleef in the Sabata role in 1970. However, the installation of Van Cleef as the lead did not pump life back into the fading series; *The Magnificent Seven Ride* was critically panned. During the same year, Lee Van Cleef returned to Europe and to the dead-serious Spaghetti Western for *The Grand Duel.*

Van Cleef had not yet touched a particular Spaghetti Western subgenre, the "East-Meets-Old-West" film, in which gunfighters and Samurais come in contact. (Charles Bronson had garnered some success in this subgenre with 1971's *Red Sun.*) In 1973, Van Cleef worked on such a film, *The Stranger and the Gunfighter,* and location shooting took the actor to Hong Kong (where he is known as Li Yun Ch'i-li-fu). This was Van Cleef's only contribution to the subgenre, but his association with the film's director, Anthony M. Dawson (a.k.a. Antonio Margheriti), continued for more than a decade.

The Spaghetti Western was coming to the end of its course, and Van Cleef started making features outside of his familiar genre. The year 1973 saw the release of *Mean Frank and Crazy Tony*, Van Cleef's first gangster picture since 1959's *Guns, Girls and Gangsters*.

However, with 1975 came *Take a Hard Ride*, another Anthony M. Dawson picture, and Van Cleef was back in the saddle again. Filmed in the Canary Islands, *Take a Hard Ride* provided Van Cleef with his last great gunslinger role. In 1976, Van Cleef made a pair of low-grade Westerns in Israel, *God's Gun* and *Kid Vengeance*. After these two, Van Cleef and the Western film went separate ways.

It seems, however, as if the genre didn't want to give up on one of its biggest stars. There was talk of Van Cleef making a Western entitled *Una desperado* in Italy with Kirk Douglas. And in 1977, a compilation film named *The Wild West*, which played briefly in the United States, Australia, and New Zealand, included a clip of Van Cleef.

During this last period of Van Cleef's Western filmmaking, the actor's personal life underwent a change. While making 1974's *The Stranger and the Gunfighter*, Van Cleef became acquainted with Barbara Hevelone, a concert pianist who was hired to do piano work for the film. By January of 1975 Van Cleef was in the process of divorcing his second wife, Joan, and announced that he would wed Barbara. On July 13, 1976, Lee Van Cleef married Barbara Hevelone.

As for his career, in 1977 an American telefilm, *Nowhere to Hide*, featured Lee Van Cleef as a present-day United States marshal named Ike Scanlon. *Nowhere to Hide* also served as a pilot for a prospective series, *Scanlon*, and although Judith Crist in a *TV Guide* review remarked that Van Cleef "does very well" in the pilot, it seems that not everybody was as impressed. *Scanlon* was never picked up for series broadcast. Van Cleef returned to film and made a 1977 Spanish crime actioner entitled *The Perfect Killer*, which was directed by Marlon Sirko.

Van Cleef stayed in the crime vein but returned to director Anthony M. Dawson for 1978's *The Squeeze*. An Italian picture, *The Squeeze* was filmed in New York City with an excellent supporting cast.

Lee Van Cleef returned to television work, and in 1979 he made *The Hard Way*, another telefilm. Unlike *Nowhere to Hide*, *The Hard Way* aired not in America but in Britain, on the ITV network. Although *The Hard Way* is far better artistically and technically than *Nowhere to Hide*, Van Cleef was again unable to use his telefilm character to initiate regular TV series work, this time because his character dies during the story.

In 1980, after nearly a decade-long absence, Lee Van Cleef returned to mainstream American cinema with his third-billed performance in *The Octagon*, a Chuck Norris martial arts feature. Although he appears in only a handful of scenes, Van Cleef gives what is perhaps the best performance of the film.

Van Cleef remained in the mainstream in 1981, supplying director John Carpenter with a supporting performance for the science-fiction picture *Escape from New York*. Van Cleef delivered another fine piece of work, and this time he was second-billed, behind action star Kurt Russell.

Things were on the upswing for Lee Van Cleef, and his first two roles of the decade clearly prove that the aging actor could have finished out his film career providing first-rate support in major releases. But it was not to be.

The early 1980s brought another hiatus in Van Cleef's career when his heart disease made it necessary for him to have a pacemaker installed. When he returned to work, Van Cleef did not continue in the direction laid out by his previous 1980s entries. Instead he made films that have been described as "grade-Z" and "lowercase." What did carry over from *The Octagon* and *Escape from New York* was his status as a supporting player; never again would Lee Van Cleef play the unshared lead of a film.

In 1983, a Mexican-Spanish picture named *The Killing Machine* was lensed in Europe with Van Cleef as the villain and Jorge Rivero as the hero. Apparently the film found a release in Spain in 1984, but it wasn't until 1986, when the American version bypassed theaters and went straight to home video, that Van Cleef could be seen spouting *Killing Machine* dialogue in his own tongue.

This type of film career — with a picture reaching his home country years later and only on home video — might have looked grim for the actor. But he got another break, and it was another chance for television stardom.

In January of 1984, a martial-arts television series began airing on NBC with the nearly 60-year-old Lee Van Cleef as the lead. *The Master*, as it was called, finally gave Van Cleef a weekly chance to enthrall prime-time viewers. Although Van Cleef had hinted earlier that television would be something of a last resort, he gave an interview for a 1984 *TV Guide* in which he implied that his *Master* character would be a welcome change from his film roles (which he inaccurately but amusingly categorized as being all heavies: "I don't necessarily like getting killed at the end of every production").

The Master's cancellation came in August of the same year, after only 13 episodes were completed. Despite its short run, the series brought Van Cleef attention — an appearance on Johnny Carson's *Tonight Show* and numerous magazine articles — that he would not have received from his fading film career.

Apparently, though, this attention wasn't enough to snare Van Cleef any roles in better films, because he returned to making unspectacular action pictures. The brevity of *The Master* allowed Van Cleef to put in work on a film that was released before the year was out. This 1984 release, a German-Italian paramilitary film entitled *Codename: Wildgeese*, is yet another film that Van Cleef made under the direction of Anthony M. Dawson. Van Cleef appears as part of an ensemble cast. Other notables making appearances are Ernest Borgnine and Klaus Kinski.

Van Cleef stuck with Dawson, and in 1985, the director's *Jungle Raiders*, an Italian rip-off of Steven Spielberg's "*Indiana Jones*" films, was released. Van Cleef had a supporting role, but this time he was not supporting any big-name stars. Others from the *Wildgeese* cast returned for *Jungle Raiders*, but Alan Collins is the only actor besides Van Cleef who is actually credited in both. Like *The Killing Machine*, *Jungle Raiders* reached American audiences only on home video.

Lee Van Cleef took a small step up by playing a starring role for Fred Olen Ray's United States film *Armed Response*, which was lensed and released in 1986. Van Cleef shared the lead with established star David Carradine, and the film was released to American theaters.

Then Van Cleef's career settled for the final time, as the actor accepted only occasional film parts and began doing product endorsements. He spoofed his villain image for a series of Cheetos snack food television commercials and also made television advertisements for Midas Mufflers and Bavarian Beer, the latter airing only in Holland. He also posed for a Japanese advertisement for Suntory whiskey.

In 1988, Van Cleef collaborated with Anthony M. Dawson for the final time, playing a small role in *The Commander*. The film is something of a follow-up to *Codename: Wildgeese*.

The actor's last two film roles were also small parts. Sources conflict as to whether Lee Van Cleef's last film appearance was in *Speed Zone* or *Thieves of Fortune*. Apparently, *Thieves of Fortune* was released in 1990, after the documented 1989 release of *Speed Zone*. Van Cleef's parts were both lensed in 1989, but they might not have been filmed in the order in which these movies were released (in fact, the actor looks older in *Speed Zone*). However, it is likely that *Thieves of Fortune* contains the last film footage of Lee Van Cleef to be released.

If *Thieves of Fortune* does indeed contain Van Cleef's last film appearance, then the actor's film finale is similar to that of another Western actor, John Wayne. In Wayne's last film, *The Shootist*, his character is dying of cancer, prophesying the subsequent death of the actor from that cause. In *Thieves of Fortune*, Van Cleef's character dies of a heart attack.

On December 16, 1989, just a few weeks shy of his 65th birthday, Lee Van Cleef died of a heart attack. His history of heart disease, had caught up with him, and he collapsed in his home in Oxnard, California. He was taken to St. John's Regional Medical Center and died in the hospital. His death certificate cited throat cancer as a secondary cause of death.

Lee Van Cleef was survived by his wife, Barbara, and his children. He was buried on December 21, 1989, at the Forest Lawn Cemetery in Hollywood Hills, California. His friend Rance Howard gave the eulogy, and colleagues such as Rory Calhoun, Anthony M. Dawson, and Harry Carey, Jr., served as casket bearers.

Nineteen years earlier, Lee Van Cleef had stated in an interview that he would never retire, and the actor did not renege on the assertion. He found an enjoyable career for which he had talent, and he was able to continue in that line of work until his last days. The length of Van Cleef's career allowed him to make a permanent mark as an actor. He had appeared in more than 80 films and had also performed as a television actor.

This is not to say, however, that Lee Van Cleef's life was not rich with other interests. One of his sidelights was music. He played a number of instruments, including trombone, guitar, and piano. In 1973, he had formed L.V.C. Music, a music production company. He also dabbled in real estate, and in the early 1980s, he considered producing a film.

However, few knew of these other interests, and it is as an actor that he is remembered.

Two exceptional qualities make Van Cleef's career stand out. First, he overcame long-standing typecasting with a single role. Prior to *For a Few Dollars More*, he was generally considered a supporting actor best cast in "heavy" or bad-guy roles. With his performance as a lead in Leone's second Spaghetti Western, he became an international star, a hero within the frame of reference of the Eurowestern genre. So complete was his image overhaul that it withstood his next role, a villain, in *The Good, the Bad, and the Ugly*, which was, in some parts of the world, more successful than *For a Few Dollars More*.

Second and perhaps more remarkable is the fact that he became a star after he had passed the age of 40. And not just any kind of star, but an action star performing in rugged action movies. Physically demanding roles that were usually offered to younger men were now available to him.

This was to become a problem. Van Cleef became known for starring in action films, and so he continued to work in that vein and had starred in little else by the time of his death. But because his breakthrough came at a late age, Van Cleef was starring in action films in his forties, fifties, and sixties. And with aging came the decline of his physical abilities, which were often needed for this line of film work. Thus it was fortunate for Van Cleef that he had such a tough-looking face; in his later years, his face was largely responsible for his continued qualification as an action star.

The unique Van Cleef face had always attracted attention and had certainly contributed to his film career success, making a strong impression on filmmakers and fans alike. Of all his remarkable features, perhaps the most striking was his eyes. They have been appropriately described as "steely," "shrewd," and "snake eyes." As part of Van Cleef's menacing expression, they allowed his characters to stare down numerous film adversaries. The fact that his eyes were so striking likely explains why Van Cleef was often known by his character name from *The Good, the Bad and the Ugly*: Angel Eyes. The Angel Eyes name was frequently used in publicity releases about Van Cleef. And in film advertisements, Van Cleef was sometimes referred to as "The Man with Gunsight Eyes."

In his younger days, however, not everything depended on his face. Van Cleef's brawny physique made him believable as a tough guy. This is especially apparent in 1957's *Joe Dakota*, which features the actor in a sleeveless shirt as an oil driller who enjoys roughhousing. Despite his health problems, the actor continued to be muscular until he was well past 50 years of age. He obviously felt it necessary to be physically fit for his newly acquired starring roles, and he was given chances to show off his physique. He appears shirtless during much of *Barquero* (1970) and *The Stranger and the Gunfighter* (1973). During part of *Captain Apache* (1971), Van Cleef's character wears nothing but a skimpy breechcloth. (However, Van Cleef never went entirely nude for a picture. He once stated that he didn't consider the nude male form to be aesthetically pleasing.)

Two minor physical details contributed to his tough look. Van Cleef was missing the end of his right-hand middle finger from the last joint. This tiny detail made him look like a man who had seen action, who had likely led a hard and dangerous life. The lack of a middle fingertip can be observed in a number of his films and is featured prominently in *The Good, the Bad and the Ugly* and *The Grand Duel*. Also, Van Cleef had an anchor tattoo, a traditional marking of navy servicemen, on his right forearm. In many of his films, the tattoo is hidden, but in several, including *The Perfect Killer* and *The Squeeze*, the adornment is in evidence.

Also inspired by the Navy was the less permanent ornamentation of a hoop earring, which Van Cleef saw worn by many of his World War II shipmates (with whom a pirate look was fashionable). In 1976, Van Cleef donned an earring for the film *Kid Vengeance*, and after that, according to the actor, all the directors seemed to desire the lobal jewelry for his characters. A hoop earring can be seen dangling from Van Cleef's ear in many of his late–1970s and 1980s films, including *The Squeeze* (1978), *The Octagon* (1980), *Escape from New York* (1981), and *The Commander* (1988).

Also, smoking has been a factor in a number of Lee Van Cleef's roles. Van Cleef was smoking as early as a teenager in the Navy, and felt comfortable using a pipe. This naturalness carried over to his film work. In a digest publication devoted to pipe smoking, an article pointed out that many actors smoked on screen, but that not all did it convincingly. Van Cleef was cited as one of the actors who smoked a pipe convincingly on screen. And in many instances, his smoking added an extra dimension to the role. In his role as Colonel Douglas Mortimer in *For a Few Dollars More*, Van Cleef's use of a pipe gave credibility to his portrayal of a man a decade older than the actor actually was.

At any rate, the unique attention-getting physical appearance gave Lee Van Cleef something all actors long for: presence. Without having to take any action, Van Cleef made mere appearances noteworthy.

However, Lee Van Cleef was very capable of carrying films with his acting. He was an effective, often brilliant actor. To William Horner (*Bad at the Bijou*) Van Cleef offered an insightful description of his job, saying that when acting, he saw from three vantage points: his own, his character's, and that of an audience member viewing his performance. Van Cleef never received much critical praise, though, and his performances were often overshadowed by the controversy surrounding some of his films.

That controversy usually sprang from the amount of violence in the films. This subject often arose during the actor's interviews, and he offered his opinions on the matter. Though he was occasionally inconsistent, he usually maintained that screen violence, if presented realistically, could act as a deterrent to actual violence. In a 1970 interview that was quoted in his *New York Times* obituary, Van Cleef said, "I believe in showing real violence, not toy violence: ... If you show violence realistic enough, people don't want to do it." In his interview with William Horner, Van Cleef complained about unrealistic violence, saying, "They make it look like fun and games, and you don't see the gore and blood."

These opinions might have been a factor when Van Cleef decided to make *Mean Frank and Crazy Tony*, a brutal gangster film that definitely does not hold back from showing any gore or blood. Certainly the final slaying of the film — the death of the principal antagonist — is totally devoid of fun and games; this villain freezes to death with a gut-wrenchingly sad expression on his face.

But there is, in the Spaghetti Western genre, the other extreme; that is, films that depict too much blood and gore to be realistic. Some of the Spaghetti Westerns, which almost qualify as "slasher-type" horror films, depict extreme brutality — sometimes to animals and children — and were banned in certain countries. Lee Van Cleef once implied in an interview that he had been offered such scripts and had rejected them because of their gratuitous violence.

However, many of Van Cleef's choices for film projects do not appear to support his opinions about screen violence. It is impossible to know exactly what the actor considered to be "toy violence," but that description seems well suited for several Van Cleef pictures, especially his two *Sabata* films.

(Controversy about violent content in Van Cleef's films continued even after the actor's death. A television tabloid-news blurb about the tragic Oklahoma City bombing of 1995 revealed that one of the alleged culprits had rented *Armed Response*—which features characters using explosive devices—shortly before the heinous crime occurred.)

In any case, it is true that a heavy dose of violence seemed to be an integral part of the Westerns of the 1960s and 1970s. But even extreme violence couldn't save the genre's popularity in the late 1970s, when Westerns all but disappeared.

In 1992, however—several years after Van Cleef's death—the Western genre became popular again when Clint Eastwood's Oscar-winning Western, *Unforgiven*, was released to box-office success and critical acclaim. Shortly afterward, other major-release Westerns appeared, including *Tombstone* (1993), *Bad Girls* (1994), *Posse* (1993), and *The Quick and the Dead* (1995). This crop of films owes more to the Spaghetti Westerns than to the classic Hollywood oaters, and naturally, Van Cleef's influence was present in this revival. The filmmaker of *Posse* even described (in the April 1993 issue of *Premiere* magazine) one of the film's important performances as being a "twisted Lee Van Cleef thing."

Van Cleef, though, will be remembered not only for his Spaghetti Western starring roles. His career as a Hollywood character actor and villain is equally important to cinema history. In fact, *The Complete Film Dictionary* uses Lee Van Cleef's name in its definition of the term "heavy."

Despite popular perception, though, not all of Van Cleef's early, supporting roles were heavies. And it was during this early film period that Van Cleef was given his first chances to bring humorous elements to his character roles (as in *Tribute to a Badman*) and even to some of his villains (as in *Kansas City Confidential* and *Pardners*). Opportunities to act in comic roles were obviously very important to Van Cleef, and as a star, he attempted humor more frequently—perhaps because he finally was in a position to hold out for comedic scripts. But the actor never seemed to get enough. In numerous interviews, Van Cleef expressed his desire to try more comedy, and in the late seventies, he announced that he would like to do situation comedy. Because Van Cleef was obviously proud of his work with comedy, any history of his life should not make the easy mistake of overlooking these humorous characters.

But of all Van Cleef's film characters, a handful of the actor's starring roles stand above the rest, exemplifying his most exciting screen persona.

During his Spaghetti Western period of the 1960s and 1970s, Van Cleef was playing most of his characters with a cool stoicism; these characters are hardened, collected, and self-contained. In a few films (e.g., *The Good, the Bad and the Ugly*), these stoic characters are presented as villains, but mostly this type of Van Cleef character appears as a protagonist.

And of these stoic protagonists, there is a heroic and an anti-heroic variety. The more anti-heroic sorts (e.g., Van Cleef's *For a Few Dollars More* character, Colonel Douglas Mortimer) are selfishly motivated and sometimes immoral, with few qualms about breaking laws or killing. They qualify as protagonists largely because their adversaries are much more dastardly. The more heroic characters, or "stoic heroes," are very selflessly motivated, unconcerned with personal danger, and interested in seeing justice served. The stoic hero is Lee Van Cleef's most exciting screen persona.

Another trait that qualifies a stoic hero as such is a certain weariness of life and of the situation with which he deals. In fact, this is one of the qualities that makes a stoic hero so exciting. In Spaghetti Westerns, a weary stoic hero seems coolly superior to the other, more petty characters, who are constantly scrambling after money and power.

Despite a stoic hero's sense of justice, this weariness would perhaps breed total apathy about the matters at hand, if the stoic hero did not feel personally obligated to guide the situation to its proper conclusion. Such an obligation usually stems from a nagging or haunting event from the stoic hero's past (when, presumably, he was of different — either less stoic or less heroic — character).

For example, Van Cleef's *Grand Duel* character, Clayton, is presented in the film as a cool, hard, world-weary former sheriff. Clayton protects Philip, a man who is wrongly accused of murdering a town leader. It is later revealed that the town leader was actually executed — lawfully but secretly — by then-sheriff Clayton. And it is revealed that an earlier effort to protect Philip (who was blamed for political reasons) cost Clayton his star. It can be surmised, then, that Clayton, as sheriff, was not a stoic hero; the hardened Clayton seen in the film is too weary and apathetic to accept a lawman's duties. Clayton's transition to the stoic hero persona probably came when he lost his star, and it is only because his actions as sheriff incriminated an innocent man that he remains involved.

In some films, Van Cleef's character only becomes a stoic hero sometime during the course of the film. This allows for the early Van Cleef character to be seen initiating the events that the stoic hero is forced to resolve. Thrice does a Van Cleef character become a stoic hero after a film's point of attack. Van Cleef's lawman character in *The Big Gundown* is first seen with zeal and fervor for law and order (he is thus less stoic), while his *Death Rides a Horse* character is introduced as a greedy revenge seeker (he is thus less heroic), and in *Beyond the Law* his character starts off as a goofy bandit (he is thus less stoic and heroic). All three transform into stoic heroes and are forced to resolve the conflicts that their earlier selves precipitated.

Today, the stoic hero is conspicuously absent from popular films. Current action heroes tend to be self-important and overbearing.

In his stoic heroes, Lee Van Cleef created a screen persona of a man who displays a cool, reserved power, is weary and hardened, and has seemingly seen it all. It is doubtful that cinema will ever have a more exciting hero.

2.
The Films

The films of Lee Van Cleef provided entertainment to theater audiences all over the world for nearly four decades. Many of his films are still presented on television and are available on home video.

There is a vast amount of incorrect and questionable information about Van Cleef's film work. This is certainly not beyond understanding; Van Cleef made films in many parts of the world and often on low budgets. Some of his films were never released theatrically in his home country. Thus, many of them have fallen into obscurity.

By concentrating on the films in which Van Cleef appears, this book hopes to present a more accurate picture of his body of work.

The films are listed in alphabetical order, each film listed under its most commonly used English-language title. All alternate titles, working titles or unused translations of titles are noted in the film's entry.

Information about each film is listed at the beginning of its entry. This includes the year of the film's initial theatrical release (as accurately as can be determined by this writer), whether it was filmed in color, and the film's running time (generally of the version reviewed by your writer). If the film is not a strictly U.S. venture, the country or countries of origin (including all countries that financed the film) are listed. Entries for entirely American films include the name of the producing company. If the film is a Western, the genre in which Van Cleef worked most frequently, it is noted as such.

Not included here are entries for two films in which Van Cleef nevertheless does actually appear:

Red Sundown: a 1956 film which merely reuses footage of Van Cleef taken from 1954's *Dawn at Socorro.*

The Wild West: a 1977 compilation film in which a Van Cleef clip is included.

The following films are not reviewed here and are not recognized by this book as Van Cleef films, although some sources purport that he appears in them. Your writer has reviewed these films (none of which give Van Cleef screen credit) and was unable to spot the actor in any of them:

Backlash (1956, with Richard Widmark)
Crime Boss a.k.a. *New Mafia Boss* (1972, with Telly Savalas)
A Fistful of Dollars (1963, with Clint Eastwood)
The Kentuckian (1955, with Burt Lancaster)
Man Without a Star (1955, with Kirk Douglas)
Shane (1953, with Alan Ladd)
The Showdown (1950, with "Wild Bill" Elliot)

Evidence is either too vague or too contradictory to conclude that Van Cleef appears in the following films:

Bite the Dust (1969)
Chameleon
Creed of Violence a.k.a. *Credo of Violence* (1968/1969)
The Four Horsemen (1986, with Johnny Crawford, Robert Forster and Jeremy Clyde). This film was apparently shot in France as a made-for-cable movie.
From Dunkirk to London (1969)
Gaucho (1969)
The Man from Far Away a.k.a. *L'Uomo che viene de lontano* (1968)
Mercenary for Any War (1968)
The Naked Street (1955, directed by Maxwell Shane)
Operation 'Nam (1990)
A Professional Gun (1968)
Scalawag (1969)
Sundown (1967)
Trieste File (1980)

Accused of Murder

1957, color, 74 minutes, Republic

Cast: David Brian (Lt. Roy Hargis), Vera Ralston (Ilona Vance), Sidney Blackmer (Hobart), Virginia Grey (Sandra), Warren Stevens (Stan), Lee Van Cleef (Sergeant Lackey), Barry Kelley (Capt. Smedley), Richard Karlan (Chad Bayliss), Frank Puglia (Caesar Cipriano), Elisha Cook, Jr. (Whitey Pollock), Ian MacDonald (Trumble), Claire Carleton (Marge), Greta Thyssen (Myra Bayliss), Hank Worden (Les Fuller), Wally Cassell (Doorman), Robert Shayne (Surgeon), Simon Scott (Day Office Cop), John Damler (Night Office Cop), Gil Rankin (Fingerprint Policeman), Joseph Corey (Sailor), Leon Tyler (Sailor), Harry Lewis (Bartender), David Bair (Parking Attendant), Bill Henry (Walt), Bob Carney (Waiter), Victor Sen Young (Houseboy)

Producer/Director: Joseph Kane

Synopsis: Police Lt. Roy Hargis (David Brian) investigates the murder of a crooked lawyer named Hobart (Sidney Blackmer). One suspect, Stan (Warren Stevens), a gangster who was assigned to kill Hobart, is proven innocent. Roy is infatuated with the case's other suspect, nightclub singer Ilona Vance (Vera Ralston). He believes that Ilona is innocent, and his hunch is confirmed when Ilona confesses that Hobart shot himself after she refused his advances.

Comment: Accused of Murder is based on the novel *Vanity Row* by crime writer W. R. Burnett. Sources conflict as to whether this film was released in 1956 or January of 1957.

Van Cleef's Role: Van Cleef plays Sgt. Lackey, Roy's partner. Unlike his partner, Lackey believes that Ilona is guilty.

Arena

1953, color, 83 minutes,
Metro-Goldwyn-Mayer (Rodeo/Western)

Cast: Gig Young (Bob Danvers), Jean Hagen (Meg Hutchins), Polly Bergen (Ruth Danvers), Henry Morgan (Lew Hutchins), Barbara Lawrence (Sylvia Morgan), Robert Horton (Jackie Roach), Lee Aaker (Teddy

Hutchins), Lee Van Cleef (Smitty), Marilee Phelps (Buster Cole), Stuart Randall (Eddie Elstead), Morris Ankrum (Bucky Hillberry)

Director: Richard Fleisher

Synopsis: Conceited rodeo star Bob Danvers (Gig Young) separates from his wife Ruth (Polly Bergen) and takes a tramp named Sylvia Morgan (Barbara Lawrence) as his mistress. But Bob patches things up with Ruth at an important rodeo in Tucson, Arizona, after his washed-up partner (Henry Morgan) sacrifices his life to save Bob from a charging Brahma bull.

Comment: Arena was the first feature issued by Metro-Goldwyn-Mayer to make use of the 3-D process. The film's rodeo footage was lensed at the annual Fiesta de los Vaqueros in Tucson, Arizona.

Van Cleef's Role: Praise has been repeatedly given to Van Cleef for giving the standout performance in *Arena*. His character, Smitty, provided the actor with an early non-villain role.

Armed Response

1986, color, 86 minutes, CineTel

Alternate Title: *The Jade Jungle*

Cast: David Carradine (Jim Roth), Lee Van Cleef (Burt Roth), David Goss (Clay Roth), Brent Huff (Tommy Roth), Mako (Akira Tanaka), Ross Hagen (Cory Thorton), Lois Hamilton (Sara Roth), Laurene Landon (Deborah Silverstein), Dick Miller (Steve), Michael Berryman (F.C.), Sam Hione (Jackie Hong), Dah've Seigler (Lauren Roth), Conan Lee (Kon Ozu), Burr DeBenning (Lt. Sanderson), Susan Stokey (Judy), Bob Hevilon (Nate), Kai Baker (Pam), Bobbie Bresee (Anna), Michelle Bauer (Dancer), Dawn Wildsmith (Thug #1), Dave O'Hara (Thug #2), Jimmy Williams (First Soldier), Fred Olen Ray (Second Soldier), Pat Culliton (Patrolman), Richard Lee Sung (Kenji), Cary Tagawa (Toshi), Brad Arrington (Dealer), Jerry Fox (Club Owner), Lisa Hayward (Mother), Lauren Hertzberg (Young Girl), Jordan Hertzberg (Young Boy), Hisako Mura (Vietnamese Girl), Mayann Zvoleff (Prostitute)

Co-Producer/Director: Fred Olen Ray

Synopsis: When Japanese gangster Akira Tanaka (Mako) is given a chance to buy back a sacred jade statuette that was stolen from him, he hires private investigator Clay Roth (David Goss) to exchange ransom money for the item. During the transaction, Clay is double-crossed and shot. Before he dies, he manages to get his hands on the statuette and deliver it to his family, which includes his father Burt (Lee Van Cleef) and his two brothers, Jim (David Carradine) and Tommy (Brent Huff). Tanaka, who desperately needs the statuette to appease a Chinese mob family, believes that Clay deliberately stole it and is ruthless in his efforts to retrieve his possession. The Roth clan holds onto the item, hoping that Clay's murderers will come looking for it, and they fend off Tanaka's attempts to retrieve it. But when Tanaka's thugs kill Tommy and capture Jim's family, Burt and Jim Roth go on the rampage, eradicating Tanaka's gang. The Japanese gangster is killed when he finally gets possession of the statuette, which Jim rigged with explosives.

Comment: Armed Response was done with an adequate amount of knowledge of the Chinese and Japanese underworlds, and although it can be categorized as low-budget, it does include some film stars and several fancy action sequences. (*Armed Response* was director Fred Olen Ray's sixth film and has a bigger budget than his five previous pictures.) But it is the poor acting that really mars this actioner. Carradine is far from being in top form (but does perform his own martial-arts-slanted fight scenes, which are mildly exciting), and most of the actors in character roles and bit parts are terrible. However, Van Cleef, Mako and Ross Hagen (whose character precipitates the trouble by double-crossing Clay) all give fine performances, and there is a cameo appearance by Dick Miller, a wonderful actor who has spent far too much time in low-budget films. *Armed Response* was filmed under the working title *The Jade Jungle,* and its Vietnam scenes (which plague the Carradine character in flashback) were filmed in an animal park in Riverside, California.

Van Cleef's Role: Despite his obviously decreased agility and his expanded midsection, Van Cleef as Burt Roth manages to look tough throughout *Armed Response,* his last outing as a full-fledged film action hero. However, Burt Roth doesn't engage in much action besides one fistfight and the climactic shootout. While the shootout at the end does not require much of the actor, the barroom fistfight, which was performed by the elderly Van Cleef himself, proved that many of Van Cleef's '70s and '80s film fights could probably have been done more convincingly if the actor himself had performed the brawls, instead of letting a stunt double fill in. Van Cleef gives appropriate characterization to the cantankerous Roth, an ex-cop widower whose gruff exterior fades when he sees his granddaughter.

Arrow in the Dust
1954, color, 79 minutes, Allied Artists (Western)

Cast: Sterling Hayden (Bart Laish), Coleen Gray (Christella), Keith Larsen (Lt. King), Tom Tully (Crowshaw), Jimmy Wakely (Carqueville), Tudor Owen (Tillotson), Lee Van Cleef (Crew Boss), John Pickard (Lybarger), Carleton Young (Pepperis)
Director: Lesley Selander
Synopsis: After he deserts his unit, calvary soldier Bart Laish (Sterling Hayden) comes upon a dying officer, and after that officer's death, Bart begins to impersonate him. Bart's new identity enables him to help a wagon train that is being attacked by Indians. He discovers that the Indians want the goods belonging to Tillotson (Tudor Owen), a wagon-train passenger who is smuggling a load of repeating rifles. After Bart destroys the rifles, the Indians retreat and the cavalry arrives to escort the wagon train to Laramie, where Bart is given the shortest prison sentence for his desertion. Christella (Coleen Gray), whom Bart met on the wagon train, promises to wait for him.
Comment: Arrow in the Dust contains footage from an earlier oater, 1951's *New Mexico*.
Van Cleef's Role: Van Cleef's character is listed simply as "Crew Boss." In 1957, Van Cleef appeared in another Sterling Hayden–starring oater, *Gun Battle at Monterey*.

Bad Man's River
1971, color, 89 minutes, Spanish-Italian-French (Western)

Alternate Titles: And They Go on Losing the Million Dollars (British), *E continuavano a fregarsi il milione di dollari* (Italian), *El hombre del río malo* (Spanish), *El ils continuaient à se volar l'un et l'autre le million de dollars* (French), *Les Quatre Mercenaires d'El Paso* (French), ... *Y seguían robndose al millón de dólares* (Spanish)

Cast: Lee Van Cleef (Roy King), James Mason (Francisco Montero), Gina Lollobrigida (Alicia), Simon Andreu (Angel), Diana Lorys (Dolores), John Garko (Pace), Aldo Sanbrell (Canales), Jess Hahn (Odie), Daniel Martin (False Montero), Luis Rivera (Orozco), Lone Ferk (Conchita), Eduardo Fajardo (Duarte), Sergio Fantoni (Fierro), Per Barclay (Reverend), Francisco Nieto, Jose Riesgo, Tito Garcia, Barta Barri, Vic Albert, Gene Collins, Tom Power, Carl Rapp, Alan Russell, Clovis Dave, Dan Van Husen, Bruno Sismondi, David Thomson, Rupert Crabb

Director: Gene [Eugenio] Martin

Synopsis: Making his getaway on a train, a bank robber named Roy King (Lee Van Cleef) is smitten with Alicia (Gina Lollobrigida), a fellow passenger. While still on the train, the two are married in an impromptu ceremony, after which Alicia takes off with all of King's bank loot. Needing more money, King goes to work for Mexican Army agent Francisco Montero (James Mason), who is scheming to swindle a million dollars from his own army. King discovers that Montero is also the new husband of Alicia. As the money-making scheme unfolds, King blows up a Mexican army arsenal, and the army gives Montero a million dollars to buy replacement weapons. Montero and Alicia try to cut King out of the deal and make off with the million, but King fights his way back in with a proposal that he and Montero share both the money and the wife. Neither man ends up with much, though, as Alicia escapes with all the money.

Comment: An uneven mix of action and comedy, *Bad Man's River* features several funny moments on the train ride at the film's opening. After that, the humor disappears from the script, and the actors' facial expressions try to carry the load. *Bad Man's River* is set against 1911 revolutionary Mexico, and this time period allows for the use of automobiles, which even figure in to a gag when Roy King and his gang build a goofy-looking armored car.

Van Cleef's Role: Van Cleef proves in *Bad Man's River* that he can look tough even in a derby hat. He is fairly convincing in this role, even though the uneven script ranges from comedy to violence. Van Cleef's talent for comedy is sometimes impressive.

The Badge of Marshal Brennan
1957, black and white, 76 minutes,
Allied Artists (Western)

Cast: Jim Davis (Stranger), Arleen Whelan (Murdock), Lee Van Cleef (Shad Donaphin), Louis Jean Heydt (Col. Donaphin), Carl Smith (Sheriff), Marty Robbins (Felipe), Harry Lauter (Dr. Steve Hale), Douglas Fowley (Marshal), Lawrence Dobkin (Chickamon)

Producer/Director: Albert C. Gannaway

Synopsis: A criminal (Jim Davis) on the run meets a dying marshal (Douglas Fowley), whose badge and job the fugitive takes. The badman-turned-lawman uses his position to battle two cattle-rustling town bosses.

Comment: A low-budget film, *The Badge of Marshal Brennan* features a cast that is almost identical to that of another 1957 oater from director/producer Gannaway, *Raiders of Old California*.

Van Cleef's Role: Van Cleef is Shad Donaphin who, with Colonel Donaphin (Louis Jean Heydt), runs the illicit cattle business until Davis' hero rids the town of their lawlessness. Van Cleef also appears in Gannaway's *Raiders of Old California*.

Bandits of Corsica
1953, black and white,
81 minutes, United Artists

Alternate Title: *Return of the Corsican Brothers* (British)

Cast: Richard Greene (Mario/Carlos), Paula Raymond (Christina), Raymond Burr (Jonatto), Dona Drake (Zelda), Raymond Greenleaf (Paoli), Lee Van Cleef (Nerva), Frank Puglia (Riggio), Nestor Paiva (Lorenzo), Peter Mamakos (Diegas), Paul Cavanagh (Dianza), Peter Brocco (Angelo), George Lewis (Arturo), Clayton Moore (Ricardo), Virginia Brissac (Maria), Francis J. McDonald (Grisha), Michael Ansara (Blacksmith), William Forrest (Marquis), John Pickard (Coachman).

Director: Ray Nazarro

Synopsis: A prominent Frenchman named Mario (Richard Greene) and a gypsy named Carlos (also Richard Greene) are Siamese twins who were separated at birth — by an operation and then by being moved to different cities — and who meet again decades later. The twin brothers, each of whom experience the emotions and sensations of the other, work together and overthrow Jonatto (Raymond Burr), the villainous ruler of the twins' homeland, Corsica. Carlos, who is in love with his brother's fiancée Christina (Paula Raymond), then tries to kill Mario, but is himself killed by his twin.

Comment: Screen adaptations of Alexandre Dumas' classic novel began in 1897.

Van Cleef's Role: Van Cleef appears as Nerva, one of Jonatto's soldiers, in this 1953 film adaptation of the Dumas novel. Nerva is present when Jonatto tortures one of the Richard Greene heroes. In 1971, another Van Cleef film character encounters twin brothers who experience each others' feelings: In *Captain Apache*, Van Cleef's title hero has a drinking contest with Corsican Brother-like twins.

Barquero
1970, color, 115 minutes,
United Artists (Western)

Cast: Lee Van Cleef (Travis), Warren Oates (Jake Remy), Forrest Tucker (Mountain Phil), Kerwin Mathews (Marquette), Mariette Hartley (Anna), Marie Gomez (Nola), Armando Silvestre (Sawyer), John Davis Chandler (Fair), Craig Littler (Pitney), Ed Bakey (Happy), Richard Lapp (Poe), Harry Lauter (Steele), Brad Weston (Driver), Thad Williams (Gibson), Armand Alzamora (Lopez), Frank Babich (Roland), Terry Leonard (Hawk), Bennie Dobbins (Encow), Rita Conde (Layeta).

Director: Gordon Douglas

Synopsis: Outlaw Jake Remy (Warren Oates) divides his gang of bandits into two groups. Remy leads one group on a pillaging mission in Buckskin, Arizona, and the other group goes to Lonely Dell to commandeer a ferry on the Paria River. When Remy's group arrives in Lonely Dell with loot from Buckskin, they expect to have a barge at their disposal, but they instead find that ferryman Travis (Lee Van Cleef) and a mountain man named Phil (Forrest Tucker) made short work of the detachment. Travis refuses to let the gang use his ferry, and without it, the outlaws can't escape pursuing lawmen by crossing the Paria and hiding in Mexico. After trying unsuccessfully to trick the ferryman, Remy and the gang build two boats. When they try to cross the river, Travis and Lonely Dell's citizenry, who are all crammed on the ferry, gun down the outlaw gang.

Comment: Warren Oates, who was terrific in the previous year's *The Wild Bunch*, is also terrific in *Barquero* as a Lee Marvin-type villain. However, anybody who has seen *The Wild Bunch* will be unimpressed with *Barquero*'s massacre scenes. *Barquero* was made with a good premise, but the resulting plot contains plenty of inconsistencies, and little effort is made to create the sense of the urgency with which Remy needs the ferry. Also annoying are *Barquero*'s many filtered day-for-night scenes.

Van Cleef's Role: Surprisingly, top-billed Van Cleef doesn't have the largest role in *Barquero*. Van Cleef's Travis is slighted as the film devotes a large amount of time to its most flamboyant character, Jake Remy. Since the heavily-featured Remy doesn't interact much with Travis (the two men are on opposite sides of the river for the duration of *Barquero*), Travis does not spend enough continuous time on screen to allow Van Cleef to present the ferryman as more than a one-dimensional character. In each of his scenes, it seems as if Travis is a slightly different character. He is always a slightly different variation of Van Cleef's starring film persona. Thus Travis is somewhat of a composite of Van Cleef's previous film roles. However, the lack of characterization in Travis is compensated for with brawn. This bargeman, or barquero, draws his craft from one bank of the river to the other by means of a rope, using only his two bare hands. Such a character would have to be strong and muscular. Van Cleef is, and the film prominently features his physique. He appears shirtless during much of *Barquero*.

The Beast from 20,000 Fathoms

1953, black and white, 80 minutes, Warner Bros.

Cast: Paul Christian (Tom Nesbitt), Paula Raymond (Lee Hunter), Cecil Kellaway (Dr. Elson), Kenneth Tobey (Col. Evans), Donald Woods

(Capt. Jackson), Jack Pennick (Jacob), Lee Van Cleef (Cpl. Stone), Steve Brodie (Sgt. Loomis), Ross Elliott (George Ritchie), Ray Hyke (Sgt. Willistead), Mary Hill (Nesbitt's Secretary), Michael Fox (Doctor), Alvin Greenman (1st Radar Man), Frank Ferguson (Dr. Morton), King Donovan (Dr. Ingersoll)

Director: Eugene Lourie

Synopsis: As part of a scientific expedition, an atomic bomb is detonated in the Arctic Circle. The bomb's explosion releases a prehistoric dinosaur from its frozen hibernation and sets it loose in the arctic region. Tom Nesbitt (Paul Christian), the only scientist to return to the United States having seen the beast, tries unsuccessfully to convince others of its existence. When sailors' sea monster sightings flood in, Tom's story gets enough credibility to prompt an expedition, but the head scientist (Cecil Kellaway) is eaten by the beast. The creature follows the arctic current and eventually reaches New York City, where the police and national guard try to stop it. When the animal is wounded by gunfire, it spills blood with prehistoric germs that cause many soldiers to perish. Tom suggests that they use a radioactive isotope to kill the beast and destroy its diseased tissue. When the isotope is shot into the beast, it dies.

Comment: The Beast from 20,000 Fathoms is very loosely based on Ray Bradbury's short story "The Foghorn," which appeared in *The Saturday Evening Post*. This film is reportedly the first "creature as a result of an atomic explosion" picture. The film's main attraction is the stop-motion effects, which were provided by special effects wizard Ray Harryhausen.

Van Cleef's Role: Van Cleef's Cpl. Stone is in the film proclaimed the finest shot in the National Guard, and it is he who kills the beast by shooting it with the radioactive isotope. Cpl. Stone is not a large role for Van Cleef; he appears only in the last few minutes of the film and wears an all-covering protective suit and hood for most of his on-screen duration.

Beyond the Law

1968, color, 110 minutes, Italian-German (Western)

Alternate Titles: *Above the Law, Al di là della legge* (Italian), *Bloodsilver, Die letzte Rechnung zahlst du Selbst* (German), *The Good Die First, The Outrider, The Outsider, Pas de pitié pour les salopards* (French)

Cast: Lee Van Cleef (Joe Billy Cudlip), Antonio Sabato (Ben Novak), Lionel Stander (Phony Preacher), Gordon Mitchell (Burton), Graziella Granata (Sally Davis), Ann Smyrner (Lola), Bud Spencer (Cooper), Carlo Gaddi, Herbert Fux, Enzo Fiermonte, Gunther Stoll, Romano Puppo, Al Hoosman, Nino Nini, Hans Elwenspoek, Adrianna Fachetti, Fernando Poggi, Valentina Arrigari

Director: Giorgio Stegani

Synopsis: A small-time bandit named Cudlip (Lee Van Cleef) and his two bandit pals steal a payroll before it reaches the mine workers of Silvertown. The man who is responsible for the money's safe arrival, Ben Novak (Antonio Sabato), agrees to make a trip for a replacement payroll and is accompanied by Silvertown's sheriff, John Ferguson. The second payroll attracts a different, more impressive group of thieves — bandits under the command of a man named Burton (Gordon Mitchell). Although Sheriff Ferguson is badly wounded, the payroll reaches the mine workers. Cudlip, who has been staying in Silvertown with his two bandit pals in hopes of swiping more money, finds that he is beginning to enjoy law-abiding town life, and he values his newly-made friendships with Novak and local girl Sally Davis (Graziella Granata). With Ferguson incapacitated, Cudlip replaces him as sheriff and is able to save the town's silver from Burton's gang. Cudlip's two bandit friends, who assume their pal's new position was taken for convenience in thievery, also try to steal the silver and, to their surprise, are gunned down by Cudlip and Novak.

Comment: Beyond the Law is a humorous, relatively non-violent Spaghetti Western, barring the overly-long shoot-out at the end. Actor Lionel Stander moved to Italy in 1967 to make this and other Italian Westerns after he was blacklisted in the United States by the House Un-American Activities Committee. Both he and Van Cleef display their aptitude for comedy, while Stegani's direction creates some exciting moments. *Beyond the Law* is marred only by its excessive number of plot developments (which seems to have made it necessary to trim down the

Poster (in French and Flemish) for *Beyond the Law* (1968), one of Van Cleef's more humorous, but still violent, European Westerns. Pictured are Van Cleef (left) and Antonio Sabato.

Sally Davis subplot), and by Mitchell's overly dramatic performance as Burton, the caped villain.

Van Cleef's Role: Beyond the Law's Cudlip sees Van Cleef in his first humorous lead. And because Cudlip undergoes a drastic transformation—one of the most drastic transformations to be featured in a Van Cleef character—the actor is able to present the transformed Cudlip as yet another of his splendid stoic heroes. As the film opens, Cudlip is a loud, scruffy-looking thief who—besides his predilection for theft—is basically good at heart. As the film progresses, Cudlip associates less with his bandit pals, and reveals an increasing preference for the company of upstanding types like Ben Novak and Sally Davis. Several scenes point to his motivation for change, including one in which Cudlip feels guilty that Novak is blamed for the payroll's disappearance, and another in which Cudlip is refused a sale by a horse breeder because of his scraggly appearance. The gradual transformation yields Sheriff Cudlip, who is clean-shaven, well-dressed and morally sound. After Cudlip runs through the last of his humorous material, his list of newly-found attributes expands to include cool, collected and hardened; Cudlip is one of Van Cleef's stoic heroes. But before Sheriff Cudlip becomes hardened and cool, he tells Sally, "Youth is for getting experience. Maturity — now *that's* for finding your place in life." When Cudlip transforms, and Van Cleef is allowed to play the character as a stoic hero, it is obvious that the actor has found his place in life.

The Big Combo
1955, black and white, 89 minutes, Allied Artists

Cast: Cornel Wilde (Lt. Leonard Diamond), Richard Conte (Brown), Brian Donlevy (Joe McClure), Jean Wallace (Susan Lowell), Robert Middleton (Capt. Peterson), Lee Van Cleef (Fante), Earl Holliman (Mingo), Helen Walker (Alicia Brown), Jay Adler (Sam Hill), John Hoyt (Nils Dreyer), Ted De Corsia (Bettini), Helene Stanton (Rita), Roy Gordon (Audubon), Whit Bissell (Doctor), Philip Van Zandt (Mr. Jones), Steve Mitchell (Bennie Smith), Baynes Barron (Young Detective), Rita Gould (Nurse), Michael Mark (Hotel Clerk), Donna Drew (Miss Hartleby), Brian O'Hara (Malloy), Tony Michaels, Bruce Sharpe

Director: Joseph Lewis

Synopsis: Police detective Leonard Diamond (Cornel Wilde) devotes all his energy to harassing a local criminal named Brown (Richard Conte). Brown's girlfriend Susan Lowell (Jean Wallace) is the object of Diamond's obsession. Brown deploys some thugs who torture Diamond. The policeman survives, though, and receives information about Brown from the criminal's repudiated wife, Alicia (Helen Walker). Alicia's information leads Diamond to a secret airplane hangar, where Brown and Susan are waiting for a getaway plane. Diamond shoots down the criminal and takes Susan for his own.

Comment: This film is noted for the controversy raised by its sadistic torture scenes. Heavy cutting was done before the film could be shown at many theaters. Principals Cornel Wilde and Jean Wallace were, at the time of the filming, real-life husband and wife.

Van Cleef's Role: Van Cleef's *Big Combo* character, Fante, is one of the thugs who tortures Cornel Wilde. One of the other torturers is Mingo (Earl Holliman), and the film implies that the two are homosexual lovers.

Probably as much has been written about Van Cleef's Fante as has been written about Van Cleef's starring roles, because of the double controversy of the violence and the homosexual implications. This sadistic role strengthened his reputation as a screen heavy, and broadened the variety of his film villain portrayals.

The performances of Tomas Milian and Lee Van Cleef helped to make *The Big Gundown* (1966) a big success.

The Big Gundown
1966, color, 84 minutes, Italian (Western)

Alternate Titles: *Account Rendered, Colorado, Der Gehetze der Sierra Madre* (German), *El Halcón y la presa* (Spanish), *The Falcon and His Prey* (unused translation of Spanish title), *La resa dei conti* (Italian), *Showdown, Un maudit de plus* (French)

Cast: Lee Van Cleef (Jonathon Corbett), Tomas Milian (Cuchillo Sanchez), Walter Barnes (Brokston), Luisa Rivelli (Lizzie), Fernando Sancho (Capt. Segura), Nieves Navarro (Widow), Benito Steffanelli (Jess), Maria Granada (Rosita), Lanfranco Ceccarelli (Jack), Robert Camardiel (Jellicol), Nello Pazzafini (Hondo), Spartaco Conversi (Mitchell), Romano Puppo (Rocky), Tom Felleghi (Chet), Calisto Calisti (Miller), Antonio Casas (Dance), Jose Torres (Nathan)

Co-Writer/Director: Sergio Sollima

Synopsis: A railroad tycoon named Brokston (Walter Barnes) promises to fund the political campaign of famous Texas lawman Jonathon Corbett (Lee Van Cleef), with the agreement that Corbett will support Brokston's railroad project. Just after their arrangement is made, a report comes about the rape and stabbing of a 12-year-old girl, and Brokston sends Corbett to capture the suspected murderer, a Mexican peon named Cuchillo Sanchez (Tomas Milian). Corbett journeys into Mexico after Cuchillo and captures him several times, but on all occasions, the Mexican escapes. Brokston comes to Mexico and, with a pack of dogs and an army of hired guns, he personally hunts Cuchillo. When these extreme measures are taken, Corbett becomes suspicious, and he learns that Cuchillo's only involvement in the crime is knowing the identity of the real culprit: Brokston's son-in-law. Corbett realizes that Brokston didn't want his family's name to be tainted by scandal and that he helped frame the Mexican, believing that nobody would bother to defend someone of Cuchillo's poor class. Corbett proves Brokston wrong, though. He and Cuchillo join forces to kill Brokston and his son-in-law. The two friends ride off in separate directions, but before Corbett is out of earshot, Cuchillo yells, "You never would have caught me!"

Comment: A Spaghetti Western with political overtones, *The Big Gundown* suggests that law and power reside in the hands of those who can pay for it. And the film also has a statement about the revolutionary activities of the oppressed Mexican peons. The Cuchillo character is not only an easy target for Brokston's personal law because he is poor,

Opposite: A Belgian poster for *The Big Gundown* (1966). Shot back-to-back with *The Good, the Bad, and the Ugly*, it provided Van Cleef with his first top-billed performance.

LEE VAN CLEEF
TOMAS MILIAN
WALTER BARNES
un maudit de plus
"the big gundown"
REGIE SERGIO SOLLIMA · PROD. ALBERTO GRIMALDI · For PEA
TECHNICOLOR® TECHNISCOPE®
EEN VERDOEMDE TE MEER

but also because he is unpopular with government officials because of his past association with revolutionary elements. *The Big Gundown*, filmed in Europe, tries admirably to seem authentic. Some Eurowesterns seem content to plop their cowboy hat-wearing characters in a desert and call it the Old West. In *The Big Gundown*, actual Western figures and events are included. In his search for Cuchillo, Van Cleef's Corbett encounters a Mormon caravan, and hears talk of Mexican revolutionary leader Juarez. When Brokston meets Corbett in Mexico, the Texas lawman is in a town that is celebrating the Day of the Dead. The internationally popular *Big Gundown* spawned a sequel, *Run, Man, Run*, which was directed by Sollima and starred Tomas Milian, but not Van Cleef.

Van Cleef's Role: Van Cleef's Jonathon Corbett is one of the actor's best characters. Van Cleef skillfully takes the character from being a man naive but zealous about law and order to a realist, weary of the situation, but forced to see it to its conclusion. Jonathon Corbett can be considered one of Van Cleef's best examples of a stoic hero.

The Bravados

1958, color, 99 minutes,
20th Century–Fox (Western)

Cast: Gregory Peck (Jim Douglas), Joan Collins (Josefa), Stephen Boyd (Bill Zachary), Albert Salmi (Ed Taylor), Lee Van Cleef (Alfonso Parral), Henry Silva (Lujan), Kathleen Gallant (Emma), Barry Coe (Tom), George Voskovec (Gus Steinmetz), Herbert Rudley (Sheriff Elroy Sanchez), Ada Carrasco (Mrs. Parral), Andrew Duggan (Padre), Ken Scott (Primo), Gene Evans (John Butler), Jack Mather (Quinn), Joe De Rita (Simms), Robert Adler (Tony Mirabel), Jason Wingreen, Robert Griffin, Juan Garcia, Jacqueline Evans, Alicia Del Lago, the Ninos Cantores De Morelia Choral Group

Director: Henry King

Synopsis: Jim Douglas (Gregory Peck) makes a trip to Rio Ariba, where four criminals are scheduled to hang. Douglas believes that these are the men who raped and murdered his wife, and he hopes to feel avenged after witnessing their execution. But the night before the scheduled hanging, the criminals escape from jail. Douglas joins the posse that chases the four but soon leaves it behind and continues the pursuit alone. He overtakes and kills three of the escaping criminals, but as he attempts to kill the last, Douglas learns that he has been after the wrong men; a miner named John Butler (Gene Evans) actually did the killing and then framed the four criminals. Jim Douglas leaves the fourth criminal with his wife and young child and returns to Rio Ariba, where he is celebrated for his work. Douglas spends his time there in church and confesses to a priest. He realizes that killing a man in revenge is not justified, and he asks the citizens of Rio Ariba to pray for him.

Comment: The Bravados' story seems to be purposefully routine until the surprise ending, but perhaps if the bulk of the film had not been done in such a perfunctory manner, the ending would not have been as effective. The withdrawn, awkward Douglas is brilliantly portrayed by Peck and is, along with the astounding enormity of Rio Ariba's church, one of the few interesting elements in this film. Joan Collins' Josefa has very little to do, and is obviously there to fulfill the mandatory love-interest role.

Van Cleef's Role: Lee plays Alfonso Parral, one of the four outlaws on the run from Douglas (and the first to be caught and killed by the revenge seeker). When Douglas overtakes the outlaw, Parral denies having seen Douglas' wife and he begs to be spared. But this doesn't dissuade Douglas, and he guns down Alfonso Parral while the outlaw is begging on his hands and knees. A *TV Guide* article from 1957, the year before *The Bravados'* release, mentioned that Van Cleef was known for creating especially evil villains, and that his heavies were the "worst of the lot." Nonetheless, Van Cleef is very effective as the most of sympathetic of this film's four outlaws.

Captain Apache

1971, color, 94 minutes,
British–Spanish (Western)

Cast: Lee Van Cleef (Captain Apache), Carroll Baker (Maude), Stuart Whitman (Griffin), Percy Herbert (Moon), Elisa Montes (Rosita), Tony Vogel (Snake), Charles Stalnaker (O'Rourke), Charlie Bravo

(Sanchez), Hugh McDermott (Gen. Ryland), Faith Clift (Abigail), Dan Van Husen (Al), D. Pollock (Ben), George Margo (Sheriff), Jose Bodalo (General), Elsa Zabala (Witch), Allen Russell (Maitre D'), Luis Induni (Ezekiel), Vito Salier (Diablo), Fernando Sanchez Pollack (Guitarist), Ricardo Palacios, X. Brands

Director: Alexander Singer

Synopsis: Captain Apache (Lee Van Cleef), a full-blooded American Indian in the U.S. Army, is assigned to investigate the murder of Indian Commissioner Collier. His only clues are the words "April Morning"—Collier's last utterance—and although Captain Apache has many leads concerning the words, all his efforts come to naught until he takes a train ride to Tucson with three suspects: Sanchez (Charlie Bravo), Griffin (Stuart Whitman) and Griffin's lover Maude (Carroll Baker). During the trip, the train picks up General Grant's personal train coach, which is named "April Morning." Captain Apache learns that Sanchez and Griffin's followers, disguised as Indians, are planning to assassinate Grant in order to incite an Indian war. Collier was murdered because he knew about the assassination plot. With help from Maude and Union soldiers, Captain Apache defeats the baddies and protects the target of their scheme. When it is over, the Captain learns that the train was actually carrying a Grant imposter, who served as a decoy, and that the President stayed behind in Tucson.

Comment: Captain Apache has a tongue-in-cheek tone, but it does not matter whether it takes itself seriously; being tedious and hard to follow, it is almost unwatchable. It is irritating to watch the Captain conduct his roundabout investigation, which does not make a bit of progress until the film's climax and is obviously just an excuse for the ridiculous, episodic happenings. In one scene, the Captain is drugged by a witch. In another, he is forced into a drinking contest with two Corsican-brother-like twins. He visits an Indian camp and strips down in order to talk to the chief. None of these disjointed episodes help to forward the plot.

Van Cleef's Role: The greatest exposure of Van Cleef's physique occurs in *Captain Apache*. On the rather thin pretext that an Indian Chief would not speak to him while Captain Apache was wearing a U.S. Cavalry uniform, the Captain strips down to a skimpy undergarment for the rest of the scene. Although pointless, the scene effectively showed off the 46-year-old actor's physical stature. This is the first film in which Van Cleef wore a toupee in order to portray a younger man. And Captain Apache looks even more different than his previous leading roles because Van Cleef's familiar mustache is missing (he obviously shaved it off to be credible as an American Indian). *Captain Apache* also features the Van Cleef–sung "April Morning," a tune which plays during the closing credits.

China Gate
1957, black and white, 97 minutes,
20th Century–Fox

Cast: Gene Barry (Sgt. Brock), Angie Dickinson (Lia "Lucky Legs"), Nat "King" Cole (Goldie), Lee Van Cleef (Major Cham), Paul Dubov (Capt. Caumont), George Givot (Cpl. Pigalle), Gerald Milton (Private Andreades), Neyle Morrow (Leung), Marcel Dalio (Father Paul), Maurice Marsac (Col. De Sars), Warren Hsieh (The Boy), Paul Busch (Cpl. Kruger), Sasha Harden (Private Jaszi), James Hong (Charlie), William Soo Hoo (Moi Leader), Walter Soo Hoo (Guard), Weaver Levy (Khuan)

Director: Samuel Fuller

Synopsis: U.S. Army Sgt. Johnny Brock (Gene Barry) leads a group of international soldiers, fighting for the French Legion, through 1950s Communist Vietnam to find and destroy an enemy bomb dump. The soldiers' guide, a Eurasian harlot named Lia "Lucky Legs" (Angie Dickinson), was once married to the Sergeant, until Brock shamefully abandoned her when he learned that their son was racially mixed. Lia has agreed to work with Sgt. Brock only on the condition that the French allow their son to leave war-torn Vietnam. Lia guides Brock's patrol safely past Communist outposts and leads them to the China Gate, a structure where the bombs are hidden. Leaving Brock and the patrol to hide in the jungle, Lia meets with the gate's commander, Major Cham (Lee Van Cleef), who wants to marry her. Lia returns to the patrol with information about the bombs' whereabouts, and before they move out to destroy them, Lia and Brock reconcile and declare their love for each other. Their mission runs into a snag, though, and Lia has to kill Major Cham and sacrifice her own life in order to make it successful. Brock returns from the mission and takes his son to America.

China Gate (20th Century–Fox, 1957), an early film treatment of the conflict in Vietnam, features Angie Dickinson as Lia "Lucky Legs." Here, Lia wins the confidence of the enemy commander, Major Cham (Lee Van Cleef), and learns the whereabouts of his bomb depot.

Comment: An early screen treatment of the conflict in Vietnam, *China Gate* is made enjoyable by its romantic subplots and the tense action behind enemy lines. The varied cast is credible as a group of international soldiers, and even includes Nat "King" Cole, who is best known for singing mellow songs such as "Unforgettable" (he also sings *China Gate*'s title song). It is rather amusing to see the sentimental singer as a soldier in this film, firing his submachinegun so vigorously that the flesh of his face ripples. *China Gate*'s ending leaves something to be desired. The film has a tragic ending (Lia sacrifices her life for the mission after finally realizing a chance for a family life with Brock and their son), but it is not treated as tragic by either the characters or the film. At the end, Brock just collects his motherless child and goes back to America.

Van Cleef's Role: Van Cleef, whose face has proved versatile enough to be convincing as American Indians and Europeans, plays a Eurasian named Cham in *China Gate*, and the actor's narrow eyes make him believable in this part. Cham, a major in the North Vietnamese Army, is the commander of the China Gate. When he receives his visit from Lia, he again asks her to marry him. His willingness to place his trust in her allows the plot to come to its conclusion, and causes the character to evoke sympathy. Unlike Brock, Cham has wanted to give Lia and her son a good life, but Lia is forced to kill Cham by pushing him off a ledge in order to save the mission. Van Cleef's excellently portrayed Major Cham is one of the film's key roles, and must have been a nice change of pace for the actor in the 1950s, when he played mostly heavies.

Codename: Wildgeese

1984, color, 101 minutes, Italian-German

Alternate Title: *Geheimcode Wildganse* (German)
Cast: Lewis Collins (Robin Wesley), Lee Van Cleef (China Travers), Ernest Borgnine (Frank Fletcher), Mimsy Farmer (Kathy Robson), Klaus Kinski (Charlton), Manfred Lehmann (Klein), Thomas Danneberg (Arbib), Frank Glaubrecht (Stone), Wolfgang Pampel (Baldwin), Hartmut Neugebauer (Brenner), Alan Collins (Priest)
Director: Anthony M. Dawson [Antonio Margheriti]

Synopsis: A team of mercenaries led by Robin Wesley (Lewis Collins) is hired by Drug Enforcement Agent Frank Fletcher (Ernest Borgnine) to wipe out opium depots in an Asian jungle. Their mission is financed by a businessman named Charlton (Klaus Kinski). Wesley and his team destroy the sites, but their escape helicopter is destroyed in the battle, and they retreat on foot. While trekking back out of the jungle, the mercenaries learn that there are other opium depots and refineries that they weren't told about, and although their supplies are dwindling, they set about destroying them also. Charlton, who secretly owns these opium sites, leads an attack disguised as a rescue mission, and he tries to stop Wesley. The mercenaries prevail, though, as the opium sites and their owner are annihilated.

Comment: Codename: Wildgeese features some very good and very tense action sequences, but they become tiresome before the film's conclusion. The performance of the usually fine Ernest Borgnine seems a little off in scenes that require him to converse with the actors who weren't speaking English during the filming.

Van Cleef's Role: Van Cleef is China Travers, a man who is released from jail to join the mercenary team as the helicopter pilot. This film is one of Van Cleef's last outings as a full-fledged action hero. By this time in Van Cleef's career, the aging actor didn't often play a ladies' man, but in *Codename: Wildgeese* China has an implied romance with a younger woman (Mimsy Farmer) who tags along with the mercenaries. She is attracted to China instead of the younger soldiers nearer her age. In an effort to appear tough, Van Cleef comes off as grumpy at first, but as he mellows a bit, his pessimistic comments becomes the film's only source of humor.

The Commander

1988, color, 96 minutes, Italian-German

Alternate Title: *The Wildgeese Commander*

Cast: Lewis Collins (Major Jack Colby), Lee Van Cleef (Colonel Mazzarini), Donald Pleasence (Henry Carlson), Manfred Lehmann (Wild Bill Hickock and Dark Mason), John Steiner (Duclaud), Brett Halsey (McPherson), Chat Silayan (Ling), Antonio Cantafora (Nick De

Carlo), Bobby Rhodes (Kong Klaus), Thomas Danneberg (Gustavson), Romano Puppo (Angelo), Hans Leutenegger, Paul Muller, Frank Glaubrecht, Christian Brockner, Wolfgang Kohne, Anita Lochner

Director: Anthony M. Dawson [Antonio Margheriti]

Synopsis: A powerful gunrunner named Colonel Mazzarini (Lee Van Cleef) facilitates a change in power in Cambodia and then expects a discount on the price of opium shipments from the new Cambodian general, Dong. To ensure that he gets the discount, Mazzarini sends as intimidation a group of mercenaries led by Major Jack Colby (Lewis Collins). The mercenaries believe that their attack will be a surprise, and they do not know of the secret arrangement between Mazzarini and General Dong. Mazzarini alerts Dong of Colby's impending arrival, and the general agrees to the gunrunner's price before the mercenaries reach the Cambodian compound. When the mercenaries arrive, they realize that Mazzarini has betrayed the mission, and Colby orders the destruction of all the opium refineries. After the mission is complete, Colby and Wild Bill Hickock (Manfred Lehmann), the mission's only other survivor, return to Europe and kill Mazzarini.

Comment: An intricately plotted action film, *The Commander* features points of exposition that are not revealed until relatively late in the film. For instance, the viewer does not know that Mazzarini put Dong in power until the film is half finished. A subplot involves an investigation to find a corrupt DEA agent, and the viewer is led to believe that the culprit is Henry Carlson (Donald Pleasence). Only in the film's last scene is it made evident that the corrupt party is actually the agent leading the investigation. Unfortunately, much of the exposition is rushed, making the film hard to follow. In both cast and musical score, *The Commander* is similar to Dawson's 1984 mercenary film, *Codename: Wildgeese.*

Van Cleef's Role: Van Cleef, who in Dawson's *Wildgeese* is part of the ensemble cast as a mercenary, has only a supporting role in *The Commander* as the man who hires the mercenaries. The film, however, does allow Van Cleef to showcase his aptitude for particularly nasty on-screen villainy. Mazzarini poisons one of his associates and promises to deliver the antidote only if a secret code is given. When Mazzarini has the code, he reveals that there is no antidote.

The character-naming of *The Commander* seems to be something of a tribute to Van Cleef. The hero of *The Commander* bears the name Jack Colby, which was Van Cleef's character name in *High Noon*. Another character is Corporal Stone, the name of Van Cleef's character in *Beast from 20,000 Fathoms*.

Commandos
1968, color, 89 minutes, Italian-German

Alternate Titles: *Sullivan's Marauders* (U.S.), *Himmelfahrtskommando el alamein* (German)

Cast: Lee Van Cleef (Sgt. Sullivan), Jack Kelly (Capt. Valli), Giampiero Albertini (Aldo), Marino Masé (Lt. Tommasini), Gotz George (German Commander), Marilu' Tolo (Adrianna), Akim Berg (Lt. Agen), Pier Palol Capponi, Ivano Staccioli, Heinz Reincke, Helmut Schmid, Otto Stern, Pier Luigi Anchisi, Gianni Brezza, Duilio Del Prete, Emilio Marchesini, Biagio Pelligra, Lorenzo Piani, Giacomo Piperno, Romano Puppo, Franco Cobianchi, Mario Ferlazzo, Mauro Lumachi, Gianni Pulone, Ivan Scratuglia

Director: Armando Crispino

Synopsis: In the deserts of World War II North Africa, Sgt. Sullivan (Lee Van Cleef) and his group of Italian-American commandos are given a new commanding officer, Capt. Valli (Jack Kelly). Sullivan dislikes Valli, who has logged little combat time, and the Sergeant believes that Valli's battle plan is overly dangerous. Nonetheless, the plan is carried out as the commandos seize an Italian-controlled oasis. By manipulating their unwilling Italian prisoners and posing as Italians themselves, they fool the Italian and German units that make daily stops at the oasis. The commandos' internal problems eventually surface, as the incensed Sergeant Sullivan tries to commit mutiny against Capt. Valli. Sullivan, who experiences frequent flashbacks to the traumatic loss of his fellow servicemen under another inexperienced commander, doesn't get his chance at insurrection, though. The commandos' identity is unmasked, and they are forced to fight it out with the Germans. The battle continues until there is only one survivor on each side, and the erstwhile enemies set down their weapons and bury the dead.

Comment: If for no other reason, *Commandos* is interesting because it's an Italian-German-made movie about World War II conflict between the Italian-German Axis and the Americans, told from the Americans'

point of view. Naturally, this leads to some subtle hints of antagonist-protagonist reversal—a reversal that probably wasn't intended to, but illustrates the moral confusion of war. This is especially evident in the Italian-prisoners'-escape scene, in which the Italians escape in a truck, the truck gets stuck in the sand and the pursuing commandos overtake them—gunning some of the helpless Italians down and driving the rest into a mine field. Also noteworthy is the final shoot-out, in which the German commander—who has been duped by the commandos' masquerade—has a hard time killing Valli, his American counterpart, whom the German befriended as an "Italian ally." A gritty film, *Commandos* sustains adequate tension, partly through Mario Nasscimbene's score, which is often just a high-pitched drone.

Van Cleef's Role: Quite a bit of aesthetic attention is drawn to Van Cleef's physical appearance in *Commandos*. His short, military haircut compliments the symmetric shape of his head, his sun-baked skin offsets his drab uniform, and the lighting during the night scenes highlights Van Cleef's tough, angular features. But it is Van Cleef's Sullivan, with his contempt for the inexperienced Valli and his paternal love for his soldiers, who is the film's most cliched character. However, his death scene is given interesting treatment, showing the Sergeant reliving his hidious flashback one final time as he dies. Sullivan, the irate-but-justified bully, is a breed apart from Van Cleef's stoic hero, the character so prevalent in this stage of Van Cleef's career.

The Conqueror

1956, color, 111 minutes, RKO

Cast: John Wayne (Temujin "Genghis Khan"), Susan Hayward (Bortai), Pedro Armendariz (Jamuga), Agnes Moorehead (Hunlun), Thomas Gomez (Wang Khan), John Hoyt (Shaman), William Conrad (Kasar), Ted De Corsia (Kumlek), Leslie Bradley (Targutai), Lee Van Cleef (Chepei), Peter Mamakos (Borgurchi), Leo Gordon (Tartar Captain), Richard Loo (Captain of Wang's Guard), Billy Curtis (Midget Tumbler)

Producer/Director: Dick Powell

Synopsis: In the 12th century, two tribes of the Gobi desert, the Merkits and the Tartars, join forces. Their union is symbolized when the Tartar chief gives his daughter Bortai (Susan Hayward) as a wife to the Merkit chief. Temijun (John Wayne), the chief of another Gobi desert tribe named the Mongols, is both threatened by the union and in love with Bortai. He steals her from the Tartar chief. Temijun's action incurs the wrath of the Merkits and the Tartars, who plan to conquer the whole Gobi desert. Temijun seeks help from a powerful ruler, Wang Khan (Thomas Gomez), but Wang Khan thinks that the Mongol is being deceptive and imprisons some of Temijun's Mongols. Temijun leads an attack, captures Wang Khan's city and uses his new acquisitions to quash the rise of the other Gobi tribes. A coronation sees Temijun become "Genghis Khan," "the perfect warrior."

Comment: John Wayne is horribly miscast as Genghis Khan, but ironically, his campy performance is the most watchable element of this tedious costumer. *The Conqueror* was filmed near Yucca Flat, Nevada, where 11 atomic test explosions occurred a year before the film's production. Ninety-one members of the film's case and crew later developed cancer.

Van Cleef's Role: Van Cleef has a bit part in *The Conqueror* as Chepei, one of the Mongol warriors. In his big scene, Chepei becomes inspired by the music of the Mongol band and begins doing a bizarre dance, with his arms and legs flailing wildly. Chepei's dance is cut off by a Mongol named Kasar (William Conrad), who suggests that Borthai should dance instead. Although brief, Chepei's dance scene is of hilarious interest to Van Cleef fans.

Dawn at Socorro

1954, color, 80 minutes, Universal (Western)

Cast: Rory Calhoun (Brett Wade), Piper Laurie (Rannah Hayes), David Brian (Richard "Dick" Braden), Kathleen Hughes (Clare), Alex Nicol (Jimmy Rapp), Edgar Buchanan (Sheriff Cauthen), Mara Corday (Lotty Diamond), Roy Roberts (Doc Jameson), Skip Homeier (Buddy Ferris), Stanley Andrews (Old Man Ferris), Richard Garland (Tom Ferris), Scott Lee (Vince McNair), Paul Brinegar (Desk Clerk), Philo McCullough (Rancher), Forrest Taylor (Jebb Hayes)

Director: George Sherman

Synopsis: In the town of Lordsburg, popular saloon owner Brett Wade (Rory Calhoun) infuriates a portion of the townspeople when he kills members of the Ferris family—one of the town's oldest families—in a showdown. Wade, who is also grappling with his declining health, decides to leave Lordsburg for the healthy climate of Colorado Springs, and on his trip, he makes a stopover in Socorro, where he waits for the dawn train to Colorado. In Socorro, he runs into Rannah Hayes (Piper Laurie), a nice girl he met near Lordsburg. He tries to dissuade Rannah from degrading herself as a saloon girl in the casino of Richard Braden (David Brian), one of Wade's enemies. When Wade tries to get Rannah out of her commitment to Braden, the casino owner hires Jimmy Rapp (Alex Nicol), a friend of the Ferris family, to murder Wade. Wade, however is faster on the draw, and after Jimmy and Braden are dead, Rannah accompanies him to Colorado Springs.

Comment: Rory Calhoun makes an exciting hero in this average oater. Footage from *Dawn at Socorro* reappears in *Red Sundown*, a 1956 Calhoun-starring western.

Van Cleef's Role: Van Cleef is impeccable in the role of Earl Ferris. This is not a large part for the actor; although Earl is the only Ferris to survive the gun deal in Lordsburg, he is killed shortly after by Brett Wade at a desert outpost. Van Cleef's death scene is among the *Dawn at Socorro* footage that is reused in 1956's *Red Sundown*, another Rory Calhoun Western.

Day of Anger

1967, color, 109 minutes,
Italian-German (Western)

Alternate Titles: *Days of Anger* (home video), *Days of Wrath* (British and home video), *Der Tod ritt dienstags* (German), *I giorni dell'ira* (Italian), *Le dernier jar de la colore* (French), *On m'appelle Saligo* (French)

Cast: Lee Van Cleef (Frank Talby), Giuliano Gemma (Scott Mary), Walter Rilla (Murph Allan Short), Lukas Ammann (Judge Cutchel), Al Mulock (Wild Jack), Pepe Calvo (Blind Bill), Yvonne Sanson (Vivien Skill), Christa Linder, Ennio Balbo, Andrea Bosic, Giorgio Gargiullo,

Anna Orso, Hans Otto Alberty, Nino Nini, Virgilio Gazzolo, Eleonora Morana, Benito Steffanelli, Franco Balducci, Christian Consola, Natale Nazareno, Ferruccio Viotti, Paolo Magalotti, Gianni Di Segni
  Director: Tonio Valerii

  Synopsis: Upon his arrival in Clifton, Arizona, master gunfighter Frank Talby (Lee Van Cleef) takes a social outcast named Scott Mary (Giuliana Gemma) as an apprentice. With Scott's help, Talby blackmails several Clifton businessmen and politicians who, ten years earlier, bilked him out of $50,000. With the key citizens under their thumbs, Talby and his apprentice find themselves the kingpins of Clifton, and Scott enjoys the respect from townspeople who had earlier shunned him. Talby, who faces quite a bit of opposition in the town, kills anybody who threatens his power, and eventually Scott realizes how sanguinary his teacher is. When Talby kills Murph Allan (Walter Rilla), one of Scott's few friends, Scott uses Murph's prized revolver to shoot Talby dead.

  Comment: Day of Anger is a tough, dead-serious Spaghetti Western which boasts several well-handled, inventive gunfights and an excellent score by Riz Ortolani (who also scored Van Cleef's *Beyond the Law* and *Mean Frank and Crazy Tony*). However, the film is marred by its predilection for pointless excesses, some of which are laughably campy. The film contains many unnecessary scenes of outrageous violence. In one scene, Talby is tied with three ropes and dragged on his stomach behind riders on three horses. Then they stop and begin to laugh until the bloody-chested Talby gets a gun and shoots all three dead. Later, Talby engages in a gun duel that requires him and his opponent to gallop on horses toward each other while loading muzzle-loading rifles with loose powder, balls and percussion caps. Even decorations that have no part in the story add to the sense of campy excess. The film's town set features a saloon with giant gold-colored revolvers — each almost the size of a full-grown man — hanging off its porch. Much has been written about *Day of Anger*'s lack of directorial style and with good reason; in close-ups throughout the film, director Valerii seems content to center the actors' heads on the screen.

  Van Cleef's Role: In *Day of Anger*, Murph Allan tells Scott that Frank Talby needs an apprentice because he is getting too old to be a gunfighter. It is a shame this fact wasn't emphasized in the film. If Talby had been shown grappling with his aging and slowed reflexes, the character would be more sympathy-evoking when Scott and Talby turn against each other, and thus the film would have been more interesting. Despite the fact that Van Cleef's anti-heroic character becomes the full-fledged antagonist during the film, Talby ranks with some of Van Cleef's more heroic, exciting characters. Van Cleef is in his tough-looking prime, and he seems to have paid special attention to his movement and speech; everything Talby does is cool, slow and deliberate. When *Day of Anger* was made, Van Cleef was the most popular Spaghetti Western star, and his first entrance in this film gets the proper treatment (a long scene of his ride into town). However, as soon as he dismounts from his horse, he begins his first exchange with Guiliano Gemma. And that conversation ranks as some of Van Cleef's worst acting.

Day of the Bad Man
1958, color, 81 minutes,
Universal (Western)

Cast: Fred MacMurray (Judge Jim Scott), Joan Weldon (Myra Owens), John Ericson (Sheriff Barney Wiley), Robert Middleton (Charlie Hayes), Marie Windsor (Cora Johnson), Edgar Buchanan (Sam Wyckoff), Eduard Franz (Andrew Owens), Skip Homeier (Howard Hayes), Peggy Converse (Mrs. Quary), Robert Foulk (Silas Mordigan), Ann Doran (Mrs. Mordigan), Lee Van Cleef (Jake Hayes), Eddy Waller (Mr. Slocum), Christopher Dark (Rudy Hayes), Don Haggerty (Floyd), Chris Alcaide (Monte Hayes)

Director: Harry Keller

Synopsis: Circuit Judge Jim Scott (Fred MacMurray) wants to marry Myra Owens (Joan Weldon), but she declines because she has fallen in love with the town's sheriff, Barney Wiley (John Ericson). Another worry comes for the Judge when he is about to pronounce sentence on killer Rudy Hayes (Christopher Dark). Four of Rudy's relatives threaten to kill him if he sentences Rudy to hang. Rudy's relatives ask Judge Scott to instead banish Rudy from town and the Judge considers this option, knowing that it would be Sheriff Wiley's hazardous duty to enforce this punishment on the dangerous killer. But the Judge decides not to jeopardize Myra's new lover, and he accepts the danger himself by sentencing Rudy to hang. When the four Hayeses attack Judge Scott, Myra begs her boyfriend sheriff to help the Judge. Wiley refuses, and so she herself goes to help him. By the time she arrives, Judge Scott has already taken care of the four attackers. Myra realizes that he is the man she wants after all.

Comment: Fred MacMurray, best known for his comedic roles, does well as the film's solemn and self-sacrificing hero. In the film, the Hayeses threaten townspeople with physical harm if they do not urge Judge Scott to banish Rudy. The frightened townsfolk comply. Thus, *Day of the Bad Man* is one of several 1950s Westerns whose story resembles that of *High Noon*; both films feature a lawman who receives no help from his town's weak citizenry when forced to deal with a small group of badmen.

Van Cleef's Role: In *Day of the Bad Man*, Van Cleef's Jake Hayes is the cousin of murderer Rudy Hayes and one of the four men who try to intimidate Judge Scott. The Hayeses hope the judge will prescribe banishment instead of death for Rudy. But when Rudy is sentenced to hang, Jake joins the three others in trying to murder the Judge. During his time as a Hollywood heavy, Van Cleef saw this sort of plot device many times. Jake Hayes resembles Van Cleef's roles in *The Lawless Breed* and *Dawn at Socorro*; all of these characters are miscreants who, with a group of kin, try to avenge an injury done to a family member. In *Day of the Bad Man*, Jake is the next-to-the-last Hayes to appear and the first to be killed.

Death Rides a Horse

1967, color, 114 minutes,
Italian (Western)

Alternate Title: *As Man to Man* (unused translation), *Da uomo a uomo* (Italian), *De hombre a hombre* (Spanish), *La mort était au rendez-vous* (French), *Von Mann zu Mann* (German)

Cast: Lee Van Cleef (Ryan), John Phillip Law (Bill), Luigi Pistilli (Walcott), Jose Torres (Pedro), Anthony Dawson (Manina), Carla Cassola (Betsy), Archie Savage (Virgo), Mario Brega, Franco Balducci, Felicita Fanny, Carlo Pisacane, Bruno Corazzari, Ignazio Leone, Angelo Susani, Guglielmo Spoletini, Vivienne Bocca, Elena Hall, Natale Nazareno, Giovanni Petrucci, Richard Watson, Walter Giulangeli, Mario Mandalari, Ennio Pagliani, Romano Puppo

Lee Van Cleef's character finds a swirling dust storm good cover in which to club an adversary with a rifle in *Death Rides a Horse* (1967).

Director: Giulio Petroni

Synopsis: Fifteen years after his family is murdered by a band of outlaws, a gunfighter named Bill (John Phillip Law) forms a loose partnership with another gunfighter, Ryan (Lee Van Cleef). They hunt down the responsible outlaws, whose leader is Walcott (Luigi Pistilli). Unbeknownst to Bill, Ryan once rode with Walcott's gang, and although he had no part in the slaying of Bill's family, Ryan was framed for those murders by the gang and served a 15-year jail sentence. Initially, Ryan tries to reach the gang members first, hoping to extort money from his former associates before Bill can kill them. But before Ryan can get any money from Walcott, the gang captures the gunfighter, and Walcott frames Ryan for yet another crime. After Bill rescues Ryan from jail, the two gunfighters have a common goal, and they annihilate the gang. But Bill learns of Ryan's past association with Walcott, and he is infuriated. Bill demands that Ryan face off with him, but Ryan refuses and begins to walk away. Bill cannot shoot him in the back, and the two gunfighters decide just to part ways.

Comment: The influence of *For a Few Dollars More* is evident in this revenge-themed Spaghetti Western. Sharp-eyed viewers will note that the outfit worn by John Phillip Law is identical to the clothes Clint Eastwood wore beneath his serape in the earlier movie. A narrative motif that appears in both films is the "all-knowing" elderly man character to whom the hero goes for information. The age relationship between the protagonists are used similarly in the two films. In *For a Few Dollars More*, Eastwood's character called Van Cleef's "Old Man," and Van Cleef's character addressed Eastwood's as "Boy." In *Death Rides a Horse*, the terms "Grandpa" and "Son" are exchanged between the characters. An exciting but overlong Spaghetti Western, *Death Rides a Horse* features a supporting performance from an actor named Anthony Dawson. Contradictary to some sources, this is not director Anthony M. Dawson (a.k.a. Antonio Margheriti), who directed Van Cleef in at least five films.

Van Cleef's Role: Van Cleef's Ryan is first seen being released from prison with a heart full of revenge and greed, and he tries to extort money from the crooks whose lies sent him to jail. But after Ryan is captured by Walcott's gang and used as the fall guy for another crime, the gunfighter abandons his greedy plans for revenge. From this point on, Ryan becomes a much more stoic character. When he does fight it out with Walcott and the gang, it is to help Bill, whose desire for revenge has made it impossible for this younger gunfighter to back out. However, the scene in which Ryan best exemplifies Van Cleef's "stoic hero" persona actually comes before his whole-hearted transition to that type of character. Early in the film, Ryan visits the graves of Bill's family. He appears weary of life and thoughtful of death as he talks with Bill and offers his condolences. Ryan rides off and reverts back to his greedy revenge-seeking, but the scene foreshadows what Ryan becomes by the end of the film.

The Desperado

1954, black and white, 79 minutes,
Allied Artists (Western)

Cast: Wayne Morris (Sam Garrett), James Lydon (Tom Cameron), Beverly Garland (Lauren Bannerman), Rayford Barnes (Ray Novack), Dabbs Greer (Jim Langley), Lee Van Cleef (Buck and Paul Creyton), Nestor Paiva (Capt. Thornton), Roy Barcroft (Martin Novack), John Dierkes (Sgt. Rafferty), Richard Shackleton (Pat Garner), I. Stanford Jolley (Mr. Garner), Charles [Richard] Garland (Trooper), Florence Lake (Mrs. Cameron)

Director: Thomas Carr

Synopsis: During the 1870s, carpetbaggers control Texas with "Bluebellies," their state policemen. Tom Cameron (James Lydon) and Ray Novack (Rayford Barnes) are amongst the many Texans who hate the carpetbaggers' oppressive rule. After assaulting two Bluebellies, Tom and Ray flee from town and join up with another fugitive, Sam Garrett (Wayne Morris). The trio does not last for long, though; Ray leaves the group on unfriendly terms. Ray then kills two Bluebellies and blames the murders on Tom. When Tom is eventually caught, he is tried for the murders. Sam arrives at the trial and frees Tom by proving that Ray is the actual culprit.

Comment: The beginning of the movie, with the historical background offered to the audience, promises more than the film delivers. It quickly becomes just another bad guys versus good guys movie, with no real effort to stay within the historical boundaries presented. Most of the portrayals are adequate, but the Sam Garrett character (played by Wayne Morris) is not really believable as a hardened gunfighter on the run.

Van Cleef's Role: For the first time in his career, Van Cleef had a dual film role when he played twin brothers for *The Desperado*. (In 1977, Van Cleef again appeared as two twin brothers in *God's Gun*.) Van Cleef first appears in *The Desperado* as Paul Creyton, one of Sam's outlaw acquaintances. Paul doesn't have a horse, but he wants to ride with Sam and Tom. Tom lets Paul ride his horse, but is forced to kill the outlaw when Paul tries to steal the animal. Van Cleef is seen later in the film as Buck Creyton, Paul's twin brother and gunfighting superior. The film takes an opportunity to draw attention to Van Cleef's unique face. When looking for his brother, Buck meets Tom and tells him that he could not have mistaken Paul, because "he looks exactly like me." After Buck learns of his brother's death and of Tom's involvement, he sets out to avenge the killing. Buck faces off with him, but Tom survives by killing this second Creyton. (Van Cleef has often played a villain whose relative was killed by the film's hero, but in this case, Van Cleef plays both parts.) It is of passing interest that Lee Van Cleef does not share a single scene with *Desperado* co-star Beverly Garland, who provided female companionship for several Van Cleef characters of subsequent film and TV productions.

El Condor

1970, color, 102 minutes,
National General (Western)

Cast: Lee Van Cleef (Jaroo), Jim Brown (Luke), Patrick O'Neal (General Chavez), Marianna Hill (Claudine), Iron Eyes Cody (Santana), Imogen Hassall (Dolores), Elisha Cook, Jr. (Old Convict), Gustavo Rojo (Col. Aguinaldo), Florencio Amarilla (Aguila), Julio Pena (Gen. Hernandez), Angel Del Pozo (Lieutenant), Patricio Santiago (Julio), John Clark (Prison Guard Captain), Raul Medoza Castro (Indian), Rafael Albaicin (Officer), George Ross (Guard), Ricardo Palacios (Chief Bandit), Charles Stalnaker, Carlos Bravo, Dan Van Husen, Peter Lenahan, Art Larkin, Per Barclay

Director: John Guillermin

Synopsis: A thief named Luke (Jim Brown) plans to capture a Mexican desert fortress which is known to contain a fortune in gold. He enlists the help of Jaroo (Lee Van Cleef), an opportunist who is friendly with the Apache Indians. When Luke, Jaroo and an army of Apaches seize the fort, the commanding officer, Gen. Chavez (Patrick O'Neal), flees into the desert, but his lover Claudine (Marianna Hill) stays behind with Luke. Luke and Jaroo divide the gold evenly and keep the Apaches ignorant of its existence; when the Apache chief (Iron Eyes Cody) accidentally stumbles upon the gold's hiding place, Jaroo kills him. With their chief dead, the Apaches desert the fort. When Chavez returns with an army, Luke worries that he and Jaroo will not be able to defend the gold without the Indians' help. Chavez, however, has come only to reclaim Claudine, and he reveals that the gold is actually plated lead; the real fortune was looted years earlier. Luke kills Chavez in their duel for Claudine. When Jaroo learns about the bogus fortune, he becomes enraged that he risked his life and ruined his relationship with the Apaches for plated lead. Jaroo faces off with Luke and is shot dead.

Comment: An American Western that imitates the style of Eurowesterns (it was even filmed in Spain), *El Condor* features a story that promises to be a light buddy yarn. But the film's apparent thirst for blood is not satisfied with such a mild tone; not only do the protagonists kill off their adversaries, but the buddy feelings fade as they wind up trying to kill each other. Killings can be counted in the scores, and gratuitous nudity is included on slim pretext, possibly hoping to attract moviegoers outside the normal crowd of Western fans.

Van Cleef's Role: In *El Condor*'s best and most tender scene, Van Cleef's Jaroo takes time to talk to a young boy who idolizes him because of his shooting skills. The boy, who has no father and is constantly called "bastard" by his mother, is encouraged when Jaroo tells him that he also is a bastard. That scene, however, is out of character for Jaroo. During most of the film Jaroo is either vicious (as when he cold-bloodedly shoots his Indian friend when the latter discovers the gold) or pathetic (as when he boasts about the puny gold nugget, which he keeps around his neck as a good luck piece and is, ironically, the only real gold in the fortress). His pathetic side is alternately humorous and sympathy-evoking. Van Cleef also helps make *El Condor*'s ending excellent, as he delivers the last line of dialogue. After Jaroo has been shot by Luke, and before he dies, he falls to his knees and asks himself confusedly, "What am I doing here?"

Escape from New York
1981, color, 99 minutes, AVCO-Embassy

Cast: Kurt Russell (Snake Plissken), Lee Van Cleef (Bob Hauk), Ernest Borgnine (Cabby), Donald Pleasence (The President), Isaac Hayes (Duke of New York), Season Hubley (Girl in Chock Full o' Nuts), Harry

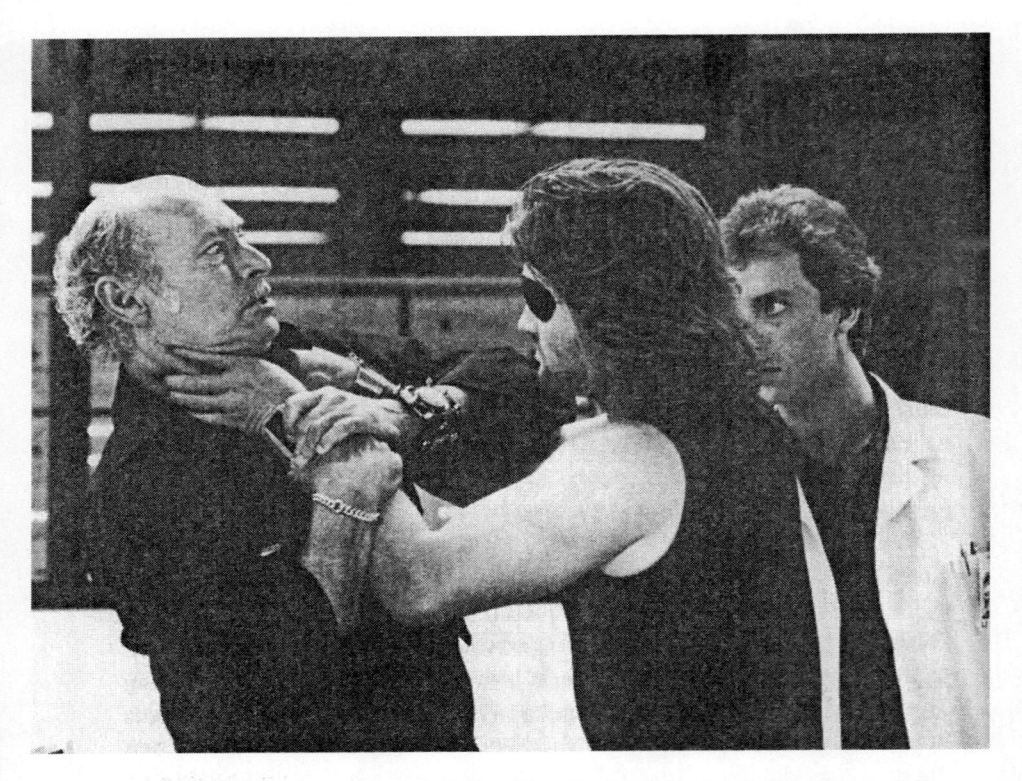

Kurt Russell attempts to strangle Lee Van Cleef as John Strobel look on in John Carpenter's science-fiction film *Escape from New York* (Avco-Embassy, 1981).

Dean Stanton (Brain), Adrienne Barbeau (Maggie), Tom Atkins (Rehme), Charles Cyphers (Secretary of State), Joe Unger (Taylor), Frank Doubleday (Romero), John Strobel (Cronenberg), John Cothran, Jr. (Gypsy #1), Garrett Bergfeld (Gypsy #2), Richard Cosentino (Gypsy Guard), Robert John Metcalf (Gypsy #3), Joel Bennett (Gypsy #4), Vic Bullock (First Indian), Clem Fox (Second Indian), Tobar Mayo (Third Indian), Nancy Stephens (Stewardess), Steven Gagon (Secret Service #1), Steven Ford (Secret Service #2), Michael Taylor (Secret Service #3), Lonnie Wun (Red Bandana Gypsy), Dale House (Helicopter Pilot #1), David R. Patrick (Helicopter Pilot #2), Bob Minor (Duty Sergeant), Wally Taylor (Controller), James O'Hagen (Computer Operator), James Emery (Trooper), Tom Liilard (Police Sergeant), Borah Silver (Theater Manager), Tony Papenfuss (Theater Assistant), John Diehl (Punk), Carmen

Filpi (Bum), Buck Flower (Drunk), Clay Wright (Helicopter Pilot #3), Al Cerullo (Helicopter Pilot #4), Ox Baker (Slag)

Co-Writer/Director: John Carpenter (who also co-scored)

Synopsis: In the near future, when the crime rate in the United States rises 400 percent, Manhattan Island is walled off, and convicted criminals are sent to this, the New York Maximum Security Penitentiary, without chance of parole. A terrorist group hijacks the plane which is carrying the President of the United States (Donald Pleasence) to an urgent peace summit meeting. The terrorists ditch the plane within the walls of the prison, and the President, who survives the crash in a protective pod, is made the property of Manhattan's ruling prisoner, the Duke (Isaac Hayes). Police Commissioner Bob Hauk (Lee Van Cleef) is put in charge of the President rescue effort, and he picks for the mission Snake Plissken (Kurt Russell), a war hero turned bank-robber. Snake is about to begin a life sentence at Manhattan Island, but Hauk offers him a full pardon if he can retrieve the President before the peace talks end. Snake enters the prison and meets a group of prisoners who help him infiltrate the Duke's inner circle, and they grab the President. The Duke and his cronies pursue the fleeing group, killing most of them, but Snake and the President escape the prison. The President immediately begins preparing for his peace talks, and when Snake tries to speak with him, the chief executive doesn't seem to appreciate the sacrifices that some of the prisoners made to bring him out alive. Snake does not let anybody know that he has the President's important cassette tape needed for the summit meeting, and as the President plays the wrong tape — a recording of "American Bandstand" — to world leaders, Snake Plissken destroys the cassette containing the secret to world peace.

Comment: An excellent piece of science-fiction, *Escape* makes a bit of social commentary. By projecting the crime rate of the time into the future, the idea of an entire city turned into a prison became plausible. Kurt Russell plays Snake as a surlier variation of the typical Clint Eastwood film persona. In 1996, 15 years after *New York*'s release, Russell reprised the role for John Carpenter's send-up sequel, *Escape from L.A.*

Van Cleef's Role: Van Cleef plays Bob Hauk, a tough police commissioner. There is a certain appropriateness in Van Cleef playing against Kurt Russell, who plays Snake like a Clint Eastwood–type hero (Van Cleef became a star after complimenting Clint Eastwood in *For a Few Dollars More*). But Russell's Snake has even more contempt for authority than the Eastwood persona, so Van Cleef plays an exceptionally stern, tough authority figure for balance. Bob Hauk is one of the roles that followed the pattern set by Van Cleef's character in the previous year's *The Octagon*. During the 1980s, Van Cleef often played a character whose narrative function was to guide a hero toward his goal.

For a Few Dollars More
1965, color, 130 minutes,
Italian-Spanish-German (Western)

Alternate Titles: *Et pour quelques dollars de plus* (French), *Für ein paar Dollar mehr* (German), *La muerte tenía un precio* (Spanish), *Per qualche dollaro in più* (Italian)

Cast: Clint Eastwood (Monco "The Man with No Name"), Lee Van Cleef (Col. Douglas Mortimer), Gian Maria Volonte (Indio), Jose Egger (Old Man Over Railway), Rosemary Dexter (Colonel's Sister), Mara Krup (Hotel Manager's Wife), Klaus Kinski (Hunchback), Mario Brega (Nino), Luigi Pistilli (Rocky), Aldo Sambrell, Benito Stefanelli, Panos Papadopoulos, Roberto Carmardiel, Luis Rodriguez, Diana Rabito, Giovanni Tarallo, Mario Menniconi, Lorenzo Robledo

Co-Writer/Director: Sergio Leone

Synopsis: Two bounty hunters, Col. Douglas Mortimer (Lee Van Cleef) and Monco (Clint Eastwood), are separately following a gang of bank robbers led by an outlaw named Indio (Gian Maria Volonte). The hunters' paths eventually converge and they decide to work together, with Monco infiltrating Indio's gang under the guise of a bank robber and Mortimer working from the outside. After Indio and his gang rob the El Paso bank — a robbery which boosts the bounty for the gang — Monco and the Colonel prepare for a shoot-out with the outlaws. Indio does not want to share the bank booty with his many gang members, so he deploys his gang, hoping that the bounty hunters and his outlaws will all die in the battle. But Monco and Mortimer are not killed. When Indio is the only member of the gang left standing, Col. Mortimer reveals that his pursuit of the gang leader is personal. Indio realizes that Mortimer is the brother of a woman he raped and killed. Monco watches as Douglas Mortimer shoots his sister's murderer dead. Satisfied with this

As Col. Douglas Mortimer — the character that provided him with his breakthrough opportunity — Van Cleef prepares for a showdown in the 1965 Spaghetti Western *For a Few Dollars More*.

revenge, Mortimer lets Monco have the valuable corpses to exchange for bounty.

Comment: For a Few Dollars More was the second in director Leone's "Dollars Trilogy," in which Clint Eastwood plays the "Man with No Name" (actually given the name "Monco" in this film). It was preceded by *A Fistful of Dollars* and followed by *The Good, the Bad, and the Ugly*. However, this film, set in post–Civil War times, can be considered chronologically as the last of the three, as the succeeding film was set during the Civil War. *For a Few Dollars More* presents a slightly surreal Old West and Ennio Morricone's score contributes to this effect. In Italy, this was the highest grossing of the trilogy.

Van Cleef's Role: With *For a Few Dollars More*, Lee Van Cleef's career was rejuvenated, and his screen image was completely overhauled. From being a supporting actor, usually a bad guy or heavy, Van Cleef was raised to star and hero status, and this film was the beginning of his long string of Spaghetti Westerns. The presence of the Douglas Mortimer character in *For a Few Dollars More* helps tighten up the "Man with No Name" formula; Van Cleef's character gives Eastwood's usually taciturn bounty hunter a business partner with whom to explain plans and motivations. Besides serving a narrative function, Mortimer is a nice compliment to Eastwood's character. Mortimer's carefully thought-out methods and fancy equipment are an interesting contrast to Monco's more crude, physical approach to bounty hunting. This contrast is evident in the early scenes that introduce the protagonists. Mortimer flushes a wanted man out from his hotel room to the street, where the Colonel uses a gun from his horse-carried arsenal to down the man. For Monco's bounty, a man is just beaten and shot. Also, Douglas Mortimer serves as a nice compliment to the mysterious "Man with No Name" because Mortimer is presented with a past. It is revealed that he was a Confederate Colonel from the Carolinas during the Civil War. Through flashbacks, scenes of the Colonel's sister are shown. (Interestingly, though, only Monco talks about his future: "When I get my hands on Indio... I'm gonna buy myself a little place, possibly retire.") But Van Cleef's Mortimer is no less exciting than Eastwood's character. Van Cleef played the Mortimer role with a steely-eyed confidence that was to become a trademark for many of his later roles.

God's Gun

1977, color, 93 minutes, Italian-Israeli (Western)

Alternate Title: *A Bullet from God* (home video); *Les impitoyables* (French); *Pistola di Dio* (Italian)

Cast: Lee Van Cleef (Father John and Lewis), Jack Palance (Sam Clayton), Leif Garrett (Johnny), Sybil Danning (Jenny), Richard Boone (Sheriff), Zila Carni (Juanita), Heinz Bernard (Judge Barrett), Didi Lukov (Rip), Ricardo David (Angel George), Chin Chin (Willy), Rafi Ben Ami (Mortimer), Robert Lipton, Cody Palance, Pnina Golan

Director: Frank Kramer [Gianfranco Parolini]

Synopsis: In Juno City, a youngster named Johnny (Leif Garrett) is befriended by Father John (Lee Van Cleef), the town's preacher. But when an outlaw gang invades Juno City, Father John is murdered by the gang leader, Sam Clayton (Jack Palance). Johnny travels to Mexico, where he locates Father John's identical twin brother, Lewis (also Van Cleef). Lewis gave up gunfighting at the request of his holy brother, but when Johnny relays the news of Father John's murder, Lewis decides to break his oath. The two return to Juno City to annihilate the gang. But Johnny learns that Sam Clayton is his father; Sam sired the boy years ago when he raped Johnny's mother, Jenny (Sybil Danning). Sam unearths a secret stash of loot, and he asks Johnny and Jenny to begin a family life with him. When Lewis meets Sam, he decides not to kill him. The appreciative outlaw reaches into a money bag to reward the gunfighter, but Lewis mistakenly thinks that Sam is reaching for a gun, and he shoots Johnny's father dead.

Comment: With its identical-twin premise, garish town sets and a drunken-like performance from Jack Palance, *God's Gun* can be appreciated for little other than its camp value. Surprisingly, the climactic showdown between Lewis (Van Cleef) and Sam Clayton (Palance) is rather memorable, and it apparently was one of two different endings that were filmed. It seems that an alternate, unused ending has Palance's Sam Clayton actually pulling out a gun from his money bag before being shot dead by Lewis. But the ending that actually appears in *God's Gun* contains — perhaps inadvertently or in hopes that audiences will not notice — a bit of this alternate resolution. In a brief shot that occurs after Lewis shoots Sam, the outlaw is seen holding the wad of money that conceals his derringer, rather than the gunless wad of cash that he is holding immediately afterwards and with which he is meant to be seen. *God's Gun*, a late Spaghetti Western filmed in Israel, contains an excellent musical score by Santa Marie Romitelli which hearkens back to the heyday of the Spaghettis.

Van Cleef's Role: Van Cleef, who played dual roles before in 1954's *The Desperado*, repeats the feat for *God's Gun*, playing both Father John and Lewis. Van Cleef, who admirably brought conviction to even his worst characters, doesn't seem to have his heart in these two roles, though. But all of this performance probably should not be credited to Van Cleef; it seems that the actor's lines were dubbed over with a different, albeit close-matching voice (Richard Boone's lines also seem to have been dubbed). Van Cleef's appearance in the film is another distraction. His neatly trimmed beard clashes with his horribly bushy shoulder length wig. *God's Gun* marked the reunion of Van Cleef with Frank Kramer, who directed the actor in *Sabata* (1969) and *The Return of Sabata* (1971 or 1972). It is one of Van Cleef's two last Westerns; the other, *Kid Vengeance*, was also filmed with former teen idol Leif Garrett in Israel.

The Good, the Bad, and the Ugly
1966, color, 162 minutes, Italian (Western)

Alternate Titles: *El bueno, el feo y el malo* (Spanish), *Il buono, il brutto, il cattivo* (Italian), *Le bon, la brute, le truand* (French), *Two Magnificent Rogues* (unused translation of German title); *Zwei glorreiche Halunken* (German).

Cast: Clint Eastwood ("Blondie"—"The Man with No Name"), Lee Van Cleef (Setenza "Angel Eyes"), Eli Wallach (Tuco Ramirez), Mario Brega (Sgt. Wallace), Aldo Giuffre (Northern Officer), Luigi Pistilli (Padre Pablo Ramirez), Al Mulloch [Mulock] (Tuco's Pursuer), Rada Rassimov, Claudio Scarchilli, Enzo Petito, John Bartho, Livio Lorenzon, Antonio Casas, Aldo Sambrell, Sergio Mendizabal, Molino Rocho, Lorenzo Robledo, Chelo Alonso, Silvana Bacci

Co-Writer/Director: Sergio Leone

Synopsis: In the American Southwest during the time of the Civil War, a paid killer named Setenza (Lee Van Cleef) learns about a missing army cash box—containing $200,000 in gold coins—from the man he was hired to kill. Setenza also learns the name of the man who disappeared with the army cash box: Bill Carson. Elsewhere, a gunslinger named "Blondie" (Clint Eastwood) deserts his partner-in-crime Tuco (Eli Wallach), and Tuco later exacts revenge by catching Blondie and trying to march him to death through a scorching desert. They come upon Bill Carson, who is dying in the desert, and he reveals that his $200,000 gold fortune is buried in a cemetery. But only Tuco hears the name of the cemetery, and only Blondie hears which grave contains the gold. Forced to work together again, Tuco and Blondie head towards the gold and cross paths with Setenza. The three men arrive at the cemetery and compete in a three-way gun duel for the loot. Setenza is gunned down. Blondie, who gets the drop on Tuco, takes half of the gold and forces his partner to stand on a grave marker with a noose around his neck.

As he rides off, Blondie stops and shoots the rope, freeing Tuco and leaving him with bags full of gold.

Comment: This was the third and last of Sergio Leone's immensely popular "Dollars" trilogy of Spaghetti Westerns. In a way, it may be considered as a "prequel" to the other two films, as it takes place in an earlier time period, that of the American Civil War. Also, Clint Eastwood's "Man with No Name" character is not seen in *The Good, the Bad, and the Ugly* wearing the trademark serape which he wears throughout the other two films (until he acquires it near the film's conclusion). A Spaghetti Western with unusually high production values (the film's budget of over $1,000,000 was more than was spent on the first two "Dollars" films put together), *The Good, the Bad, and the Ugly* is an excellent but sprawling and overlong picture. It has remained popular for decades after its release, but even so, the popularity of the film's catchy title and memorable score — by Ennio Morricone — may well outlast that of the film itself.

Van Cleef's Role: Van Cleef is at his most villainous as "The Bad" of this film; Setenza (known better in the film as "Angel Eyes") is the role for which he is perhaps best remembered. His introduction in the film is as a paid killer who takes pride in always finishing his jobs. Hired for $500, Setenza tracks down a farmer, who offers him $1,000. After murdering the farmer, he takes the money, goes back and also murders his employer. Later, Setenza is seen as a Union army sergeant (the scene showing his transition from hired killer to soldier was cut from the American version) at a prison camp, where he is robbing the Confederate soldiers. It is at the prison that Setenza comes across Tuco and Blondie, who have been caught by Union troops while wearing the uniforms of dead Confederate soldiers. Setenza invites Tuco into one of the prison's cabins for dinner and asks if he would like music with his meal. "Music? Yes," Tuco says, "Very good for the digestion," not knowing that Setenza is forcing the nearby Confederate prison band to play so as to cover the screams that will result from his impending torture session. "Angel Eyes" watches as Tuco is brutally beaten and interrogated about the gold's whereabouts. After his character watches blood drip from Tuco's face and mouth, Van Cleef brilliantly delivers a line with utter coldness: "How's your digestion now?" Van Cleef does not play this part as a greedy bully, but as an intelligent, almost impassive man who goes into the final shootout without fear. The actor played many villains during his career, but the Setenza "Angel Eyes" character is in a class of its own.

Van Cleef in *The Good, the Bad, and the Ugly* (1966).

The Grand Duel

1972, color, 92 minutes,
Italian-German-French (Western)

Alternate Titles: *Big Showdown*, *Drei Vaterunser für vier Halunken* (German), *El gran duelo* (Spanish), *Hell's Fighters* (British), *Il grande duello* (Italian), *Le grand duel* (French), *Stormrider* (home video)

Cast: Lee Van Cleef (Clayton), Peter O'Brien (Philip Premeire), Marc Mazza (Eli Saxon), Jess Hahn (Big Horse), Horst Frank, Klaus Grunberg, Antony Vernon, Dominique Darel, Sandra Sardini, Gastone Pescucci, Elvira Cortese, Anna Maria Gherardi, Hans Terofal, Salvatore Baccaro, Ray O'Connor, Meme Perlini, Giancarlo Badessi, Luigi Antonio Guerra, Maria Teresa Piaggio, Franco Balducci, Giovanni Filidoro,

Giovanni Cianeriglia, Angelo Susani, Gianni De Segni, Clemente Cipriano, Mimmo Rizzo, Giorgio Testrini, Furio Meniconi
Director: Giancarlo Santi

Synopsis: The Saxons, three politically-motivated brothers, wrongly blame Philip Premeire (Peter O'Brien) for killing their father, Saxon City's "Patriarch." They chase Philip out of Saxon City and prevent him from becoming one of the town's leaders. Philip is later chased by Saxon-hired bounty hunters but receives help from Clayton (Lee Van Cleef), a former sheriff who knows the identity of the Patriarch's real murderer. When Philip is captured by the Saxons and faces a hanging, Clayton rescues him from the gallows and reveals that he, as sheriff, lawfully executed the villainous Patriarch. Clayton, who realizes that the three Saxons are as evil as their father was, shoots all three brothers dead in a grand duel.

Comment: The Grand Duel has a subtly surreal, often dusky quality, and the film manages to be exciting, despite what appears to have been a shoestring budget (historical purists may be offended that the film tries to pass off a World War II German machine gun as being accurate for the time period). The superb direction and Sergio Bardotti's excellent score help to create some stirring moments, most notably the climactic gallows scene. But *The Grand Duel*'s far-fetched acrobatic-type stunts seem out of place in this otherwise serious Spaghetti Western. They are possibly evidence of the influence of Spaghetti director Frank Kramer, who put acrobatics in many of his films (such as *Sabata* with Van Cleef). *The Grand Duel* has undergone many significant changes in making the jumps to its home video versions. Different versions of the film, including the gore and nudity-containing unedited version, have been released on video as *Stormrider*. One *Stormrider* version contains added synthesized music which even overlaps the original score in places. Like his mentor Sergio Leone, director Giancarlo Santi seemed to like extreme facial close-ups; *Grand Duel* theater audiences might have grown tired of seeing the screen filled entirely with an actor's two eyes. However, home video viewers, watching the film on a different shaped screen, will not run that risk; to handle these close-ups, some video versions show little more than the bridges of the actors' noses, and others pan quickly from one eye to the other.

Van Cleef's Role: Van Cleef's Clayton at first appears to be a bounty hunter chasing wrongly-accused fugitive Philip Premeire. Soon after catching Philip, though, Clayton reveals that he only intends to protect the framed man from the Saxons and their trigger-happy hired guns and bounty hunters. Later, Philip learns that Clayton was once a sheriff and that he lost his star when he accused the Saxons of bribing the judge who condemned Philip. The situation is resolved when Clayton kills the evil Saxon brothers. Unlike some of Van Cleef's other roles (*The Big Gundown*, *Death Rides a Horse* and *Beyond the Law*), Clayton does not transform to a stoic hero during the course of the film; he is this type of character throughout the film. From his first scene, in which he says, "I'm thirsty" and calmly walks through a contingent of bounty hunters to get to a cantina, to the last scene, in which he faces down the three brothers, Clayton is world-weary, unconcerned about personal danger. It can be assumed that the Clayton featured in *The Grand Duel* became as he is—weary, hardened—because of the loss of his sheriff's star prior to the beginning of the film. He could not have possessed these qualities while serving as sheriff; the Clayton of the film is too apathetic to want to be sheriff. Clayton is involved only to see that innocent Philip doesn't hang for Clayton's actions as sheriff, when he was a markedly different man. Van Cleef is superb in this role, aided by sharp dialogue (and overcoming the occasional hokey lines).

Gun Battle at Monterey

1957, black and white, 67 minutes
Allied Artists (Western)

Alternate Title: *Gun Battle of Monterey*

Cast: Sterling Hayden (Turner), Pamela Duncan (Maria), Ted De Corsia (Reno), Mary Beth Hughes (Cleo), Lee Van Cleef (Kirby), Charles Cane (Mundy), Pat Comiskey (Frank), Byron Foulger (Carson), Mauritz Hugo (Charley), I. Stanford Jolley (Idwall)

Directors: Carl K. Hittleman (who also produced) and Sidney A. Franklin, Jr.

Synopsis: During a bank robbery, outlaw Turner (Sterling Hayden) is shot in the back by his partner Reno (Ted De Corsia). After a woman named Maria (Pamela Duncan) helps Turner to recover, he sets out to kill Reno.

Van Cleef's Role: Van Cleef, who appears as a character named Kirby in this film, had previously been in another Hayden-starring oater, *Arrow in the Dust.*

Gunfight at the O.K. Corral
1957, color, 122 minutes, Paramount (Western)

Cast: Burt Lancaster (Wyatt Earp), Kirk Douglas (John "Doc" Holliday), Rhonda Fleming (Laura Denbow), Jo Van Fleet (Kate Fisher), John Ireland (Johnny Ringo), Earl Holliman (Charlie Bassett), DeForest Kelley (Morgan Earp), Lyle Bettger (Ike Clanton), Lee Van Cleef (Ed Bailey), Dennis Hopper (Billy Clanton), Jack Elam (Tom McLowery)

Director: John Sturges

Synopsis: Marshal Wyatt Earp (Burt Lancaster) develops a friendship in Dodge City with a gambler named Doc Holliday (Kirk Douglas). Holliday accompanies his friend when Wyatt moves to Tombstone. In Tombstone, the marshal helps his lawmen brothers put an end to the cattle rustling schemes of Ike Clanton (Lyle Bettger). When Clanton's gang murders one of Wyatt's brother's, Doc Holliday joins the remaining members of the Earp clan for a showdown with the Clanton bunch at the O.K. Corral. Wyatt and Doc survive the bloody gunfight but part ways.

Comment: Generally considered one of the finest Westerns ever made, this recounting of the events surrounding this historical event is actually rather tedious at times, but there are enough face-offs, showdowns and shoot-outs to generate an adequate amount of tension. All of the acting is excellent, and Kirk Douglas as Doc Holliday gives the film's standout performance. The subplot about Holliday and Johnny Ringo (John Ireland) fighting for possession of Kate Fisher (Jo Van Fleet) is the most engaging part of the story. The Frankie Laine–sung title song is memorable.

Van Cleef's Role: Van Cleef plays Ed Bailey, a man who wants to avenge his dead brother and tries to shoot his brother's killer, Doc Holliday, at the beginning of the film. The death of Ed's brother is not shown, but characters mention that Holliday was justified in killing the brother, who was drunk and cheating at cards. Even if the brother had not been described, it may be assumed that the dead Bailey was of bad disposition, as we have the example of Van Cleef's Ed Bailey. Ed Bailey storms into a saloon where he is to meet Holliday, then sits drinking, becoming more pugnacious with time. Several good shots of him appear in the reflection in the bar mirror after Holliday enters the saloon. Holliday throws a knife which pierces Bailey's chest and kills him. Van Cleef played this villainous "avenging kin" type of character many times during the 1950s.

Guns, Girls and Gangsters
1959, black and white, 70 minutes, United Artists

Cast: Mamie Van Doren (Vi Victor), Gerald Mohr (Chuck Wheeler), Lee Van Cleef (Mike Bennett), Grant Richards (Joe Darren), Elaine Edwards (Ann Thomas), John Baer (Steve Thomas), Carlo Fiore (Tom Abbott), Paul Fix (Lou Largo), W. Beal Wong (Mr. Wong)

Director: Edward L. Cahn

Synopsis: While gangster Mike Bennett (Lee Van Cleef) is incarcerated, his unfaithful wife Vi Victor (Mamie Van Doren) becomes involved with other criminals and a scheme to rob an armored car. Bennett escapes from prison and reclaims his wife.

Van Cleef's Role: Apparently Van Cleef has a substantial part in *Guns, Girls and Gangsters*, as gangster Mike Bennett. It also seems as though this character is somewhat of the protagonist, a role that Van Cleef rarely played in 1950s productions.

Gypsy Colt
1954, color, 72 minutes, Metro-Goldwyn-Mayer

Cast: Donna Corcoran (Meg MacWade), Ward Bond (Frank MacWade), Frances Dee (Em MacWade), Lee Van Cleef (Hank), Larry Keating (Wade Y. Gerald), Bobby Hyatt (Phil Gerald), Nacho Galindo (Pancho), Rodolfo Hoyos, Jr. (Rodolfo), Bobby Dominguez (Pedro), Joe Dominguez (Tony), Jester Hairston (Carl), Peggy Maley (Pat)

Director: Andrew Marton

Synopsis: When a drought hits the MacWade farm, the family needs money and is forced to sell their beloved horse Gypsy to race horse owner Wade Gerald (Larry Keating). Gerald is a kind man, but the trainer he employs, Hank (Lee Van Cleef), is rough and ill-tempered. Gypsy twice escapes from Hank and returns home to the MacWade family, but on both occasions, the saddened MacWades return the horse to Gerald. Hank and Gerald take Gypsy 500 miles away for a horse race, but the homesick horse again escapes Hank's abusive treatment, making an arduous journey across a desert and finding its way home. This time, Gerald allows the MacWades to keep Gypsy, and he is not worried about settling monetary matters until the drought passes and the family again has success with farming. Just then it begins to rain.

Comment: A pleasant, well-acted family film, *Gypsy Colt* is essentially a remake of 1943's *Lassie Come Home*, with the obvious change from a canine to an equestrian homeward-bound pet. The film's best scene has Gypsy outrunning a pursuing motorcycle gang that is hoping to catch and make a profit on the thoroughbred horse.

Van Cleef's Role: Van Cleef's Hank is the trainer whose mean-spirited horse handling prompts Gypsy to flee Gerald's ranch. At the film's end, Hank complains when his boss decides to leave Gypsy with the MacWades, and Gerald fires his unsympathetic employee. Van Cleef does well at making the overly-ambitious, success-oriented Hank look foolish when sharing scenes with the easygoing older characters played by Ward Bond and Larry Keating.

High Noon

1952, black and white, 85 minutes
United Artists (Western)

Cast: Gary Cooper (Will Kane), Grace Kelly (Amy Kane), Thomas Mitchell (Jonas Henderson), Lloyd Bridges (Harvey Pell), Katy Jurado (Helen Ramirez), Otto Kruger (Percy Mettrick), Lon Chaney, Jr. (Martin Howe), Henry Morgan (William Fuller), Ian McDonald (Frank Miller), Eve McVeagh (Mildred Fuller), Harry Shannon (Cooper), Lee Van Cleef (Jack Colby), Robert Wilke (James Pierce), Sheb Wooley (Ben

Miller), Tom London (Sam), Ted Stanhope (Station Master), Larry J. Blake (Gillis), William "Bill" Phillips (Barber), Jeanne Blackford (Mrs. Henderson), James Millican (Baker), Cliff Clark (Weaver), Ralph Reed (Johnny), William Newell (Drunk), Lucien Prival (Bartender), Guy Beach (Fred), Howland Chamberlin (Hotel Clerk), Morgan Farley (Minister), Virginia Christine (Mrs. Simpson), Paul Dubov (Scott), Jack Elam (Charlie), Harry Harvey (Coy), Tim Graham (Sawyer), Nolan Leary (Lewis), Tom Greenway (Ezra), Dick Elliot (Kibbee), John Doucette (Trumball).

Director: Fred Zinnemann

Synopsis: Marshal Will Kane (Gary Cooper) marries a Quaker woman named Amy (Grace Kelly) on a Sunday morning in Hadleyville. He gives up his star — leaving the town in need of a replacement lawman — at the request of his peace-loving bride. But before they can leave on their honeymoon, Kane learns that an outlaw named Frank Miller (Ian McDonald) will be arriving in Hadleyville on the noon train. Miller had been caught by Kane, tried, sentenced to death and then pardoned. With Miller looking for revenge and on his way to town, Kane resumes his lawman duties, causing his disappointed wife to abandon him. Kane knows that three outlaws are waiting at the Hadleyville train depot to help the coming Miller, and so the marshal tries to recruit some temporary deputies for assistance in confronting Miller. Most all of the townsfolk are grateful for the fine service that Kane has given Hadleyville over the years, but few are eager to help the lawman, and some think the situation will be calmed if Kane leaves town. Kane is left to face Miller and his three henchmen alone. The noon train comes, and a gunfight ensues. The marshal receives some last-minute help from his new wife, and he kills the four badmen. Silently, he drops his star into the dirt of the street and rides off with his wife.

Comment: *High Noon* ushered in the popularity of a new type of Western, called the "thinking" or "adult" Western. There had been adult Westerns before, but *High Noon* caught the attention of audiences in a new way because of the interpersonal relationships of the characters and the internal struggles of its hero. The film won several Academy Awards. Gary Cooper won an Oscar for his performance as Will Kane, one of the cinema's most memorable martyrs. The film also includes several fine performances by then-rising stars whose characters are involved in the film's subplots. Lloyd Bridges plays Kane's deputy who refuses to help because he was not chosen as the marshal's successor. Katy Jurado plays one of Kane's old flames who talks with Amy Kane after she leaves her new husband. Of interest is the fact that the movie takes place in "real time" (the time elapsed during the film's story is about the same as the length of the film). The fine musical score by Dmitri Tiomkin and the song based on it, "Do Not Forsake Me, Oh My Darlin'" (sung by Tex Ritter) have become classics. The musical theme is repeated in many ways during the film.

Van Cleef's Role: Van Cleef made his film debut in *High Noon*. He is, in fact, the first character to be seen in the film, waiting during the opening credits for his two outlaw pals to join him. He rides into town with them, and when Miller arrives with the train, the four go after Marshal Kane. His character, Jack Colby, is the second of the four badmen to be killed. His is not a large part, and Jack Colby doesn't utter a single line of dialogue in the film. The character does, however, emit sound; at the train station, Jack Colby plays the harmonica, and Colby's song is one of the many recurrences of the film's musical theme. It is his facial expressions and eye movements, though, that really convey what is needed to be known about his sinister character. Van Cleef also used this technique of letting his face and eyes project his character to good advantage in many later films.

How the West Was Won

1962, color, 155 minutes
Metro-Goldwyn-Mayer/Cinerama (Western)

Cast: James Stewart (Linus Rawlings), George Peppard (Zeb Rawlings), Debbie Reynolds (Lilith Prescott), Carroll Baker (Eve Prescott), Henry Fonda (Jethro Stuart), Gregory Peck (Cleve Van Valen), Richard Widmark (Mike King), Walter Brennan (Col. Hawkins), Eli Wallach (Charlie Gant), Lee J. Cobb (Lou Ramsey), Karl Malden (Zebulon Prescott), John Wayne (Gen. William T. Sherman), Harry Morgan (Gen. Ulysses S. Grant), Andy Devine (Scotsman), Lee Van Cleef (Marty), Agnes Moorehead (Rebecca Prescott), Carolyn Jones (Julie Rawlings), Robert Preston (Robert Morgan), Brigid Bazlen (Dora Hawkins).

Directors: Henry Hathaway, John Ford, George Marshall and Richard Thorpe (uncredited)

Synopsis: The Prescott family builds a raft and heads west down a river to find a new life and new land to farm. Their raft is wrecked in the rapids, and the mother and father die. One of the daughters, Eve (Carroll Baker), vows never to move from the spot where her parents are buried, and she settles down to farm with a mountain man named Linus Rawlings (James Stewart). The other daughter, Lilith (Debbie Reynolds), heads farther west with a wagon train and eventually marries a riverboat gambler named Cleve Van Valen (Gregory Peck). The Civil War intervenes, and Zeb Rawlings (George Peppard), son of Linus and Eve, goes off to war. Surviving the war, he returns home to learn that both of his parents have died, and then he heads west again with the army. He encounters Indians, buffalo, buffalo hunters and the transcontinental railroad. Later, as a lawman, he has one last adventure when he fights an outlaw gang. In a more placid west, Zeb finally settles down with a family of his own, and he is joined by his widowed aunt Lilith, the only living member of his family's original westward journey. The west has been won.

Comment: This was the first film to be shown using the Cinerama process, a simultaneous three-projector, wide-screen projection method. This method produced a great deal of excitement with the action scenes, as it gave an almost three-dimensional effect. The scenes of the raft shooting the rapids, the stampede of the buffalo, logs breaking loose from the railroad cars and the train derailment are particularly memorable. The story depicted three generations of a family heading west, covering their history over six decades. The narration by Spencer Tracy helped smooth the transitions from one period to the next. From the early push into the midwest, through the Civil War, across the plains, the family ends up in a civilized west where law and order prevail. An interesting ending, bringing the audience abruptly up-to-date, is provided by the final scene. A westward-moving rapid aerial view of the plains and mountains suddenly gives way to views of the densely-populated present-day California coast, with its expressway system and traffic snarls. It is a decided contrast with the sparsely-settled west of the film, and is considered inappropriate by some. Some versions of the film did not include this ending.

Van Cleef's Role: Although this is Van Cleef's last film role before his three-year film dry spell, his inclusion in *How the West Was Won* (which boasts an all-star Western cast) speaks to his status as a Western veteran. His character, a pirate named Marty, has only a few lines and a short time on screen. Marty is killed by Linus Rawlings (Jimmy Stewart) when the pirate and his family are in the process of robbing the Prescotts and other settlers.

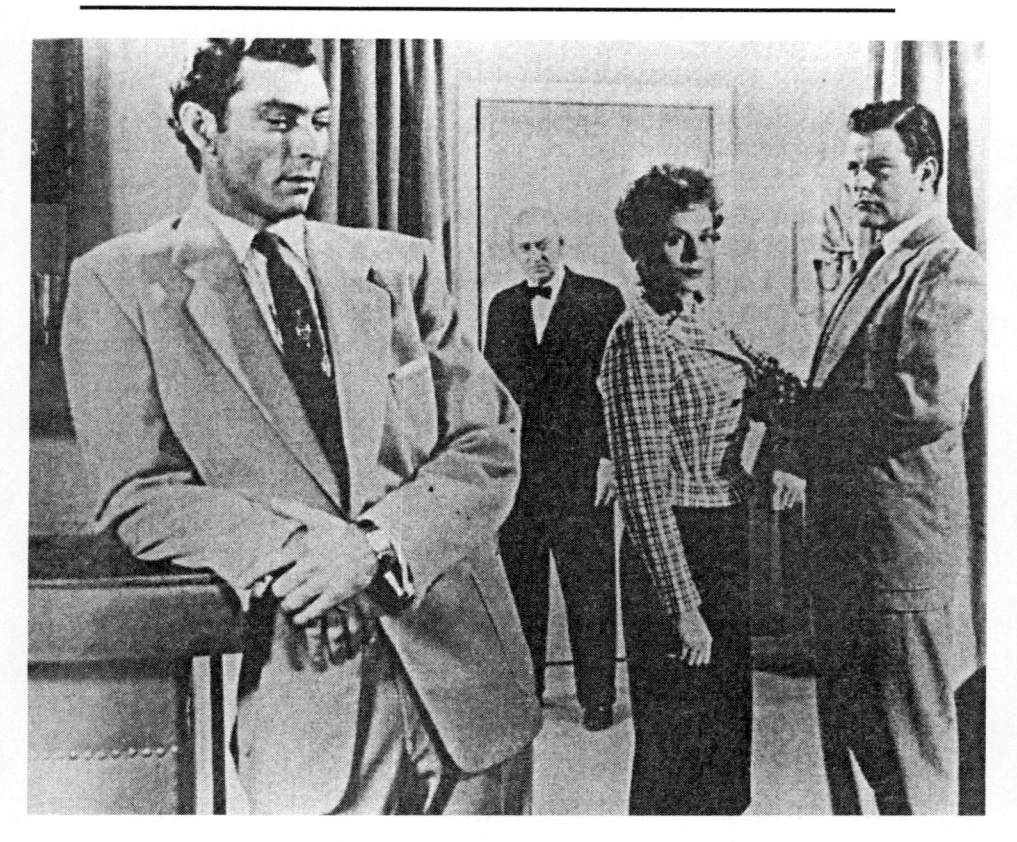

A young Van Cleef (left) in Republic's 1955 crime film *I Cover the Underworld*, with (left–right) Harry Tyler, Jaclynne Greene, and Sean McClory.

I Cover the Underworld
1955, black and white, 70 minutes, Republic

Cast: Sean McClory (John O'Hara and Gunner O'Hara), Joanne Jordan (Joan Marlowe), Ray Middleton (Police Chief), Jaclynne Green

(Gilda), Lee Van Cleef (Flash Logan), James Griffith (Smiley Di Angelo), Hugh Sanders (Tim Donovan), Roy Roberts (District Attorney), Peter Mamakos (Charlie Green), Robert Crosson (Danny Marlowe), Frank Gerstle (Dum-Dum Wilson), Willis Bouchey (Warden Lewis L. Johnson), Philip Van Zandt (Jake Freeman)

Director: R.G. Springsteen

Synopsis: Divinity student John O'Hara (Sean McClory) convinces the city police chief (Ray Middleton) to delay the parole of his gangster brother, Gunner O'Hara (also Sean McClory). Then, by impersonating his criminal sibling, John infiltrates his brother's gang in hopes of having the whole bunch incarcerated. He begins a romance with a nightclub performer named Joan Marlowe (Joanne Jordan), but it is Gunner's girlfriend, Gilda (Jaclynne Greene) who helps John acquire the evidence he needs. Just before he succeeds, his brother Gunner escapes from prison, but before he can expose John's plan, one of the gangsters accidentally kills Gunner. After a shootout with the police, the gangsters are jailed, and John is forced to end his relationship with Joan when he returns to divinity school.

Van Cleef's Role: In *I Cover the Underworld*, Van Cleef plays a character named Flash Logan. His other crime film of 1955 was *The Big Combo*.

It Conquered the World

1956, black and white, 68 minutes,
American International

Cast: Peter Graves (Paul Nelson), Beverly Garland (Claire Anderson), Lee Van Cleef (Tom Anderson), Sally Fraser (Joan Nelson), Charles B. Griffith (Pete Shelton), Russ Bender (Gen. Patrick), Jonathan Haze (Priv. Manuel Ortiz), Richard [Dick] Miller (Sgt. Neil), Karen Kadler (Ellen Peters), Paul Blaisdell (Visitor from Venus)

Producer/Director: Roger Corman

Synopsis: One of the world's most brilliant scientists, Tom Anderson (Lee Van Cleef), uses his radio equipment to communicate with a life form on Venus. Convinced that it is a benevolent creature, Tom makes arrangements for the creature to visit his hometown, Beechwood,

This publicity shot for Roger Corman's *It Conquered the World* (AIP, 1956) shows Van Cleef, as the film's hero, posing with the conquering alien. This feature provided Van Cleef with his first starring role.

and agrees to help the visitor with its plans to improve life on Earth. When the alien arrives, it uses mind-control devices to master some of Beechwood's key citizens, and it disables the town's power generators. Believing that the alien's methods will eventually yield good, Tom continues to assist the Venutian, despite pleas from his wife Claire (Beverly Garland) and from fellow scientist Paul Nelson (Peter Graves). When the alien kills Claire, Tom realizes that he has been duped, and he sacrifices his own life to rid Earth of the invader.

Comment: Critics of the time pointed out that it probably would have been better to have had the alien's presence an implied one, without actually showing it. Certainly the appearance of the monster, created and played by Paul Blaisdell, did nothing to improve the film. It looked like a giant squash with lobster claws, antennae and large pointed teeth.

Van Cleef's Role: Van Cleef's first starring role was in *It Conquered the World*. His Tom Anderson is portrayed in believable fashion as a scientist misled by his desire to see mankind's lot improved. Later, he is torn between continuing with his original ideas or accepting the fact that he has been deluded. Van Cleef appeared with actress Beverly Garland, his screen wife in this film, in another 1956 production, the "Measure of Faith" episode of TV's *Ford Theatre*.

Jack Slade

1953, black and white, 89 minutes
Allied Artists (Western)

Alternate Title: *Slade* (British)

Cast: Mark Stevens (Jack Slade), Dorothy Malone (Virginia Dale), Barton MacLane (Jules Reni), John Litel (Judge), Paul Langton (Dan Traver), Harry Shannon (Tom Carter), John Harmon (Hollis), Jim Bannon (Farnsworth), Lee Van Cleef (Toby MacKay), Sammy Ogg (Joey Slade), Nelson Leigh (Alf Slade), Ron Hargrave (Ned Prentice), David May (Tump), John Halloran, Richard Reeves, Dorothy Kennedy, Duane Thorsen, Harry Landers, Ann Navarro

Director: Harold Schuster

Synopsis: Jack Slade (Mark Stevens), a murderer since age 13, becomes a gunslinger who helps the law take action against stagecoach bandits. Slade is in love with a woman, but when the relationship sours, he becomes a drinking, murdering killer until a friend guns him down.

Comment: Real-life western figure Jack (Joseph Alfred) Slade (1829–1864) was a soldier, stage driver and killer. Slade did help the Overland stage line deal with stage robberies and Indian attacks, but sources claim that his film is an entirely fictional story of his life.

Van Cleef's Role: Van Cleef is Toby MacKay in this film. Reportedly, the story in *Jack Slade* is unrelated to that of real-life western killer Jack Slade, and thus the film should not be considered one of Van Cleef's fact-based Westerns, a category which makes up a sizable portion of the Western genre. Examples of Van Cleef's participation in this subgenre can be found in 1953's *The Lawless Breed* (about Texas outlaw John Wesley Hardin), a 1954 TV episode of *Stories of the Century* entitled "Frank and Jesse James" (in which Van Cleef portrays Frank James) and 1957's *Gunfight at the O.K. Corral*.

Joe Dakota

1957, color, 79 minutes
Universal (Western)

Cast: Jock Mahoney (Joe Dakota), Luana Patten (Jody Weaver), Charles McGraw (Cal Moore), Barbara Lawrence (Myrna Weaver), Claude Akins (Aaron Grant), Lee Van Cleef (Adam Grant), Anthony Caruso (Marcus Vizzini), Paul Birch (Frank Weaver), George Dunn (Jim Baldwin), Steve Darrell (Sam Cook), Rita Lynn (Rosa Vizzini), Gregg Barton (Tom Jensen), Anthony Jochim (Claude Henderson), Jeane Wood (Bertha Jensen), Juney Ellis (Ethel Cook)

Director: Richard Bartlett

Synopsis: Former Cavalry officer Joe Dakota (Jock Mahoney) travels to a small, unfriendly town named Arborville, looking for an Indian friend who once served as his scout. Joe finds the Indian's house on a piece of property near Arborville, but instead of finding his friend, he finds Cal Moore (Charles McGraw) and other Arborville citizens drilling an oil well on the land. Joe is told that the Indian sold the land to Cal before moving away. Finding this dubious, he checks with the county recorder's office and learns that the land hasn't legally changed hands. He also learns that the Indian signed the deed with the only English name he could write: "Joe Dakota." Taking advantage of the deed's misnomer, Joe claims the land and promises to disrupt the drilling until someone tells him the truth. Joe is visited by a shy young woman named Jody Weaver (Luana Patten) who tells him that the Indian was hanged because of bogus criminal charges made by land-grabbing Cal, an oil expert who promised jobs to the nearby townspeople. Jody relates that the Arborville citizens, who were eager to make some money, readily believed the charges. Joe convinces the townspeople that they have let Cal commit a heinous crime. Once they get rid of the oil man, the people have no more secrets to hide, and Arborville again becomes a friendly town.

Comment: Although its story bears a resemblance to that of 1954's *Bad Day at Black Rock*, *Joe Dakota* is a wonderful, pleasant film whose hero, actor-stuntman Jock Mahoney's title character, is laid-back and memorable. The film has been incorrectly called a Western which does not feature a single gunshot; actually, Cal fires a warning shot during the film's climax. The small size of Arborville allows for most of the townspeople to have distinct personalities and to be used to good effect. A notable scene occurs after Joe learns the disposition of his Indian friend: Joe hangs a noose from Arborville's town sign. This type of action, done for aesthetic value rather than for narrative function, would later feature heavily in Spaghetti Westerns.

Van Cleef's Role: Van Cleef appears in *Joe Dakota* as Adam Grant, a brawny Arborville citizen who helps Cal drill for oil on the Indian's land. Adam and his brawny brother Aaron (Claude Akins) have devised a silly roughhousing game, and they invite Joe to play with them. Joe accepts their invitation, even though the people of Arborville have not yet accepted him as a friend, and the two Grant brothers use the game as an excuse to beat on the unwelcomed stranger. After the townspeople realize their mistakes and befriend Joe, the Grant brothers are no longer menacing; they actually become one of the film's sources of comedy, as they continue to refer to the rules of their silly game.

Jungle Raiders

1985, color, 102 minutes, Italian

Alternate Titles: *Captain Yankee, La legenda del rudio malese*

Cast: Christopher Connelly (Duke "Captain Yankee" Howard), Marina Costa (Maria Yanez), Lee Van Cleef (Warren), Alan Collins (Gin Fizz), Dario Pontonutti, Mike Monty, Rene Abadeza, Cirillo Vitali, Francesco Arcuri

Director: Anthony M. Dawson [Antonio Margheriti]

Synopsis: Museum curator Maria Yanez (Marina Costa) hires two adventurers, Duke Howard (Christopher Connelly) and Gin Fizz (Alan Collins), to help her locate the Ruby of Gloom, an old and valuable artifact. Their expedition leads them through the jungles and underground caverns of Malaysia, and when they do finally find the ruby, it is stolen from them by a smuggler named Da Silva and a Borneo pirate named Tiger. Duke, Fizz and Maria follow the ruby to a jungle fortress where they fight against Tiger's pirates and Da Silva's mercenaries. Trade Inspector Warren (Lee Van Cleef), who arranged Maria's expedition, has an interest in capturing Da Silva and Tiger, and he lends a hand as Maria and the adventurers retrieve the Ruby of Gloom.

Comment: Made after the success of the similar and far better *Raiders of the Lost Ark, Jungle Raiders* is an unimpressive imitation. The film's most exciting scenes are during the fiery cavern sequences (and even they aren't great), but a surprisingly small portion of this film is spent in that locale, as the ruby is found there with disappointing ease. The few interesting elements of the film, including a mysterious race of cavern "guardians," are slighted in order to make time for the long, nondescript action sequences near the film's end. "Lucky for You," the Karen A. Jones–sung theme song, is one of the few pleasant aspects of the film.

Van Cleef's Role: With his gray hair colored black, his voice unusually guttural, and his attire alternating between an all-white outfit and an all-black outfit, Van Cleef plays Trade Inspector Warren. The character serves mainly to help direct the film's heroes toward the action. Inspector Warren is part of the "advising oldster role" trend in Van Cleef's characters that started with McCarn (*The Octagon*) and Bob Hauk (*Escape from New York*). Like the other characters, Warren has a small amount of (seemingly obligatory) action; the film sees Warren firing a few shots and then twirling his gun back into his holster.

Kansas City Confidential
1952, black and white, 98 minutes, United Artists

Alternate Title: *The Secret Four* (British)

Cast: John Payne (Joe Rolfe), Coleen Gray (Helen Foster), Preston Foster (Timothy Foster), Dona Drake (Teresa), Jack Elam (Pete Harris), Neville Brand (Boyd Kane), Lee Van Cleef (Tony Romano), Mario Seletti (Timaso), Howard Negley (Andrews), Ted Ryan (Morelli), George Wallace (Olson), Vivi Janiss (Mr. Rogers), Helen Kleeb (Mrs. Crane), Kay Wiley (Woman), Harry Hines (News Vendor), Don Orlando (Diaz), Joe Ray (Houseman), Paul Hogan (Bouncer), Paul Dubov (Eddie), Ric Roman (Brother), Sam Pierce (Workman), Eduardo Coch (Airline Clerk), William Haade (Detective Barney), Charles Cane (Detective Mullins), Ray Bennett (Prisoner), Orlando Beltran (Porter), Carleton Young (Assistant District Attorney Martin), Phil Tead (Collins), Lee Phelps (Jailer)

Director: Phil Karlson

Synopsis: Timothy Foster (Preston Foster), a criminal mastermind and former Kansas City police captain, arranges the heist of a Kansas City bank. He hires three small-time criminals to do the job. The criminals aren't allowed to see their employer's face, and Foster requires them to wear masks so they will be unable to rat on each other if caught. The criminals successfully pull off the heist with their getaway vehicle disguised as a floral delivery truck, and they agree to meet later in a city named Borados to divide the bank loot. The investigating police arrest Joe Rolfe (John Payne), a floral delivery truck driver, and although Joe is found to be innocent, his arrest causes him to lose his job. Unable to find other work, Joe wants to clear his name, and he tracks down one of the robbers, Pete Harris (Jack Elam), who is on his way to Borados. Pete is shot to death by the police before he can board the Borados-bound plane, and so Joe poses as Pete and goes in his place. In Borados, Joe tries to convince the other two criminals, Boyd Kane (Neville Brand) and Tony Romano (Lee Van Cleef), that he was one of the masked rob-

Lee Van Cleef holds a gun to John Payne's head in *Kansas City Confidential* (United Artists, 1952). Neville Brand sits with Van Cleef as Preston Foster drives.

bers. When Joe learns that he stands to receive part of the bank loot, he considers abandoning his name-clearing attempt and taking the money instead. Foster, though, has no intention of giving the money to the three bank robbers; he tries to turn them in to the police for reward money. But Tony shoots Foster, and the mastermind lays dying when the police barge in. Foster, who knows that Joe is not actually Pete, tells the cops that Joe helped to bring the crooks to justice. Joe is in line to get reward money and has begun a romance with Foster's daughter.

Comment: Kansas City Confidential, done in *film noir* style, does create some good moments of suspense. John Payne's performance is good. In order for his character to be believable as a floral delivery truck driver who is able to infiltrate the criminal underworld, the character is introduced as an ex-convict who has gone straight and taken the delivery job. The film is notable for bringing together Van Cleef, Jack Elam and Neville Brand, three of the top "heavies" of the 1950s.

Van Cleef's Role: The three criminals are introduced when each has his own interview with Foster (Pete Harris actually has an earlier telephone scene), and the distinguishing personality trait of each crook becomes apparent in these scenes. Pete is nervous, Boyd Kane is taciturn and Tony Romano is girl-crazy. Van Cleef gets an early chance to prove his comedic ability in his interview scene when Foster lays down the rule: "no dames." Tony responds with a sleazy smile while straightening his bow tie: "Look, friend, if you don't like it, don't knock it." Tony Romano provided Van Cleef with the actor's largest role of 1952, his first year in pictures. Tony was also Van Cleef's first non–Western film role.

Kid Vengeance

1977, color, 94 minutes,
Italian-U.S.-Israeli (Western)

Alternate Titles: *Les cavaliers du diable* (French), *Vendetta* (Italian), *Vengeance*

Cast: Lee Van Cleef (McClain), Jim Brown (Isaac), Leif Garrett (Tom Thurston), John Marley (Jesus), Matt Clark (Grover), Glynnis O'Connor (Lisa Thurston), David Loden (Matthew Thurston), Dalia Penn (Beth Thurston), Tim Scott (Ned), Richard Vanstone (Dewey), Joseph Shiloah (Lupe)

Director: Joe Manduke

Opposite: Van Cleef donned a headband and earring for the part of a raping, murdering bandit named McClain in the 1977 Western *Kid Vengeance*, which was filmed in Israel.

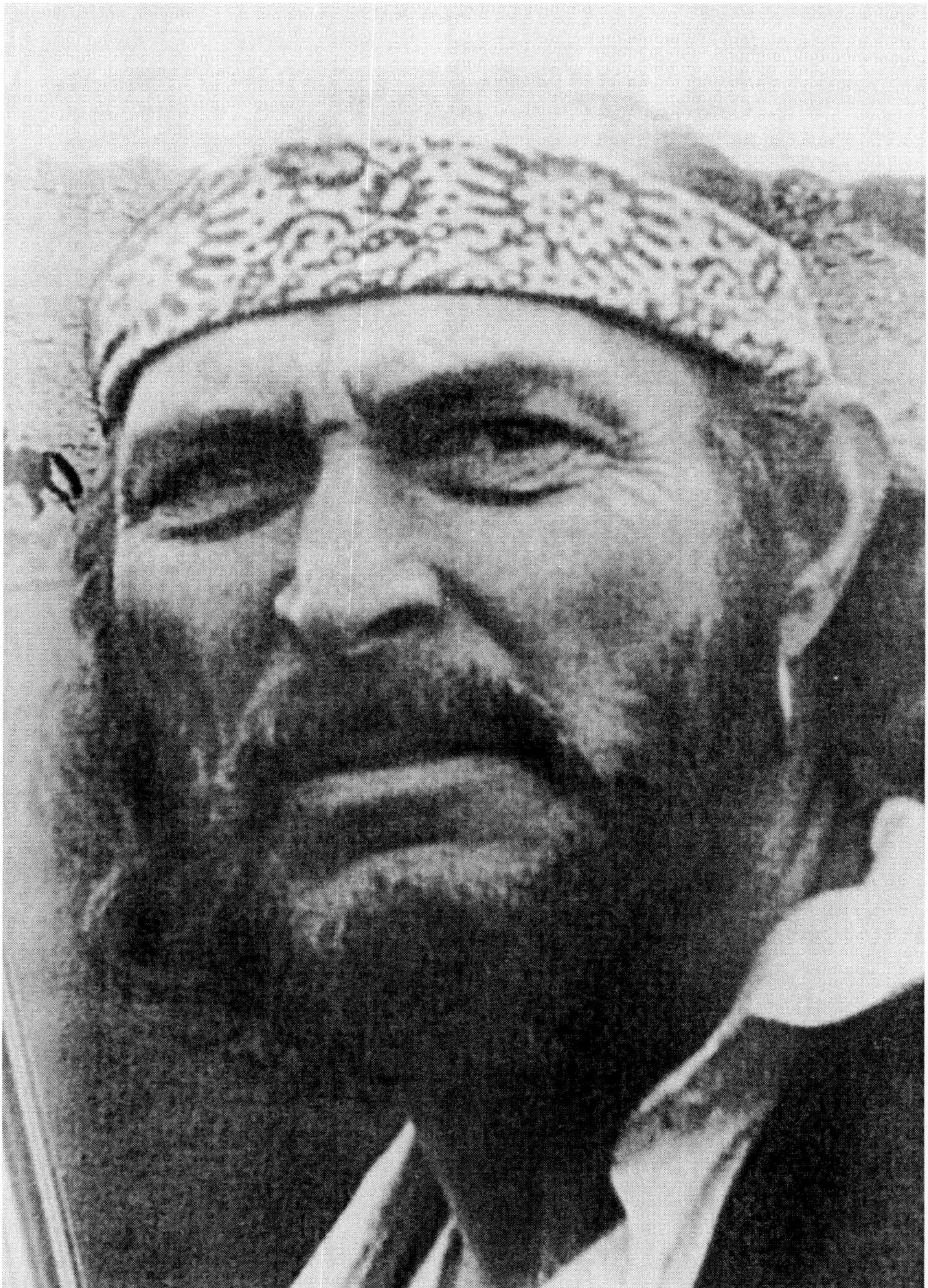

Synopsis: A gang of bandits led by McClain (Lee Van Cleef) learns that gold miner Isaac (Jim Brown) has struck it rich, and they ride out to rob him. On their way, the gang encounters the Thurston family camped out in the desert. The bandits murder the parents and ride off with the daughter, Lisa (Glynnis O'Connor), but fail to kill Tom (Leif Garrett), the adolescent Thurston son. Tom trails the gang until they reach Isaac's mine, stealthily killing some of McClain's men along the way. After they steal Isaac's gold and leave him bound, Tom unties the plundered miner. The two combine their efforts and attack McClain's village, where the head outlaw lives with his young son. Tom finds McClain, kills him and pumps his dead body full of lead. Isaac frees Lisa but is shot dead by the bandits. After the battle is over, McClain's son picks up a gun and contemplates killing Tom, but the two boys decide that too much violence has already taken place, and Tom rides away.

Comment: There is little to recommend *Kid Vengeance.* There are few solid characterizations, as the unintelligent script keeps most characters one-dimensional. The film's revenge theme is undistinguished. The novelty of Tom's young age doesn't really work; there are only a few moments when Tom's actions are different than those of many older revenge-film heroes. But the story is mildly interesting in that it has McClain and his gang first learn of Isaac's gold and premeditate the crime before encountering the Thurston family. This causes the murders of Tom's parents, their major offense, to be seen as merely incidental from McClain's viewpoint.

Van Cleef's Role: During the 1970s, Van Cleef was generally playing the hero of his films. McClain, his character in *Kid Vengeance,* is one of the actor's few villains of the 1970s. And of all the heavies that Van Cleef played after becoming a star, only McClain seems to resemble an older version of Van Cleef's grubby heavies from his Hollywood Western period. McClain gives us an idea what some of Van Cleef's earlier villains might have been like had they survived to grow older (but not much wiser). *Kid Vengeance* is one of Van Cleef's last two Westerns; the other, *God's Gun,* was also filmed in Israel with former teen idol Leif Garrett. *Kid Vengeance* was the actor's last teaming with pro football star-turned-actor Jim Brown, who appeared with Van Cleef in *El Condor* and *Take a Hard Ride.*

The Killing Machine
1984, color, 95 minutes, Spanish-Mexican

Alternate Titles: *Goma 2, La máquina de matar* (Spanish)

Cast: Jorge Rivero (Chema), Margaux Hemingway (Jacqueline), Lee Van Cleef (Maître Julot), Willie Aames (Tony), Richard Jaeckel (Martin), Ana Obregon (Liza), Hugo Stiglitz (Picot)

Director: J. Anthony Loma [Jose Antonio de la Loma]

Synopsis: Chema (Jorge Rivero), a truck driver, takes his pregnant wife along for his last trip, a Spain-to-France drive. In France, Chema's truck is set afire by angry French farmers who have connections to organized crime, and Chema's wife dies in the blaze. After crime boss Maître Julot (Lee Van Cleef) helps get the guilty men acquitted, Chema sets out to avenge his wife's murder and gets his hands on several crates of plastic explosive. Chema receives help from his brother-in-law Tony (Willie Aames), but Tony is killed for associating with the truck driver. Chema moves in with Jacqueline (Margaux Hemingway), who helps him locate the guilty men, and he uses plastic explosives to annihilate them. Chema then places explosives under Maître Julot's car and confronts the criminal. Julot is allowed to drive away, believing that he is getting off the hook, before Chema uses a remote control detonator switch to blow him up.

Comment: Whereas some revenge pictures distinguish themselves by having the avenger killing his or her maltreaters in clever or especially brutal manners, *The Killing Machine* has Chema kill each of the three transgressors in the exact same way: with plastic explosive. Many banal motifs from the revenge-film formula surface in *The Killing Machine*, including the flashbacks that come to the avenger just before he or she decides to kill, and the new love interest that replaces the avenger's murdered spouse.

Van Cleef's Role: Maître Julot is one of Van Cleef's last and definitely one of his nastiest film villains. In his last scene, Van Cleef goes out in top villain form: Chema allows Julot to believe that he will be permitted to leave without retribution. As Julot leaves in his car, he rubs his hands and displays the expression of a fiendishly happy little child. This perfectly evil facial expression is one of the most memorable moments of the film. *The Killing Machine* gives rise to an interesting coincidence in Van Cleef's career. Actor Willie Aames, playing the supporting role of Tony, was also a regular as the son on Dick Van Patten's TV series *Eight Is Enough*. Van Cleef, after having appeared in this film with Van Patten's screen son, began his weekly TV series *The Master*, co-starring Timothy Van Patten, Dick Van Patten's real-life son.

The Last Stagecoach West
1957, black and white, 67 minutes, Republic (Western)

Cast: Jim Davis (Bill Cameron), Mary Castle (Louise McCord), Victor Jory (Rand McCord), Lee Van Cleef (Steve Margolis), Grant Withers (Ben Gibson), Roy Barcroft (Pa Ketchum), John Alderson (George Bryson), Mary Treen (Miss Feeney), Percy Helton (Telegraph Operator), Glenn Strange, Willis Bouchey

Director: Joe Kane

Synopsis: Railroad detective Bill Cameron (Jim Davis) investigates sabotage of the mail-carrying Chicago and Pacific Transcontinental Railroad. Cameron finds the saboteur to be Rand McCord (Victor Jory), who operates the competition — a mail stagecoach — which is losing its government contracts and going out of business. Louise McCord (Mary Castle), Rand's daughter and business partner, is ignorant of her father's nefarious doings, and after Rand's scheme is exposed, Bill consoles Louise.

Comment: The Last Stagecoach West was issued theatrically in 1957 by Republic. Some sources indicate that it was originally released on television in 1954, as the pilot film for Republic's first television series, *Stories of the Century*. It is true that *Stories* also stars *Last Stagecoach West*'s Jim Davis as a railroad detective, but his character's name is Matt Clark, not Bill Cameron. Similarly, Mary Castle, who appears in this film, is also a regular in *Stories of the Century*, but as a character with a different name.

Van Cleef's Role: In *The Last Stagecoach West*, Van Cleef plays a heavy named Steve Margolis. Van Cleef also appeared in an episode of *Stories of the Century*, as real-life outlaw Frank James.

The Lawless Breed
1953, color, 83 minutes, Universal (Western)

Cast: Rock Hudson (John Wesley Hardin), Julia [Julie] Adams (Rosie), John McIntire (J.C. Hardin and John Clements), Mary Castle (Jane Brown), Hugh O'Brian (Ike Hanley), Forrest Lewis (Zeke Jenkins), Lee Van Cleef (Dirk Hanley), Tom Fadden (Chick Noonan), William Pullen (Joe Hardin), Dennis Weaver (Jim Clements), Glenn Strange (Ben Hanley), Richard Garland (Joe Clements), Race Gentry (Young John Hardin), Carl Pitti (Sheriff Conlon), Michael Ansara (Gus Hanley)

Director: Raoul Walsh

Synopsis: Notorious killer John Wesley Hardin (Rock Hudson) is released from prison in Huntsville, Texas, and delivers a manuscript containing his life story to a publisher. As the story goes, Hardin gambled at cards and hoped to win enough money to buy a horse ranch for himself and his fiancée Jane Brown (Mary Castle). During one game, Hardin was accused of cheating and was forced to kill Gus Hanley (Michael Ansara) and several Army soldiers. Before he could prove that the shootings were in self-defense, Hardin was being chased by lawmen and Hanley's brothers. Each time he killed in order to protect himself, Hardin was further incriminated. In a shoot-out, Jane was accidentally killed by Hardin's pursuers, and when the fugitive did eventually establish his horse ranch, it was with his next lover, Rosie (Julia Adams), who became his wife. When the Texas Rangers eventually captured Hardin, the killer was sentenced to 25 years of imprisonment but was pardoned after 16 years. After John Wesley Hardin leaves this story with the publisher, he returns to his ranch, just in time to save his 16-year-old son from making the same mistakes that he did.

Comment: Based loosely on the autobiography of real-life outlaw John Wesley Hardin (1853–1895), *The Lawless Breed* is a watchable and occasionally exciting recounting of the gunman's life. It contains a very early starring performance by Rock Hudson.

Van Cleef's Role: Van Cleef plays Dirk Hanley, the most feared killer of the Hanley brothers. After Hardin kills Gus Hanley, the remaining Hanleys get on Hardin's trail, hoping to kill the young gunslinger. Van Cleef is the first revenge-seeking Hanley to be killed by Hardin. The Dirk

Hanley character is the first part in a trend of Van Cleef film roles. Many times has the actor played a villain who tries to avenge the death of his villainous sibling by killing the film's hero (e.g., *Dawn at Socorro*, *The Desperado* and *Gunfight at the O.K. Corral*).

The Lonely Man

1957, black and white, 87 minutes,
Paramount (Western)

Cast: Jack Palance (Jacob Wade), Anthony Perkins (Riley Wade), Neville Brand (King Fisher), Robert Middleton (Ben Ryerson), Elaine Aiken (Ada Marshall), Elisha Cook, Jr. (Willie), Claude Akins (Blackburn), Lee Van Cleef (Faro), Harry Shannon (Dr. Fisher), James Bell (Judge Hart), Adam Williams (Lon), Denver Pyle (Sheriff)

Director: Henry Levin

Synopsis: Jacob Wade (Jack Palance), a notorious outlaw beginning a law-abiding life, visits Riley (Anthony Perkins), the son he abandoned more than a decade earlier. Jacob is too late to rectify his relationship with his estranged wife, though; she committed suicide five years earlier. Riley blames Jacob's abandonment for his mother's suicide, but he tries a new life with his reformed father. Jacob's reputation keeps the two from settling in any town, and as a last resort, Jacob takes Riley to Monolith, his old ranch-home hideout. While at Monolith, Riley begins to respect his father, and he learns the truth about his parents' schism. (Riley's mother refused to accompany Jacob on a move, and this pushed Jacob into lawlessness.) Jacob's eyesight begins to fail and, barely able to defend himself, he is shot by his enemy King Fisher (Neville Brand), who knew Jacob during his outlaw days. After Riley arrives and helps his father kill King and his cronies, all the obstacles to a peaceful life are eliminated. But Jacob isn't able to enjoy it, because he dies from King Fisher's bullet.

Comment: The Lonely Man is a well-acted drama but is a bit too contrived. Jack Palance creates a sympathy-evoking hero, playing Jacob Wade with a stopped posture and a soft voice. The subplot about Jacob's attempts to catch and break wild horses supplies *The Lonely Man* with its mandatory action scenes.

In *The Lonely Man* (Paramount, 1957), Faro (Lee Van Cleef) attempts to restrain hot-tempered head villain King Fisher (Neville Brand), who is trying to beat a crony, Willie (Elisha Cook, Jr.). Lon (Adam Williams) looks on from a distance.

Van Cleef's Role: Faro, Van Cleef's character, is one of King Fisher's outlaw cronies. He helps Fisher in the effort to kill Jacob Wade. But Faro is killed by the near-blind gunfighter. Faro is one of Van Cleef's more reserved heavies, and the black attire worn by the sharply-dressed Faro resembles the outfits of later Van Cleef heroes Mortimer (*For a Few Dollars More*) and Sabata (*Sabata*). Van Cleef appeared in another 1957 Western with Anthony Perkins and Neville Brand, *The Tin Star*.

Machete

1958, black and white, 75 minutes, United Artists

Cast: Mari Blanchard (Jean), Albert Dekker (Don Luis Montoya), Joano Hernandez (Bernardo), Carlos Rivas (Carlos), Lee Van Cleef (Miguel), Ruth Cains (Rita)

Producer/Director: Kurt Neumann

Synopsis: Jean (Mari Blanchard) is married to sugar cane plantation owner Don Luis Montoya (Albert Dekker), but she wants to have a liaison with a foreman named Carlos (Carlos Rivas). Jean's scheme does not force Don Luis to end his friendship with Carlos, whom the plantation owner raised from birth, because the unfaithful wife dies in a field fire.

Comment: Machete was filmed in Puerto Rico.

Van Cleef's Role: In this film, Van Cleef plays Miguel, a trouble-making cousin.

The Magnificent Seven Ride

1972, color, 100 minutes,
United Artists (Western)

Cast: Lee Van Cleef (Chris), Stefanie Powers (Laurie Gunn), Mariette Hartley (Arilla), Michael Callan (Noah Forbes), Luke Askew (Skinner), Pedro Armandariz, Jr. (Pepe Carral), William Lucking (Walt Drummand), James B. Sikking (Hayes), Ed Lauter (Scott Elliott), Melissa Murphy (Madge Buchanan), Darrell Larson (Shelly Donovan), Allyn Ann McLerie (Mrs. Donovan), Ralph Waite (Jim MacKay), Carolyn Conwell (Martha), Jason Wingreen (Warden), Elizabeth Thompson (Skinner's Woman), Rita Rogers (De Toro's Woman), Robert Jaffe (Bob Allen), Gary Busey (Hank Allan), Rodolfo Acosta (Juan De Toro)

Director: George McGowan

Synopsis: A recently-married lawman named Chris (Lee Van Cleef) refuses to help Marshal Jim MacKay (Ralph Waite), who asked Chris to help defend the town of Magdalena from a gang of bandits. After his

Left–right: Chris (Lee Van Cleef), Skinner (Luke Askew), Pepe Carral (Pedro Armandariz, Jr.), and Walt Drummand (William Lucking) are four of the seven who dig in to defend a village from an onslaught of bandits in ***The Magnificent Seven Ride*** (United Artists, 1952).

wife is murdered, though, Chris decides to help, and he travels to Magdalena with a journalist named Noah Forbes (Michael Callan). When they arrive, Chris and Noah find that the bandits have slaughtered Marshal MacKay and all of the townsmen, but that the women—raped and ravaged—have been kept alive for future visits. Chris and Noah travel to a nearby prison, where they offer pardons to five prisoners who agree to help protect Magdalena from the bandits. But before the seven men return to the village, they visit the house of Juan De Toro (Rodolfo Acosta), the bandits' leader, and nab De Toro's woman. The seven men retreat to Magdalena, which they fortify, and when De Toro arrives, the village becomes a battlefield. The defenders prevail, but of the seven men, only three—Chris, Noah and one of the prisoners—are left alive.

The three defenders settle down in Magdalena with the remaining women.

Comment: When you consider that *The Magnificent Seven Ride* is the third sequel in a series of films that uses essentially the same formula in each entry (perhaps to please audiences who are watching the sequels because they enjoyed the very popular original film), this fourth film does not seem all that bad. The series began in 1960 with *The Magnificent Seven* and continued with 1966's *Return of the Seven* and 1969's *Guns of the Magnificent Seven.* Yul Brynner starred as the leader in the first two films, and George Kennedy took over for one installment before Van Cleef assumed the role. Eli Wallach played the lead villain for the original film and received praise for his excellent performance. The principal heavy of *The Magnificent Seven Ride*, Juan De Toro (Rodolfo Acosta), is filling a necessary role but isn't given much chance for characterization. By the end of *The Magnificent Seven Ride*, most of the cast has been killed off, but fortunately viewers are not subjected to what could have been a too-coincidental-to-swallow Hollywood ending: having an equal number of men and women survivors. Instead, there are five women and three men left alive after the battle. And the script was able to wrap it up neatly from there with a touch of humor, as Skinner (Luke Askew), one of the surviving men, grabs three women and announces, "I'm a Mormon," in obvious reference to his plans to wed anyone left over.

Van Cleef's Role: The Magnificent Seven Ride is the only Van Cleef-starring Western that has the feel of a traditional American Western. Besides this film, Van Cleef starred in only two other strictly American Western films, *El Condor* and *Barquero* (both 1970), but both of those films borrowed heavily from the Spaghetti Western style. Van Cleef does fine in the role of Chris, the leader of the seven. He doesn't seem to be trying to imitate any of his predecessors, but rather adapts his hardened, lone gunfighter persona to this leadership and team role.

A Man Alone

1955, color, 95 minutes, Republic (Western)

Cast: Ray Milland (Wesley Steele), Mary Murphy (Nadine Corrigan), Raymond Burr (Stanley), Ward Bond (Sheriff Gil Corrigan), Arthur

Space (Dr. Mason), Lee Van Cleef (Clantin), Alan Hale, Jr. (Deputy Jim Anderson), Grandon Rhodes (Luke Joiner), Martin Garralaga (Ortega), Kim Spalding (Sam Hall), Howard J. Negley (Wilson), Julian Rivero (Tio Rubio), Lee Roberts (Higgs), Minerva Urecal (Mrs. Maule), Thorpe Whiteman (Boy), Dick Rich (Kincaid), Frank Hagney (Dorfman)

Director: Ray Milland

Synopsis: In the town of Mesa, ambiguous events surround the arrival of famed gunfighter Wesley Steele (Ray Milland). This makes it possible for Stanley (Raymond Burr), the town's crooked banker, to frame Steele for several recent crimes. The crimes, including a stagecoach robbery and the murders of its passengers, were actually committed by Stanley's hired gun Clantin (Lee Van Cleef) and were overlooked by Mesa's corrupt Sheriff Corrigan (Ward Bond). Seeking refuge from angry townspeople, Steele hides in the house of Sheriff Corrigan, who has been rendered delirious by yellow fever. Steele convinces Corrigan's daughter Nadine (Mary Murphy) of his innocence. When the sheriff awakens, he is forced to choose between defending Steele, with whom Nadine has fallen in love, or siding with his secret partner, Stanley. Making his decision, Gil gives Steele safe passage out of town. When the angry townspeople learn of this, they try to lynch their sheriff. Steele returns to Mesa in time to save Corrigan, and together they rid the town of Stanley's villainy.

Comment: A Man Alone begins in exciting fashion. The hero, Wesley Steele (Ray Milland), is presented in a confusing light, being a seemingly benevolent man and yet gunning down a deputy for no apparent reason (it is later revealed that he is paranoid because of his reputation as a gunfighter). Also exciting is the surprisingly quick way that the story gets Steele entangled in all of his troubles. However, once Steele establishes a relationship with Nadine, the sheriff's daughter, *A Man Alone* falls into routine channels, the only unpredictable element being the wild-card character of Sheriff Corrigan. *A Man Alone* is competently directed (by Milland himself — his debut as a director). The film's fine cast, including Raymond Burr (famous as TV's Perry Mason) and Ward Bond (a John Wayne film regular), overcomes the lack of realism in the dialogue.

Van Cleef's Role: Van Cleef's Clantin is actually one of the actor's more intelligent heavies, but Clantin spends most of the film acting like most of Van Cleef's other 1950s heavies: antagonistic and none-too-bright. Clantin's true character can be observed in his first scene of the film, in which he has a secret meeting with his criminal boss, Stanley. But during most of *A Man Alone*, Clantin is out in public in Mesa, where he not only has to keep secret the fact that he is a killer but also pretend to believe that Steele is guilty and deserving of punishment.

The Man Who Shot Liberty Valance
1962, black and white, 123 minutes
Paramount (Western)

Cast: John Wayne (Tom Doniphon), James Stewart (Ransom Stoddard), Vera Miles (Hallie), Lee Marvin (Liberty Valance), Edmond O'Brien (Dutton Peabody), Andy Devine (Link Appleyard), Ken Murray (Doc Willoughby), John Carradine (Major Cassius Starbuckle), Jeanette Nolan (Nora Ericson), John Qualen (Peter Ericson), Willis Bouchey (Jason Tully), Carleton Young (Maxwell Scott), Woody Strode (Pompey), Denver Pyle (Amos Carruthers), Strother Martin (Floyd), Lee Van Cleef (Reese), O.Z. Whitehead (Hasbrouck), Anna Lee (Passenger), Charles Seel (President, Election Council)

Director: John Ford

Synopsis: Senator Ranse Stoddard (Jimmy Stewart) returns with his wife Hallie (Vera Miles) to his hometown of Shinbone for the funeral of Tom Doniphon (John Wayne). Shinbone's newspaperman does not understand why the important senator is paying respect to an obscure man like Doniphon, who is being buried in a pine box. The reporter wants a scoop. Ranse asks to be undisturbed in his grieving but is finally persuaded to tell the story: Ranse first came to Shinbone as a tenderfoot eastern attorney, hoping to establish a law practice in the West. He quickly made enemies with Liberty Valance (Lee Marvin), a gunman who worked for cattle barons, keeping Shinbone citizens from supporting the territory's push for statehood. Legal action did not affect Liberty, so Ranse received gunfighting lessons from Tom Doniphon, whose girlfriend was Hallie. When Ranse met Liberty in the middle of town for a gunfight, Tom was standing in a dark alley. Ranse missed his target, but Tom shot Liberty dead and slipped away unnoticed. Ranse, who thought he had killed the gunman, became a reluctant celebrity, and Hallie fell in love with him. After the attorney's political career began to take off, Tom told Ranse the truth about the shooting but stressed that it should remain a secret, because Ranse's popularity was needed for the statehood campaign. Ranse married Hallie and eventually became a U.S. senator. After Ranse Stoddard tells this story, he and his wife leave on the train. Stoddard thanks the conductor for the special arrangements that have been made on his behalf, and is told, "Nothing's too good for the man who shot Liberty Valance."

Comment: An understated Western of the time, *The Man Who Shot Liberty Valance* explored the idea of the dying of the Old West. At the beginning of Stoddard's story, he arrived by stagecoach, and only strong men such as Tom Doniphon could stand up against the lawlessness of outlaws like Liberty Valance. When Stoddard's story ends, the setting is one in which such heroes have been forgotten, and the stagecoach could be a museum relic. To emphasize the change, Stoddard and his wife depart by train. This idea of the dying of the Old West was to become a major theme in a number of Westerns in the 1960s and 1970s. The film does contain some clichéd dialogue, mostly in Ranse and Tom's arguments about "Western law" residing in skill with a gun. But the fine cast overcomes all of the story's shortcomings and helps to make this film, one of director John Ford's last Westerns, a classic.

Van Cleef's Role: Van Cleef plays Reese, one of Liberty's outlaw pals, and was obviously not allowed to upstage Lee Marvin, who played Valance, the film's principal heavy. Thus Van Cleef plays Reese as a more reserved heavy. (Reese even restrains Valance from administering a brutal beating to Stoddard in one scene.) However, Van Cleef's Reese is shown being really nefarious during a scene in which Liberty's gang robs a stagecoach. In the robbery, Reese has the job of snitching the passengers' wallets and valuables. He grabs the purse of an elderly woman and demands to have the ornamental pin that she is wearing. The woman begs to keep it, saying, "My dead husband gave it to me." Reese replies with false compassion, "Oh, a widow woman, huh?" before shouting, "I'll take it anyways!" *The Man Who Shot Liberty Valance* was Van Cleef's last film to be shot entirely in black and white.

Mean Frank and Crazy Tony

1973, color, 93 minutes, French-Italian

Alternate Titles: *Dio, sei proprio un padreterno* (Italian), *Escape from Death Row* (home video), *Gangster Story, The Gun, Il suo nome faceva Tremare ... Interpol in allarme!, Johnny le fligueur* (French), *Power Kill*

Cast: Lee Van Cleef (Frank Diomedes a.k.a. Frankie Dio), Tony LoBianco (Tony Breda), Edwige Fenech (Orchid), Jean Rochefort (Annunziata), Jess Hahn (Jeannot), Joe Scedi, Adolfo Lastretti

Director: Michele Lupo

Synopsis: American crime boss Frankie Dio (Lee Van Cleef) arrives in Italy to kill his European underboss. Dio, needing an alibi for this murder, arranges with local police for the public to presume him jailed while he is actually out killing his associate. All does not go as planned, though, as a rival family, controlled by Annunziata (Jean Rochefort), gets involved and forces the police to keep Dio incarcerated. One of Annunziata's men attempts an in-prison assassination, but Dio's life is saved by Tony Breda (Tony LoBianco), a fellow inmate who idolizes the American gangster. With his organization crumbling and his presence no loner awing the other prisoners, Dio accepts the trivial gangster as his only friend. As soon as Tony's release and Dio's jailbreak put the two on the loose again, Annunziata and his thugs are dealt a finishing stroke.

Comment: A slightly uneven mixture of violent gangster film and mild spoof, *Mean Frank and Crazy Tony* is nevertheless almost thoroughly enjoyable. The film's two musical themes — a bright, brassy blues and somber horn piece — signify the changes between the film's two tones. Similarly, the title characters are different. Van Cleef's stony Frankie Dio is responsible for the gory violence. LoBianco, whose Tony character at times resembles the nervous Woody Allen persona, aptly handles the humorous material. Despite its occasional flashiness, Lupo's direction is superb, but an overlong car chase and shoot-out drag the film out near the end. *Mean Frank and Crazy Tony* is a film from prolific producer Dino de Laurentiis. It was released in Europe in 1973 and was given both the *Mean Frank* name and the title *Power Kill* for its release elsewhere in the mid–1970s. *Escape from Death Row*, a severely edited home video version, credits the following actors with appearing in the supporting cast: Guy De Sac, Barbara More, James Lane and Alice Belios. *Escape from Death Row* also credits Benet Spector with directing and Fred O'Bryan with scripting.

Van Cleef's Role: Frankie Dio, a hardened anti-hero, is less personable than most of Van Cleef's protagonists, although Van Cleef's portrayal of Dio is little different from the way he offers most of his heroic incarnations. The only drastic difference in Dio is his sadistic manner of killing, forcing a drill bit into a man's neck in one instance, and electrocuting a bather in another. What really keeps Dio from being as likable as the bulk of Van Cleef's heroes is the lack of justification for Dio's violent behavior. The film tries to justify his violent raid against Annunziata by earlier having Annunziata's thugs kill Dio's brother, who had no involvement with crime. This justification is not effective, though, and Dio just seems to be a gangster killing other gangsters. Moreover, Dio doesn't learn from his experiences. He doesn't denounce organized crime at the end of the story as expected — even though a massive amount of carnage was required to settle his personal grudges (only then does he recommend that Tony stay clear of the gangster life). It should be mentioned that Van Cleef made a noticeable alteration in his normal mannerisms by slowing his speech, which is very fitting for his cool crime-boss role.

The Nebraskan

1953, color, 68 minutes, Columbia (Western)

Cast: Phil Carey (Wade Harper), Roberta Haynes (Paris), Wallace Ford (McBride), Richard Webb (Ace Eliot), Lee Van Cleef (Reno), Maurice Jara (Wingfoot), Regis Toomey (Col. Markham), Jay Silverheels (Spotted Bear), Pat Hogan (Yellow Knife), Dennis Weaver (Capt. DeWitt), Boyd "Red" Morgan (Sgt. Phillips)

Director: Fred F. Sears

Synopsis: U.S. Army scout Wade Harper (Phil Carey) protects his Indian guide Wingfoot (Maurice Jara), wrongly accused of murdering one of his tribal elders. In an old house, Harper and other soldiers hold off the furious Indians who are after Wingfoot.

Comment: The Nebraskan was originally issued in 3-D.

Van Cleef's Role: The Nebraskan is another early Van Cleef film which features the actor as a baddie. Reno, Van Cleef's character, is a deserter who causes dissent amongst Harper and crew. In *The Motion Picture Guide*, Van Cleef's appearance in *The Nebraskan* is declared the "saving grace" of the film. In the book *The Western*, author Phil Hardy surmises that Van Cleef used Richard Widmark's character in 1947's *Kiss of Death* as a model for his role of Reno.

The Octagon

1980, color, 103 minutes, American cinema

Cast: Chuck Norris (Scott James), Karen Carlson (Justine), Lee Van Cleef (McCarn), Art Hindle (A.J.), Carol Bagdasarian (Aura), Tadashi Yamashita (Seikura), Kim Lankford (Nancy), Kurt Grayson (Doggo), Yuki Shimoda (Katsumoto), Larry D. Mann (Tibor), John Fujioka (Isawa), Jack Carter (Sharkey), Richard Norton (Kyo and Longlegs), Redmond Gleeson (Duffy), Alan Chappuis (Pierre), Brian Libby (Deadwyler), Michael Norris (Scott at 18), Brian Tochi (Seikura at 18), Kevin Brando (Scott at 8), Darrin Lee (Seikura at 8), Ken Gibbel (Meat), Cheyenne Rivera (Greek), Ted Duncan, Alan Marcus (Truckdrivers), Gerald Okamura (Ninja Instructor), Jo McDonnell (Amy Lee), Ernie Hudson (Quinine), Robert B. Loring (Johann), Fenton Jones (Square Dance Caller), Crane Jackson (House Detective), Clarke Gordon (Drunk), Ben Freedman (Newsvendor), Shannon Scott David (Waitress), Elizabeth Carder (Desk Clerk), Kitty Beau (Hostess), Keh Lesco (Stunt Ninja), Aaron Norris (Hatband), John Barrett (Justine's Killer), Bill Beau (Aide), Enrique Lucero (One-Armed Man), Eric F. Valdez (Scott's Taxi Driver), Gasper A. Henaine (A.J.'s Taxi Driver), Carlos Romano (Pilot), Mario Valdez (Hotel Clerk), John Shields (1st Lieutenant), Thad Geer (2nd Lieutenant), Haven Earle Haley (Diplomat), Ben Perry (Male Assassin), Janette Jiliano (Female Assassin), Don Pike (Chauffeur), Janell Twomey (Nanny), J. Ross Imler (French Policeman)

Director: Eric Karson

Synopsis: When former karate champion Scott James (Chuck Norris) witnesses a murder, he observes the assailants using an outlawed form of martial arts that only he and his estranged half-brother, Seikura (Tadashi Yamashita), are capable of teaching. Scott suspects Seikura of running a terrorist-affiliated assassin training camp, and his interest becomes more than personal when a rich woman named Justine (Karen Carlson) offers him the job of finding and disbanding Seikura's operation. Scott declines but continues to collect information about his half-brother with help from an anti-terrorist named McCarn (Lee Van Cleef) and one of Seikura's former pupils, Aura (Carol Bagdasarian). When Scott's close friend, A.J. (Art Hindle) gets involved and is taken prisoner by Seikura, Scott accepts Justine's assignment, and he infiltrates his half-brother's camp. A.J. is killed, but Scott prevents further evil by killing Seikura.

Comment: The 1980 entry in Norris' long list of martial arts films, *The Octagon* features a Norris character whose actions are guided by voices in his head, which are effectively eerie during the title sequence and annoying thereafter. Norris does, however, fight with seemingly effortless fluidity and the exciting sets (in the giant octagonal training arena) keep the violence from getting tiresome towards the end.

Van Cleef's Role: Van Cleef plays a resourceful, much-talked-about anti-terrorist named McCarn, who — although his main function in the film is to direct Norris' character towards the action — engages in a bit of combat himself in an alley shoot-out. With an underlying softness not found in even the nicest of Van Cleef's heroes, McCarn genuinely hates terrorism and has created an organization that is, in a movie full of truly evil enemies, a seemingly invincible force for goodness. This film could not have worked as anything but a vehicle for Norris' martial-arts prowess but, had McCarn been played more mysteriously and had his organization made a bigger impact on the storyline, Van Cleef might have stolen the picture.

Pardners

1956, color, 90 minutes
Paramount (Western)

Cast: Dean Martin (Slim Mosely Sr. and Jr.), Jerry Lewis (Wade Kingsley Sr. and Jr.), Lori Nelson (Carol Kingsley), Jeff Morrow (Pete

Rio), Jackie Loughery (Dolly Riley), John Baragrey (Dan Hollis), Agnes Moorehead (Mrs. Mathilda Kingsley), Lon Chaney, Jr. (Whitey), Milton Frome (Hawkins), Richard Aherne (Chauffeur), Lee Van Cleef (Gus), Stuart Randall (Carol's Cowhand), Scott Douglas (Salvin), Jack Elam (Pete), Bob Steele (Shorty), Mickey Finn (Red), Douglas Spencer (Smith), Philip Tonge (Footman), Emory Parnell (Col. Hart), Dorothy Ford (Amanda), Frances Mercer (Sally), William Forrest (Hocker), James Parnell (Bank Teller), Mary Newton (Laura), Len Hendry (Cowboy), Charles Stevens (Indian)

Director: Norman Taurog

Synopsis: Two best friends, Slim Mosely (Dean Martin) and Wade Kingsley (Jerry Lewis), are killed while trying to defend their ranch from masked raiders. Years later, Slim, Jr. (also Dean Martin), is trying to keep the ranch in business but is facing financial difficulties and more masked raiders. Wade, Jr. (also Jerry Lewis), who has become a New York millionaire, goes out west to help the rancher, and although Slim appreciates the financial help, he doesn't like the tenderfoot easterner hanging around. But Wade is out West to stay, and he even becomes the sheriff of nearby Carson Valley after a banker named Dan Hollis (John Baragrey) nominates him. Slim and the sheriff eventually unmask the raiders' ringleader, Hollis, who had implemented Wade as a lawman because he thought the newcomer would be a pushover.

Comment: Pardners is the usual Martin and Lewis fare, with Dean Martin playing it straight and Jerry Lewis engaging in his often funny antics. The bit about Wade Jr.'s false confidence as a lawman is a gem. *Pardners* is a remake of the 1936 Bing Crosby film *Rhythm on the Range.*

Van Cleef's Role: Van Cleef is Gus, one of Hollis' many masked raiders. Gus has only a few lines of dialogue, but Van Cleef's distinct facial features once again help the actor stand out amongst the other heavies. Gus' big scene comes in a saloon: Wade knocks a table over, which sends a beer bottle flying through the air. The bottle lands on and smashes over Gus' head, leaving him soaking wet and the other saloon patrons laughing hysterically.

The Perfect Killer
1977, color, 93 minutes, Spanish

Alternate Titles: *Bye Bye Darling, The Killers, Quel pomeriggio maledetto* (Italian), *Verano sangrieto* (Spanish)

Cast: Lee Van Cleef (Harry Chapman), Tita Barker (Krista), John Ireland (Benny), Robert Widmark (Luc), Karen Well, Al Landi, Diana Polakov, Paolo Manincor, Jean Pierre Clarain, Fabian Lopez Tapia, Fernando Sancho

Director: Marlon Sirko [Mario Siciliano]

Synopsis: After a botched attempt to rob a greyhound race track, Harry Chapman (Lee Van Cleef) is double crossed by his partner Krista (Tita Barker) and incarcerated. While serving time, Harry and his cellmate choose the alternative to imprisonment: working as assassins for the mysterious "Organization." Harry gains a reputation as an excellent killer. But when he is assigned to kill his former cellmate, he quits — much to the chagrin of the Organization, which dispatches a younger killer named Luc (Robert Widmark) to put Harry out of the way. Dodging Luc's murderous attempts, Harry lands a job as a free-lance assassin, on assignment to kill his former partner, Krista. Because of his romantic feelings for her, Harry's reunion with Krista does not end with death but instead leads to a renewed partnership, in which she uses Harry in a phony arms-selling scheme and betrays him again. Finally, when hired by the party that was swindled in the arms deal, Harry kills Krista.

Comment: An undistinguished and very dated action film, *The Perfect Killer* is nearly saved by its fast pacing. Both Widmark's reckless Luc and Van Cleef's cool Harry make convincing professional killers and, fortunately for the film, the impetuousness-of-youth angle is not overdone. Third-billed John Ireland gives the film its most solid performance in the insignificant role of Benny, Harry's pal who forges passports and loves pet birds.

Van Cleef's Role: Trendy and sleazy, Harry Chapman is one of Van Cleef's most anti-heroic protagonists. The one quality that distinguishes Harry from such miscreants as Luc and Krista is his undying perseverance. Harry is indeed in a bad position; he is betrayed by his lover and the Organization, can trust scarcely anybody, and is constantly in danger of losing his life. Through all of this Harry pushes, and he does not rest until he reaches a satisfying resolution. Mostly, though, *The Perfect Killer*'s manipulative violence is responsible for establishing Harry Chapman as the film's protagonist. The violence, when performed by Luc, the villain, is brutal and repulsive. But violence on the part of Harry, the "nice" killer, seems routine and desensitizing.

Posse from Hell
1961, color, 89 minutes,
Universal (Western)

Cast: Audie Murphy (Banner Cole), John Saxon (Seymour Kern), Zohra Lampert (Helen Caldwell), Vic Morrow (Crip), Robert Keith (Capt. Brown), Ward Ramsey (Marshal Webb), Rudolph Acosta (Johnny Caddo), Frank Overton (Burt Hogan), Royal Dano (Uncle Billy Caldwell), James Bell (Benson), Paul Carr (Jack Wiley), Lee Van Cleef (Leo), Ray Teal (Larson), Forrest Lewis (Dr. Welles), Charles Horvath (Hash), Harry Lauter (Russell), Henry Wills (Chunk), Stuart Randall (Luke Gorman), Alan Lane (Burl Hogan)

Director: Herbert Coleman

Synopsis: Four escaped prisoners ransack and murder in the western town of Paradise, and they abduct a woman named Helen Caldwell (Zohra Lampert) before leaving. Gunslinger Banner Cole (Audie Murphy) whose friend was amongst the murdered, leads a posse that pursues the four outlaws and retrieves Helen, but not before she is raped by all four of her captors. During the chase, some of the posse members are killed and abandon the hunt, but Banner Cole persists until all four outlaws are dead. He returns to Paradise, and he gives hope to rape-victim Helen, who is being shunned by the townspeople.

Comment: Posse from Hell doesn't maintain the exciting level apparent in the film's beginning, when the four outlaws hold the citizens of Paradise in a state of terror. The posse is filled out by some very obviously contrived characters, including the tenderfoot easterner, the show-off gunslinger who folds under pressure, and the retired army captain who wears his uniform on the hunt. The only interesting aspects of these men are their treatments of rape victim Helen Caldwell; each posse member has a different approach to the subject. Although steadily paced, *Posse from Hell* doesn't succeed in being anything more than a mediocre chase film.

Van Cleef's Role: Van Cleef, who later mentioned his disdain for *Posse from Hell*, is Leo, one of the four badmen who ransacks Paradise and rapes Helen. Second of the four to die, Leo has only two large scenes. The first serves to establish the character as ruthless and dangerous. In a Paradise saloon, Leo draws a knife and cuts the wrist of an unsuspecting bar patron in order to take the drinker's bottle of whiskey. Leo's next big moment is his death scene. After being wounded in the chest by Banner Cole's gunshot, Leo begins whimpering and whining when he realizes that Cole and the posse are going to leave him in the desert to die.

Princess of the Nile
1954, color, 71 minutes, Twentieth Century–Fox

Cast: Debra Paget (Princess Shalimar/Taura), Jeffrey Hunter (Prince Haidi), Michael Rennie (Rama Khan), Dona Drake (Mirva), Wally Cassell (Goghi), Edgar Barrier (Shaman), Michael Ansara (Capt. Kral), Jack Elam (Basra), Lester Sharpe (Babu), Lee Van Cleef (Hakar), Billy Curtis (Tut), Robert Roark (Capt. Hussein)

Director: Harmon Jones

Synopsis: In the thirteenth century, Prince Haidi (Jeffrey Hunter) begins a trip home to Baghdad with a friend after fighting in a war. Along the way, they stop at the Egyptian city of Halwan, which is under the oppressive rule of Rama Khan (Michael Rennie). During their stay, Prince Haldi's friend is murdered. Haidi stays in Halwan to find the murderer, and he meets Princess Shalimar (Debra Paget), the daughter of Rama Khan. When Halwan's ruler become increasingly tyrannical, Prince Haidi enlists the help of the city's thieves, and Rama Khan is overthrown. A royal wedding follows for Haidi and Shalimar.

Comment: This costumer was shot partly on sets used in the previous year's *The Robe*, which also features a performance by Michael Rennie.

Van Cleef's Role: Van Cleef has a role as Hakar, one of the film's scimitar-wielding toughs.

Private Eyes

1953, black and white, 64 minutes, Allied Artists

Alternate Title: *Bowery Bloodhounds* (production title)

Cast: Leo Gorcey (Terence Aloysius "Slip" Mahoney), Huntz Hall (Horace Debussy "Sach" Jones), David Condon (Chuck), Bennie Bartlett (Butch), Bernard Gorcey (Louie Dumbrowski), Rudy Lee (Herbie), Joyce Holden (Myra Hagen), Robert Osterloh (Prof. Damon), William Forrest (John Graham), William Phillips (Soapy), Gil Perkins (Al), Peter Mamakos (Chico), Lou Lubin (Oskar), Emil Sitka (Wheelchair Patient), Chick Chandler (Eddie the Detective), Tim Ryan (Andy the Cop), Edith Leslie (Aggie the Nurse), Lee Van Cleef, Myron Healey, Carl Saxe.

Director: Edward Bernds

Synopsis: Sach (Huntz Hall) becomes able to read minds after being punched in the nose, and his friend Slip (Leo Gorcey) tries to capitalize on this talent by opening a detective agency. The boys' first client is Myra Hagen (Joyce Holden), and her case requires Sach and Slip to tangle with the mob. The boys infiltrate the mob's hideout, disguised as a Viennese physician and a rich old woman, and they run off the gangsters.

Comment: Private Eyes has been recognized as one of the fastest-paced entries in the long-running Bowery Boys film series. One of the film's writers, Ellwood Ullman, also worked for such comedy teams as the Three Stooges, Martin and Lewis and Abbott and Costello.

Van Cleef's Role: Most sources list Van Cleef's character's name as Karl, but the book *The Films of the Bowery Boys* credits another character, Myron Healey, with the part of Karl and lists Van Cleef's part as "Bit." Another book, *The Psychotronic Encyclopedia of Film*, describes Van Cleef's *Private Eyes* character as a spy.

The Quiet Gun

1957, black and white, 77 minutes,
Twentieth Century–Fox (Western)

Cast: Forrest Tucker (Sheriff Carl Brandon), Mara Corday (Irene), Jim Davis (Ralph), Kathleen Crowley (Teresa), Lee Van Cleef (Sadler), Tom Brown (Reilly), Lewis Martin (Hardy), Hank Worden (Sampson), Gerald Milton (Lesser), Everett Glass (Judge), Edith Evanson (Mrs. Merric), Vince Barnett (Undertaker)

Director: William Claxton

Synopsis: Sheriff Carl Brandon (Forrest Tucker) investigates trouble involving his rancher friend, Ralph (Jim Davis). Rumors are spread that Ralph has been having an affair with an Indian girl named Irene (Mara Corday) while his wife Teresa (Kathleen Crowley) is out of town. Ralph is so enraged by the rumors that he kills a man, and when a lynch mob is assembled, Ralph is hanged. Sheriff Brandon discovers that a saloonkeeper named Reilly (Tom Brown) and a killer named Sadler (lee Van Cleef) started the rumors and instigated the lynching. The sheriff also learns that the two bad men grabbed Ralph's land when the rancher was dead. Carl faces off with Reilly and Sadler and kills them both.

Van Cleef's Role: The Quiet Gun is one of Van Cleef's 11 films in 1957, and Sadler, a killer who is part of the scheme to grab Ralph's land, is one of the many Van Cleef heavies who does not live until the film's end. In *The Quiet Gun* Van Cleef supports star Forrest Tucker, but by 1970 the roles had reversed, and Tucker played a supporting role for the Van Cleef starrer *Barquero*.

Raiders of Old California

1957, black and white, 72 minutes
Republic (Western)

Cast: Jim Davis, Arleen Whelan, Faron Young, Marty Robbins, Lee Van Cleef, Louis Jean Heydt, Harry Lauter, Douglas Fowley, Larry Dobkin, Bill Coontz, Don Diamond, Ric Vallin, Tom Hubbard

Producer/Director: Albert C. Gannaway

Synopsis: In 1850s California, after the Mexican War, villainous cavalry officers try to establish their own domain in a Mexican-inhabited area of the state. A brave pioneer joins the Mexicans in trying to stop the officers' plan.

Comment: This film contains a cast which is almost identical to that of another 1957 Gannaway Western, *The Badge of Marshal Brennan*. In *Raiders*, singer Faron Young also appears with Country and Western star Marty Robbins.

Van Cleef's Role: Van Cleef, who reportedly plays a character named Damon Parde in *Raiders of Old California*, also appears in *The Badge of Marshal Brennan*.

Rails into Laramie
1954, color, 80 minutes
Universal (Western)

Cast: John Payne (Jefferson Harder), Mari Blanchard (Lou Carter), Dan Duryea (Jim Shanessy), Joyce MacKenzie (Helen Shanessy), Barton MacLane (Lee Graham), Harry Shannon (Judge Pierce), Ralph Dumke (Mayor Brown), Lee Van Cleef (Ace Winton), Myron Healey (Con Winton), James Griffith (Orrie Sommers), Alexander Campbell (Higby), George Chandler (Grimes), Charles Horvath (Pike Murphy), Stephen Case (Gen. Auger), Douglas Kennedy (Telegraph Operator), George Cleveland

Director: Jesse Hibbs

Synopsis: In Laramie, Wyoming, a local bartender named Jim Shanessy (Dan Duryea) leads an effort to keep railroad workers from completing their job in Laramie, because the workers bring needed business to town. Army Sgt. Jefferson Harder (John Payne) is sent to Laramie to see that the railroad is completed, and Harder captures Shanessy and his gang of sabotaging crooks. Since previous all-male juries acquitted Shanessy on other charges, an all-female jury is assembled. The jury convicts Shanessy.

Van Cleef's Role: In *Rails into Laramie*, Van Cleef is Ace Winton. Van Cleef had supporting roles in two other films starring John Payne, *Kansas City Confidential* (1952) and *The Road to Denver* (1955).

Return of Sabata
1971 or 1972, color, 106 minutes
Italian-French-German (Western)

Alternate Titles: È tornato Sabata, hai chiuso un'altra volta (Italian), Il ritorno di Sabata (Italian), Le retour de Sabata (French), Sabata kehrt zurück (German)

Cast: Lee Van Cleef (Sabata), Reiner Schone (Clyde), Annabella Icontrera (Maggie), Gianni Rizzo (Jeremy Sweeney), Gianpiero [Giampiero] Albertini (Joel McIntock), Jacqueline Alexandre (Jackie), Pedro Sanchez [Ignazio Spalla] (Bronco), Nick Nordan [Aldo Canti] (Angel), Karis Vassili (Acrobat), Annibal Venturi (McIntock's Henchman), Benito Vasconi (Bouncer), Sylvia Alba (Saloon Girl), Gunther Stoll

Co-Writer/Director: Frank Kramer [Gianfranco Parolini]

Synopsis: When a traveling circus sideshow arrives in Hobsonville, Sabata (Lee Van Cleef), the circus trick shooter, spots his Civil War pal Clyde (Reiner Schone), who owes him $5000. Clyde can't pay the debt, but when Sabata quits the circus, Clyde agrees to help his war pal swipe the fortune of Joel McIntock (Gianpiero Albertini), Hobsonville's greedy kingpin who levies outrageous taxes. The two men get their hands on McIntock's stash of money but find that it is counterfeit. They offer to return McIntock's counterfeit decoy money — which was printed by the circus' sleight-of-hand artist, Mr. Pickles — in exchange for ten percent of the town boss' real fortune. McIntock does not agree to those terms. With another plan in mind, Sabata and Clyde use circus make-up to fake their own bloody deaths. McIntock is fooled, and he tells the whereabouts of his hidden fortune to what he believes are two corpses. Sabata and Clyde arise, and McIntock is surprised and then killed. Sabata retrieves the fortune, which sat in the late Joel McIntock's chimney.

Comment: Return of Sabata begins with a mysterious council in a smoke-filled room commissioning a team of gunfighters to murder Sabata. Sabata enters and shoots down the men one by one, often using showy methods. Only after Sabata has finished off all the gunfighters and after circus clowns enter the room is it apparent that this is Sabata's sideshow act. Critics have accurately stated that the main part of *Return of Sabata* never quite matches the surprisingly good surreal effect of this interesting opening sequence. The film is full of gadgetry that was prevalent in *Sabata*, and it features the acrobatics that seem to form a part of most of Kramer's (Parolini's) films. After the opening, the story line degenerates and the film becomes a hard-to-follow vehicle for lots of killing and maiming.

Van Cleef's Role: After other actors portrayed the character he made popular, Van Cleef resurrects his 1969 character Sabata for this early '70s sequel. He is first seen as a trick-shot artist in the traveling circus. This role is not much of an acting challenge for Van Cleef; all Sabata has to do is look expressionless and kill people. However, a few moments of intentional humor, not evident in the original *Sabata*, are provided to allow Van Cleef to use his talent for humor to add to the character.

Ride Lonesome

1959, color, 73 minutes, Columbia (Western)

Cast: Randolph Scott (Ben Brigade), Karen Steele (Carrie Lane), Pernell Roberts (Sam Boone), James Best (Billy John), Lee Van Cleef (Frank), James Coburn (Wid), Dyke Johnson (Charlie), Boyd Stockman (Indian Chief)

Producer/Director: Budd Boetticher

Synopsis: Bounty hunter Ben Brigade (Randolph Scott) captures outlaw Billy John (James Best) and travels with his prisoner towards Santa Cruz. Along the way, Ben and Billy are joined by two reforming outlaws and a widow whose husband was killed by hostile Indians. Ben's companions eventually learn that the bounty hunter has no intention of handing Billy John over to the law. Ben is using his prisoner as bait, hoping to lure Billy's brother Frank (Lee Van Cleef), the man who murdered the bounty hunter's wife. Frank arrives to rescue his brother but is gunned down by Ben while making the attempt. With no more use for Billy John, Ben gives the wanted man to the two reforming outlaws, who can exchange Billy for a pardon.

Comment: A visually appealing film, *Ride Lonesome* is a simple, tightly-plotted Western with an excellent supporting cast. The rocky desert scenery gives way to sandy desert and finally to wooded area, treating the viewer to a variety of outdoor splendor as the story progresses. Scott handles the part of revenge-seeking Ben Brigade well, and James Best, Pernell Roberts and Karen Steele are believable in their roles. Roberts especially is convincing as the outlaw who wants a chance to go straight, and who has his eye on the attractive widow. *Ride Lonesome* marks the film debut of actor James Coburn.

Van Cleef's Role: Van Cleef appears as Frank, the brother of the wanted man Brigade is bringing in. Frank chases Brigade with four of his cronies. After a while, it dawns on Frank that Brigade is not even trying to elude his pursuers. He realizes that Brigade is setting a trap for him, using his brother Billy John as bait. Van Cleef's Frank is anticipated but is not seen until near the picture's end. In his final scene, Frank seems remorseful about his previous crime. He pleads with Ben to set his brother free; Frank makes it obvious that he does not want to kill the bounty hunter, and he does not want the uninvolved Billy to be harmed. Van Cleef is superb as Frank, and he plays the character with an interesting mixture of responsibility toward his brother and fatalism concerning his meeting with Brigade. Frank is a more noble character than most of the Western screen villains played by Van Cleef during the 1950s.

Road to Denver
1955, color, 90 minutes
Republic (Western)

Cast: John Payne (Bill Mayhew), Mona Freeman (Elizabeth Sutton), Lee J. Cobb (Jim Donovan), Skip Homeier (Sam Mayhew), Andy Clyde (Whipsaw), Lee Van Cleef (Pecos Larry), Karl Davis (Hunsaker), Glenn Strange (Big George), Buzz Henry (Pete), Daniel White (Joslyn), Robert Burton (Kraft), Anne Carroll (Miss Honeywell), Tex Terry (Passenger), Ray Middleton (John Sutton)

Director: Joseph Kane

Synopsis: Bill Mayhew (John Payne) leaves behind his trouble-making younger brother Sam (Skip Homeier) and moves to Colorado, where he gets legitimate work setting up a stagecoach line to Denver. Sam also moves to Colorado, but he joins a band of criminals led by Jim Donovan (Lee J. Cobb). The two brothers eventually end up on opposite sides in a shoot-out, and older brother Bill comes out victorious.

Van Cleef's Role: Van Cleef appears as Pecos Larry.

Sabata (Lee Van Cleef) smiles as Carrincha (Pedro Sanchez, a.k.a. Ignazio Spalla) exults over a fistful of dollars in *Sabata* (1969).

Sabata

1969, color, 107 minutes,
Italian (Western)

Alternate Titles: *Ehi, amico ... c'e Sabata, Hai Chiuso!* (Italian); *Sabata's Here ... Close Everything* (British)

Cast: Lee Van Cleef (Sabata), William Berger (Banjo), Pedro Sanchez [Ignazio Spalla] (Carrincha), Nick Jordan (Alley Cat), Franco Ressel (Stengel), Anthony Gradwell [Antonio Gradoli] (Fergusson), Linda Veras (Jane), Robert Hundar [Claudio Undari] (Oswald), Gianni

Rizzo (Judge O'Hara), Alan Collins (False Father Brown), Romano Puppo (Rocky Bendato), Mimmo Poli (Hotel Workman)

Co-Writer/Director: Frank Kramer [Gianfranco Parolini]

Synopsis: When the Texas town of Daugherty stores $100,000 of U.S. Army money in its bank's safe, one of its most prominent citizens, Stengel (Franco Ressel), masterminds a robbery. The heist is carried out by Stengel's men, but during their getaway, a stranger named Sabata (Lee Van Cleef) kills the robbers and returns the safe to the Army. After receiving a $5000 reward, Sabata tries to become richer by blackmailing Stengel, and the respected citizen deploys many gunfighters to kill the drifter. But Sabata receives help from two rag-tag friends, a knife-throwing beggar named Carrincha (Pedro Sanchez) and an acrobat named Alley Cat (Nick Jordan). Stengel's gunmen are no match for Sabata, who kills Stengel and makes off with a lot of money.

Comment: It's quick-draw after quick-draw in this over-the-top, internationally successful Spaghetti Western; some of the gun duels are well handled and clever while others serve only to drag out the film's length. Kramer (Parolini) liked plenty of gadgets and acrobatics in his films, and *Sabata* is well supplied with both. Trick guns, especially, are in evidence. A pistol that shoots from its handle, a rifle with barrels of different lengths, a shooting banjo and other oddities caused one reviewer to comment that no one ever seemed to get shot with anything ordinary. On the whole, *Sabata* is a fun film.

Van Cleef's Role: Sabata is not a demanding character for Van Cleef. The self-assured gunfighter keeps either an impassive look or a slight grin of smug confidence on his face throughout the whole film. Van Cleef's portrayal was very well-received in Europe, and a number of sequels, mostly unauthorized, were spawned. Van Cleef himself did a sequel, *Return of Sabata*, a few years later.

Speed Zone

1989, color, 95 minutes, Entcorp/Orion

Alternate Title: *Cannonball Run III*

Cast: John Candy (Charlie Cronyn), Donna Dixon (Tiffany), Matt Frewer (Alec), Joe Flaherty (Vic), Tim Matheson (Jack), Mimi Kuzyk

(Heather), Melody Anderson (Lee), Shari Belafonte (Margaret), Brian George (Valentino), Art Hindle (Flash), Dick Smothers (Nelson Van Sloan), Tom Smothers (Randolph Van Sloan), Peter Boyle (Chief Spiro T. Edsel), Don Lake (Whitman), Lee Van Cleef (Grandfather), Harvey Atkin (Gus Gold), Eugene Levy (Leo Ross), Michael Spinks (Bachelor), Brooke Shields (Stewardess), Alyssa Milano (Truck Driver), Louis Del Grande (Salesman), Carl Lewis (Jogger)

Director: Jim Drake

Synopsis: Professional drivers meet in Washington, D.C., to begin the Cannonball Run, a cross-country road race, but Police Chief Spiro T. Edsel (Peter Boyle) has the drivers arrested in a preemptive strike. With amateur drivers filling in, the race is given the green light. Chief Edsel follows them across the country, but most of the problems the drivers encounter are from dirty tricks employed by the other greedy drivers. As the drivers converge near the finish line on the Santa Monica Pier, Chief Edsel, in an attempt to apprehend the racers, passes the other drivers and crosses the finish line first, becoming the winner.

Comment: Speed Zone, full of flat-falling shopworn gags, is at its funniest when it pokes fun at itself. Most of the humor is intended to come from the tricks the drivers use to win, but the film makes a self-deprecating joke when two racing partners (played by the Smothers Brothers) go as far as to bribe an airline pilot and begin taxiing down the nation's highways in a jet airplane. Part of the fun is just trying to pick out all the semi-famous people who make brief cameo appearances. John Candy is fine as usual as a likable loser.

Van Cleef's Role: Lee Van Cleef has a small cameo at the film's beginning. He plays an oldster who is trying to teach his uninterested grandson how to skip stones on a lake. Nearby, police cruisers are chasing a Lamborghini, a car whose shape resembles the flat stones that the grandfather is skipping. Obviously, the stage is set for the first gag of *Speed Zone*, and it comes about when the Lamborghini eludes the cops by skipping across the lake while the grandson watches with mouth agape. As the Lamborghini roars off on the other side of the lake, the boys turns to Van Cleef and asks to be shown stone-skipping again. This is one of Van Cleef's last two roles.

The Squeeze

1978, color, 100 minutes, Italian

Alternate Titles: *The Big Rip-Off, Controrapina, The Heist, The Rip-Off*

Cast: Lee Van Cleef (Chris Gretchko), Karen Black (Clarisse Saunders), Edward Albert (Jeff Olavson), Lionel Stander (Sam Epstein), Robert Alda (Donati), Angelo Infanti (Inspector), Antonella Murgia (Jessica), Peter Carsten (Van Stratten), Rudolf Van Husen (Hans), Dyane Silverstein (Cashier), Steve Burche (Fred), Ron Van Clief (Duke), Bob Avalone (Lieutenant), Roy Brocksmith (Warehouse Owner), Ewald G. Spader (Electrician)

Director: Anthony M. Dawson [Antonio Margheriti]

Synopsis: Master safecracker Chris Gretchko (Lee Van Cleef) comes out of hiding in Mexico in order to help his friend's son Jeff Olafson (Edward Albert), who is in debt to a German criminal named Van Stratten (Peter Carsten). Chris flies to New York City, where Jeff presents the safecracker for Van Stratten's use and, in doing so, absolves his debt. Van Stratten needs Chris to open a safe and steal $6,000,000 worth of diamonds, but before the heist gets underway, Chris learns that his associates intend to kill him when the job is done. Chris alters the plan and steals the diamonds for himself, but while fleeing from Van Stratten's thugs, he is badly wounded in the leg. The New York police, who recognize the heist as Gretchko's work, comb the city for the safecracker. This police search confines Chris to his hideout in a vacant apartment, where his leg wound is cared for by another tenant, Clarisse Saunders (Karen Black). Eventually, Clarisse learns the whereabouts of the diamonds, which the safecracker had hidden in a bottle of beer, and she tries to kill him. When Clarisse's secret partner Jeff Olafson believes that Chris is dead, he arrives to kill her and take the diamonds but instead finds that Chris had discovered their secret betrayal. Chris kills Jeff and leaves with the diamonds just before the police arrive.

Comment: Van Cleef works well with Edward Albert, Lionel Stander and Karen Black, and all four actors turn in terrific performances. It is their performances that carry most scenes of *The Squeeze* and make it watchable, despite its all-too-familiar plot of a criminal called back for one last job. It's only when Gretchko becomes confined to his hideout that the performances can't redeem *The Squeeze*, as it plods through scenes of Gretchko moping around his apartment and introduces a needless, hard-to-follow subplot about thugs who murder Van Stratten. The film wraps up in good order, though, with its neatly constructed surprise ending. *The Squeeze* also boasts a knowledgeable handling of safecracking and an infectious pop-tinged score.

Van Cleef's Role: Like Van Cleef's Harry Chapman character in the previous year's *The Perfect Killer*, Chris Gretchko is the film's protagonist and is also on the wrong side of the law. Gretchko is also similar to Harry Chapman in his ability to overcome giant odds and to persevere in hostile situations. Van Cleef turns in a good performance (under the direction of Dawson, who directed Van Cleef in at least five films), and his physical appearance helps him to look convincingly tough. For many of his films of this time period, the aging Van Cleef wore a bad-looking toupee and looked very craggy. In *The Squeeze*, he remains bald but sports long hair, and also an earring, a goatee and suave attire. This is Van Cleef's last outing as a film's principal protagonist.

The Stranger and the Gunfighter

1974, color, 100 minutes,
U.S.-Italy-Spain-Hong Kong (Western)

Alternate Titles: *Blood Money* (British), *In meiner Wut weig' ich vier Zentner* (German), *La brute, le colt, et le karate* (French), *Là, dove non batte il sole* (Italian), *Moneda Sangrienta* (Spanish)

Cast: Lee Van Cleef (Dakota), Lo Lieh (Wang Ho Kiang), Karen Yeh [Yeh Ling Chih] (Lia), Julian Ugarte (Yancy Hobit), Goyo Peralta (Indio), Al Tung (Mr. Wang), Patty Shepard (Russian), Erika Blanc (American), Femi Benussi (Italian), George Rigaud (Barclay), Richard Palacios (Calico), Alfred Boreman (Laundryman), Bart Barry (Sheriff), Paul Costello (Lawyer)

Director: Anthony M. Dawson [Antonio Margheriti]

Synopsis: A bank robber named Dakota (Lee Van Cleef) uses dynamite to open the bank vault of a wealthy Chinese man named Mr. Wang (Al Tung), who came to the West hoping to invest his family's fortune in American businesses. But before Dakota can open the vault, Mr. Wang arrives to stop the break-in and is accidentally killed as the dynamite explodes. Once the vault is opened, Dakota finds that Wang's fortune is not there; the vault was used by Wang only to hold photographs of four women. When Wang's kung fu–fighting nephew Ho Kiang (Lo Lieh) is sent from China to retrieve the family fortune, he teams with Dakota and together they search for the four photographed women, all of whom have had clues to the fortune's whereabouts tattooed on their buttocks by the late Mr. Wang. Ho Kiang falls in love with the fourth woman, Lia (Karen Yeh), and before he can find a tactful way to ask to see her bare buttocks, she is abducted by a madman named Yancy Hobit (Julian Ugarte), who knows about the fortune and the gluteal clues. Dakota and Ho Kiang rescue Lia from Yancy's clutches, and all three depart for China, where the late Mr. Wang's fortune was kept hidden all the while.

Comment: A small subgenre of the Spaghetti Western contains films in which martial arts–fighting Asians come to the Old West. *The Stranger and the Gunfighter*, a film falling into this category, brings together likable martial arts film star Lo Lieh and Western star Van Cleef. The tone is humorous, but the successful jokes are few. Also, some of the fight scenes involving protagonist Ho Kiang (Lo Lieh) are intended to be humorous. They are not, however, and since they are too one-sided in favor of Ho Kiang, they also are not very exciting. For its climax, *The Stranger and the Gunfighter* takes a decidedly heavier tone.

Van Cleef's Role: Van Cleef plays Dakota, a bank robber. His is supposed to be a humorous role, but the script is not particularly funny, making the part a difficult one. But Van Cleef is effective in portraying Dakota as a man enjoying himself with his new-found foreigner friend. Dakota's best scene comes at a roulette table, where Ho Kiang is using an abacus to figure out probabilities in order to beat the game. After Ho begins a sustained winning streak, the gambling house owner looks worried, but the laughing Dakota just pounds his fist on his table and shouts, "Pay! Pay! Pay!" Viewers are also treated to the sound and spectacle of the Western actor singing "Rye Whiskey" during one scene. Van Cleef's character is presented as a tough action hero only after the film's tone becomes serious near the conclusion. Attempting to rescue Lia (Karen Yeh), Dakota is captured, given a whipping and thrown in a temporary jail cell. Before Dakota is freed to gun down the villain, the film takes time to show the tough hero peering from the shadows of his cell, shirtless, bleeding from the whipping, and ready to wreak destruction upon those who mistreated him. This is the first film that Van Cleef made with Anthony M. Dawson, who directed other Van Cleef films such as *Take a Hard Ride, The Squeeze, Codename: Wildgeese* and *Jungle Raiders*.

Take a Hard Ride
1975, color, 103 minutes
U.S.-Italian-German (Western)

Alternate Title: *La parola di un fuorilegge ... è legge* (Italian)

Cast: Jim Brown (Pike), Lee Van Cleef (Kiefer), Fred Williamson (Tyree), Catherine Spaak (Catherine), Jim Kelly (Kashtok), Barry Sullivan (Sheriff Kane), Dana Andrews (Morgan), Harry Carey, Jr. (Dumper), Robert Donner (Skave), Charles McGregor (Cloyd), Leonard Smith (Cangey), Ronald Howard (Halsey), Ricardo Palacios (Calvera), Robin Levitt (Chico), Buddy Joe Hooker (Angel)

Director: Anthony M. Dawson [Antonio Margheriti]

Synopsis: After delivering a herd of cattle, trail boss Morgan (Dana Andrews) succumbs to illness. Before he dies, his head cowboy, Pike (Jim Brown), promises to deliver the $86,000 payroll to Morgan's family and employees in Mexico. Pike begins his journey and is joined by a rag-tag group of travelers, including a gambler named Tyree (Fred Williamson), a widow named Catherine (Catherine Spaak) and a martial arts–fighting mute named Kashtok (Jim Kelly). They are trailed by ruthless bounty hunter Kiefer (Lee Van Cleef), who knows about an old bounty that is still outstanding on Pike, and is aware that Pike is carrying a large quantity of money. The group is also trailed by a lawman named Kane (Barry Sullivan). Near the end of their journey, Tyree decides he has helped Pike defend the payroll for long enough, and he tries to fight the cowboy for the money. The fight is interrupted by the approaching of Kiefer and other greedy pursuers. Pike gives the money to a little boy who carries it into Mexico. Tyree again decides to help Pike, and the two create a large explosion which keeps their pursuers from closing in. Pike and Tyree walk to Mexico.

Comment: Take a Hard Ride boasts a fine cast, solid performances and four very interesting Spaghetti Western characters: Pike, Tyree, Kane and Kiefer. However, the yarn spun in *Hard Ride* doesn't allow for enough of the needed interaction amongst the four (Kane and Kiefer aren't given chances to make their motivations obvious). Also, the film becomes full of inconsistencies near the end. *Hard Ride* contains many overlong action sequences, and although some stuntmen take some terrific spills, the action consists mainly of nondescript chase scenes and large-scale shoot-outs. The film has few man-to-man quick draws, an element that made earlier Spaghetti Westerns so exciting. Filmed in the Canary Islands, *Take a Hard Ride* is enhanced by interesting scenery and by Jerry Goldsmith's wonderful score.

Van Cleef's Role: An exciting character, Van Cleef's bounty hunter is marred only by his lack of apparent motivations. This is a result of the limited script. Near the film's beginning, Kiefer gives a speech about the importance of law and order (as per Van Cleef's character in *The Big Gundown*) after Sheriff Kane questions Kiefer's killing of a wanted but reformed man. Later, Kiefer seems to be after Pike's payroll. But *Take a Hard Ride* seems to be trying to present Kiefer as a protagonist; he never openly states that he is after the payroll money, and the film constantly offsets Kiefer by surrounding him with obnoxious, greedy moneychasers. These other characters are introduced when Kiefer recruits them to ride on the hunt. This action further clouds Kiefer's motivations, because the bounty hunter obviously does not like these other riders, and he is lessening his potential share of the money by recruiting them. (Kiefer obviously does not need them, because his closest attempt to capturing Pike comes when the bounty hunter is alone.) Kiefer, though irritatingly mysterious, is well-played by Van Cleef to be the most intelligent extreme of his hardened tough guy persona. In fact, this is probably Van Cleef's last great Western role. It is fitting, then, that Kiefer is seen to be a harmonica player like Van Cleef's first Western character, Jack Colby, in *High Noon*.

Ten Wanted Men

1955, color, 80 minutes,
Columbia (Western)

Cast: Randolph Scott (John Stewart), Jocelyn Brando (Corinne Michaels Stewart), Richard Boone (Wick Campbell), Alfonso Bedoya

(Hermando), Skip Homeier (Howie Stewart), Leo Gordon (Frank Scavo), Lester Matthews (Adam Stewart), Dennis Weaver (Sheriff Clyde Gibbons), Donna Martell (Maria Segura), Clem Bevans (Tod Grinnel), Minor Watson (Jason Carr), Tom Powers (Green), Lee Van Cleef (Al Drucker), Denver Pyle (Dave Weed), Francis McDonald (Warner), Pat Collins (Bartender), Louis Jean Heydt (Tom Baines)

Director: Bruce Humberstone

Synopsis: Arizona businessman Wick Campbell (Richard Boone) makes unwanted advances towards his love interest Maria Segura (Donna Martel), prompting Maria to flee for safety at the ranch of prosperous cattleman John Stewart (Randolph Scott). Campbell, who has always envied John, is enraged and hires approximately ten gunslinging outlaws to help him feud with the cattle rancher. John, who is aided by local friends and his relatives from Cincinnati, puts Campbell and his hired guns to rest.

Comment: Ten Wanted Men is a dull and predictable film, with the players giving only passable performances. Star Randolph Scott was also the co-producer.

Van Cleef's Role: Van Cleef is Al Drucker, one of Campbell's hired gunfighters. Drucker tries to kill John Stewart when John comes looking for businessman Campbell in a hotel room where Drucker is waiting. A weak attempt is made to establish a second motivation for Drucker's attempted murder when Drucker tells John that he's not only killing for the money but also because John's nephew killed Al's outlaw chum. Because it is hard to tell whether Drucker believes his own words, it is uncertain whether the feebleness of this motivation comes from Drucker or from the scriptwriter. Either way, John is quicker on the draw, and he kills Drucker. Van Cleef gives *Ten Wanted Men* one of its few consistently good performances but isn't given many chances to foul it up; he has only a handful of scenes.

Thieves of Fortune

1990, color, 100 minutes, Skouras Pictures

Alternate Title: *May the Best Man Win*

Cast: Michael Nouri (Juan Luis), Lee Van Cleef (Sergio Danielo

Christophero), Shawn Weatherly (Peter Christopher), Craig Gardner (Henry Horatio Christopher), Liz Torres (Big Rosa), Russel Savadier (Miguel), John Hussey (Sir Nigel), Toni Caprari (Chief Priest), Joe Ribiero (Police Inspector), Nadia Bilchik (Isabella), Nobby Clark (Sput McGuigan), Claudia Udy (Marissa), Danie Voges (Gomez), Graham Weir (Pirana), Jon Maytham (Flagstead), Kenneth Hendel (Loony Professor), Charles Kinsman (Nunzio), Michael Fisher (Mr. Forstman), Stuart Parker (Prospector), Pamela Perry (Mrs. Christopher), Alan Pierce (Mr. Christopher), Koos Strauss (Senior Peasant), Tom Hoskins (Jim Haines), Gary Ford (Bank Manager), Martin James (Clockston), Anthony Wilson (Barman), Peter Tobin, John Lesley, Paddy Lyster, Toni Caprari, Robert Trevallyan

Director: Michael McCarthy

Synopsis: Aware of his threatening heart disease, millionaire Sergio Danielo Christophero (Lee Van Cleef) arranges a competition to determine which of his only two living blood relatives, Peter (Shawn Weatherly) or Henry (Craig Gardner), will inherit his $28,000,000 fortune. When Sergio dies of a heart attack, the competition begins near his home in Mexico and is monitored by Sergio's trusted friend Juan Luis (Michael Nouri). The competition tests the manly powers of the two heirs, and since Peter is actually a woman with a masculine name, she disguises herself as a man in order to qualify. Although her true sex is revealed during the competition, Peter bests Henry, and Juan Luis decides that the rules' "may the best man win" clause is just a figure of speech. Peter inherits the fortune and marries Juan Luis.

Comment: Thieves of Fortune, with its mindless violence and exploitative nudity, was obviously meant to appeal to home video audiences. Shawn Weatherly, who plays the film's heroine, was once Miss Universe.

Van Cleef's Role: Although some sources list 1989's *Speed Zone* as Van Cleef's last film appearance, much evidence suggests that this distinction belongs to *Thieves of Fortune*, which was apparently released in 1990. Van Cleef is in fine acting form as usual, and his character, millionaire Sergio (possible a Leone allusion) Danielo Christophero, is rather colorful. Before the film's midpoint, Sergio suffers a fatal heart attack, just as Van Cleef later did in reality. Making it especially poignant is an earlier scene in which Sergio fakes a heart attack in order to be alone with his voluptuous nurse. Van Cleef fans might have liked to see the actor finish his career in a full-fledged Western, but at least the Mexico-based Sergio character provided the character with the familiar tasks of shooting a revolver (as a joke on some of his friends) and wearing Western garb.

The Tin Star
1957, black and white, 93 minutes
Paramount (Western)

Cast: Henry Fonda (Morgan Hickman), Anthony Perkins (Ben Owens), Neville Brand (Bart Bogardus), Betsy Palmer (Nona Mayfield), Michael Ray (Kip Mayfield), John McIntire (Dr. McCord), Lee Van Cleef (Ed McGaffey), Mary Webster (Millie Parker), Peter Baldwin (Zeke McGaffey), Richard Shannon (Buck Henderson), James Bell (Judge Thatcher)

Director: Anthony Mann

Synopsis: Inexperienced Sheriff Ben Owens (Anthony Perkins) solicits advice from bounty hunter and former sheriff Morgan Hickman (Henry Fonda). Hickman, a disillusioned lawman, is reluctant to help — advising Ben to instead give up his star — but he does eventually give the sheriff advice. When the town's beloved doctor is murdered by two half-breeds (Lee Van Cleef, Peter Baldwin), Ben tries to bring the two killers to justice with a fair trial. The town's citizens don't help to uphold their sheriff's decision, though, when town bully Bart Bogardus (Neville Brand) tries to lynch the two murderers. With no help from the townspeople, the young sheriff stands alone against Bogardus, until Hickman puts on a star and helps Ben quell the lynching. With this experience, Ben becomes a confident lawman. Hickman rides off with a renewed faith in law and order, hoping to find work as another town's sheriff.

Comment: An intelligent Western from prolific director Anthony Mann, *The Tin Star* features a story which contains some similarities to the influential *High Noon*. The ending, which has Hickman finally put on a deputy's star, is manipulative and predictable but is, nonetheless, effective.

Van Cleef's Role: Ed McGaffey (Van Cleef) and his brother Zeke are two murderous half-breeds (Bogardus uses their racial mixture to

Fledgling sheriff Ben Owens (Anthony Perkins) gains experience by rounding up two wanted brothers, Zeke and Ed McGaffey (Peter Baldwin and Lee Van Cleef), in *The Tin Star* (Paramount, 1957).

convince the townspeople that the McGaffeys aren't deserving of a trial). The two kill a man in a robbery, and Zeke is severely wounded. Ed finds the town's doctor and gets medical attention to Zeke, but Ed realizes that the doctor knows why Zeke is wounded. Ed kills the doctor. Later, the brothers are seen waiting in a jail cell, fearing that they will be lynched by Bogardus. Ed McGaffey is one of Van Cleef's most sympathetic heavies, partly because of the actor's realistic portrayal, but also because both his murders occurred off-screen.

Treasure of Ruby Hills

1955, black and white, 71 minutes,
Allied Artists (Western)

Cast: Zachary Scott (Haney), Carole Mathews (Sherry), Barton MacLane (Reynolds), Dick Foran (Doran), Lola Albright (May), Gordon James (Voyle), Raymond Hatton (Scotty), Lee Van Cleef (Emmett), Steve Darrell (Hull), Charles Fredericks (Payne), Stanley Andrews (Garvey), James Alexander (Burt), Rick Vallin (Vernon)

Director: Frank McDonald

Synopsis: An outlaw's son named Haney (Zachary Scott) tries to establish a ranch but must contend with two groups of crooked cattle ranchers, whose greedy quarrels threaten Haney's water rights.

Comment: Treasure of Ruby Hills is based on a story by famous Western writer Louis L'Amour.

Van Cleef's Role: Van Cleef plays Emmett in *Treasure of Ruby Hills*. Besides this film, Van Cleef appears in another production based on a Louis L'Amour story: the "Man Down, Woman Screaming" TV episode of *City Detective*.

Tribute to a Bad Man

1956, color, 95 minutes,
Metro-Goldwyn-Mayer (Western)

Cast: James Cagney (Jeremy Rodock), Don Dubbins (Steve Miller), Stephen McNally (McNulty), Irene Papas (Jocasta Constantine), Vic Morrow (Lars Peterson), James Griffith (Barjack), Onslow Stevens (Hearn), James Bell (L.A. Peterson), Jeanette Nolan (Mrs. L.A. Peterson), Chubby Johnson (Baldy), Royal Dano (Abe), Lee Van Cleef (Fat Jones), Peter Chong (Cooky), James McCallion (Shorty), Clint Sharp (Red), Carl Pitti (Tom), Tony Hughes (1st Buyer), Roy Engel (2nd Buyer), Bud Osborne, John Halloran, Tom London, Dennis Moore, Buddy Roosevelt, Billy Dix

Director: Robert Wise

Synopsis: While drifting out West from his home in Pennsylvania,

Steve Miller (Don Dubbins) comes upon rancher Jeremy Rodock (James Cagney), who is defending his life in a shoot-out against a gang of horse rustlers. Steve saves Rodock's life, and the rancher returns the favor by giving Steve a job as a wrangler on his ranch. The young man enjoys being a wrangler but is disturbed by Rodock's affinity for hanging rustlers. Steve has romantic feelings for the rancher's live-in lover Jocasta Constantine (Irene Papas), who also hates Rodock's "hanging fever." Steve convinces Jocasta to leave the ranch with him, but before they get their chance, Rodock tasks Steve to help him deal with a gang of rustlers, including Lars Peterson (Vic Morrow), the son of Rodock's former partner. After he administers severe punishment to Lars, Rodock sees the error of his way and returns with Steve to Jocasta, who decides to stay with the reformed rancher.

Comment: Because Jeremy Rodock and Steve Miller both manage to win the audience's sympathy, the ending, which forces Jocasta to choose between the two, is somewhat unsatisfying. The film was originally intended for stars Spencer Tracy and Grace Kelly.

Van Cleef's Role: Lean actor Van Cleef has a bit part as Fat Jones, an especially randy wrangler on Rodock's ranch. Fat's big scene comes in the bunkhouse when Steve first meets his bunkmates, and Fat asks the newcomer if he has any catalogues with pictures of women in corsets. Steve doesn't, and the scene ends somewhat humorously, with Fat Jones releasing his frustrations by violently knifing a piece of wood and muttering, "Corsets."

Tumbleweed
1953, color, 79 minutes
Universal (Western)

Cast: Audie Murphy (Jim Harvey), Lori Nelson (Laura), Chill Wills (Sheriff Murchoree), Roy Roberts (Nick Buckley), Russell Johnson (Lam), K.T. Stevens (Louella Buckley), Madge Meredith (Sarah), Lee Van Cleef (Marv), I. Stanford Jolley (Ted), Ross Elliott (Seth), Ralph Moody (Aguila), Eugene Iglesias (Tigre), Phil Chambers (Trapper Ross), Lyle Talbot (Weber), King Donovan (Wrangler), Harry Harvey (Prospector)

Director: Nathan Juran

Synopsis: While Jim Harvey (Audie Murphy) is escorting a wagon train to the town of Borax, Yaqui Indians attack, massacre most of the passengers and make Jim their captive. When he is freed, Jim travels to Borax, where he is accused of abandoning the wagons. Jim flees, narrowly escaping a lynching. A posse is formed to hunt Jim, but when the posse members catch him, the group is attacked by Yaquis. Jim saves the lives of his pursuers and clears his name by exposing the real culprit, Lam (Russell Johnson). Lam had persuaded the Indians to massacre the wagon passengers so that he could snatch the land belonging to one of the deceased.

Comment: Tumbleweed is a routine Western, and Audie Murphy's limitations as an actor keep it from being very good. The film's title refers to the name of Jim's often unlucky horse, to which the hero relates.

Van Cleef's Role: Van Cleef's Marv is first seen becoming a temporary deputy in order to help the Borax sheriff prevent the lynching of Jim. It is soon evident that Marv has taken the job in hopes of enabling the hanging to proceed when the sheriff's back is turned. Although Marv is putting on a facade, it is interesting to see an early Van Cleef character perform the duties of a lawman (a Van Cleef character in a similar position can be seen in the "Missing Hacienda" TV episode of *The Adventures of Kit Carson*). Marv later joins the posse that hunts Jim, but after the fugitive saves his life, Marv tries to return the favor when Jim is held at gunpoint by Lam. But Lam kills Marv. Van Cleef is fine as the easily influenced, none-too-bright Marv, and good characterization comes when Marv attempts to impress the posse by trying to cross some rough terrain and falls off his horse. The other posse members begin to laugh, and the embarrassed Marv laughs also, to hide his humiliation.

Untamed Frontier

1952, color, 75 minutes
Universal (Western)

Cast: Joseph Cotten (Kirk Denbow), Shelley Winters (Jane Stevens), Scott Brady (Glenn Denbow), Suzan Ball (Lottie), Minor Watson (Matt Denbow), Katherine Emery (Camilla Denbow), Antonio Moreno (Bandera), Douglas Spencer (Clayton Vance), John Alexander (Max Wickersham), Lee Van Cleef (Dave Chittun), Richard Garland (Charlie Fentress), Robert Anderson (Ezra McCloud), Fess Parker (Clem McCloud), Ray Bennett (Sheriff Brogan)

Director: Hugo Fregonese

Synopsis: In Texas, the powerful Denbow family owns a giant piece of ranch property that surrounds free U.S. government lands, and the family won't allow homesteaders to pass over their land in order to claim the free range. The family's profitable setup is threatened when Glenn Denbow (Scott Brady) murders a man in front of a witness, Jane Stevens (Shelley Winters), and faces a hanging. Knowing that Texas law won't allow a woman to testify against her husband, Glenn quickly cajoles Jane into marriage. But soon after the wedding, Jane realizes why they were married, and she falls in love with his cousin, Kirk Denbow (Joseph Cotten). Glenn begins to resent his family, and when he resorts to rustling the family cattle, he is killed. Jane is now able to persuade Kirk to allow the homesteaders to pass over the Denbow land.

Comment: The main attraction of this well-acted oater is Joseph Cotten, whose character eventually realizes how wrong his family is.

Van Cleef's Role: Filmgoers saw Van Cleef in color for the first time in *Untamed Frontier*. His character, Dave Chittun, is a licentious Denbow employee who refuses to take orders from anyone but his friend Glenn Denbow. When Glenn has a falling-out with his family, Dave leaves the Denbow ranch. He then blackmails Glenn and forces his friend to join him in a scheme to rustle Denbow cattle. After Glenn, Dave and the other rustlers are discovered by Denbow cowhands, they try to escape, and Dave falls off his horse. But Glenn knows he can't pick up his friend *and* escape, so he refuses. Dave shoots Glenn in the back, but before the coward can take Glenn's horse, he is killed by the pursuing cowhands. In a film with no clear-cut heavy, Van Cleef is effective in presenting Dave Chittun as being less than likable. For the part, the actor wears for the first time in a film a full mustache; this facial hair would become an integral part of the later film star Lee Van Cleef. Van Cleef also had to learn some Spanish, a language with which the actor would again come into contact when he filmed his Westerns in Spain.

The Vanishing American

1955, black and white, 90 minutes,
Republic (Western)

Cast: Scott Brady (Blandy), Audrey Totter (Marian Warner), Forrest Tucker (Morgan), Gene Lockhart (Blucher), Jim Davis (Glendon), John Dierkes (Friel), Gloria Castillo (Yashi), Julian Rivero (Etenia), Lee Van Cleef (Jay Lord), George Keymas (Coshonta), Charles Stevens (Quah-Tain), Jay Silverheels (Beeteia), James Millican (Walker), Glenn Strange (Beleanth)

Director: Joseph Kane

Synopsis: A Navajo brave named Blandy (Scott Brady) defends his people's land from crooks, including Blucher (Gene Lockhart), an Indian agent who is trying to monopolize the territory's waterholes. Blandy is aided by and falls in love with Marian Warner (Audrey Totter), a farmer whose land is also threatened.

Comment: This film is something of a remake of the 1925 silent classic of the same name.

Van Cleef's Role: Van Cleef plays the part of Jay Lord, one of two henchmen (the other played by Jim Davis) in the employ of villainous trading post owner Forrest Tucker.

Vice Squad

1953, black and white, 88 minutes, United Artists

Alternate Title: *The Girl in Room 17* (British)

Cast: Edward G. Robinson (Capt. Barnaby), Paulette Goddard (Mona), K.T. Stevens (Ginny), Porter Hall (Jack Hartrampf), Adam Williams (Marty Kusalich), Edward Binns (Al Barkis), Jay Adler (Frankie Pierce), Joan Vohs (Vickie Webb), Lee Van Cleef (Pete Monte), Dan Riss (Lt. Imlay), Mary Ellen Kay (Carol Lawson), Barry Kelly (Hartrampf's Lawyer)

Director: Arnold Laven

Synopsis: A Los Angeles policeman is killed when he tries to apprehend two crooks, Al Barkis (Edward Binns) and Pete Monte (Lee Van Cleef). An undertaker named Jack Hartrampf (Porter Hall) witnesses the crime. Hartrampf, who was near the crime scene because he was visiting a prostitute, doesn't want to ruin his reputation by helping the police. Capt. Barnaby (Edward G. Robinson) uses instead the less reliable information of Mona (Paulette Goddard), the manager of the escort service that Hartrampf patronized. Mona's information leads Barnaby to an innocent man named Marty Kusalich (Adam Williams), but when crooks Al and Pete turn up at a bank robbery, Marty becomes useful, as he tells Barnaby where their hideout is. The crooks are found, justice is served, and Capt. Barnaby returns to the often menial tasks of police work.

Comment: Vice Squad reportedly uses a pseudo-documentary style to help illustrate an average day in the life of a police officer. The picture marks the cinematic return of Edward G. Robinson, whose blacklisting by anti–Communist hearings in 1949 kept him from film work.

Van Cleef's Role: Van Cleef's Pete Monte, with his criminal partner, set the story in motion by killing the policeman who catches the two crooks trying to steal a car. (The car was for use in the bank robbery which occurs later in the film and is eventually responsible for their being caught by the police.) Pete's partner Al is killed, but Van Cleef's crooked character survives to be arrested.

White Lightning

1953, black and white, 61 minutes, Monogram

Cast: Stanley Clements (Mike), Steve Brodie (Jack), Gloria Blondell (Ann), Barbara Bestar (Margaret), Lyle Talbot (Rocky), Frank Jenks (Benny), Paul Bryar (Stew), Lee Van Cleef (Brutus), Myron Healey (Nelson), Riley Hill (Norwin), Tom Hanlon (Announcer), Jane Easton (Girl), John Bleifer (Tailor), Duncan Richardson (Davey), Joel Marston

Director: Edward Bernds

Synopsis: The Red Devils hockey team begins a winning streak after they acquire a talented player named Mike (Stanley Clements), but the team has to endure Mike's egotism. One of Mike's teammates, Nelson (Myron Healey), is being paid by the mob to throw the games, and when Nelson is suspended for his cheating, mobsters proposition Mike with the same scheme. Since he is having spats with the coach, Mike considers the mob's offer but decides instead to stay clear of such illegal activities, and he helps the team win an important game.

Van Cleef's Role: Van Cleef plays Brutus Allen, a member of the crooked investment syndicate that tries to bribe Mike.

The Yellow Tomahawk
1954, color, 82 minutes
United Artists (Western)

Cast: Rory Calhoun (Adam), Peggie Castle (Katherine), Noah Beery, Jr. (Tonio), Warner Anderson (Major Ives), Peter Graves (Sawyer), Lee Van Cleef (Fireknife), Rita Moreno (Honey Bear), Walter Reed (Keats), Dan Riss (Sgt. Bandini), Adam Williams (Cpl. Maddock), Ned Glass (Willy)

Director: Lesley Selander

Synopsis: A group of Indian warriors led by Chief Fireknife (Lee Van Cleef) attacks Major Ives (Warner Anderson) and his cavalry troops. An Indian guide named Adam (Rory Calhoun) is Fireknife's friend but is forced to kill the chief in order to save Ives and prevent an Indian attack on settlers in the area.

Van Cleef's Role: Van Cleef's unique features allowed him to believably portray the Indian chief Fireknife. Van Cleef would again play an American Indian in the title role of *Captain Apache* (1971).

The Young Lions
1958, black and white, 170 minutes,
20th Century–Fox

Cast: Marlon Brando (Christian Diestl), Montgomery Clift (Noah Ackerman), Dean Martin (Michael Whiteacre), Hope Lange (Hope Plowman), Barbara Rush (Margaret Freemantle), May Britt (Gretchen Hardenberg), Maximilian Schell (Capt. Hardenberg), Dora Doll (Simone), Lee Van Cleef (Sgt. Rickett), Liliane Montevecchi (Francoise), Parley Baer (Brant), Arthur Franz (Lt. Green), L.Q. Jones (Pvt. Donnelly), Doris Wiss (Nurse), John Gabriel (Burn)

Director: Edward Dmytryk

Synopsis: During World War II, the lives of three soldiers — one German, two American — are set to converge. German soldier Christian Diestl (Marlon Brando) becomes an officer in the Africa Korps. Diestl had initially supported Hitler, but was not a Nazi. Two Americans, Noah Ackerman (Montgomery Clift) and Michael Whiteacre (Dean Martin), are drafted and become friends. Ackerman is a Jew, a quiet store clerk, and Whiteacre is a brash Broadway entertainer. Meanwhile, Diestl becomes increasingly disillusioned with the purposes and methods of the Nazi regime. In the United States, Ackerman is the subject of anti–Semitism, and is taunted and beaten up during basic training. Whiteacre tries to avoid military service altogether, and when that is not possible, he transfers away from Ackerman's unit into special services as an entertainer to avoid combat. Ackerman proves himself to the men and becomes a superior soldier. Whiteacre begins to question his own character and decides to transfer back into Ackerman's combat unit, now in Europe. Diestl is in Europe when the Americans advance, and the German comes upon a concentration camp, seeing for himself for the first time the horrors the Nazi system has brought about. Shortly afterward, Ackerman and Whiteacre's unit discovers the same concentration camp. Shocked, they go for a walk together and talk. The disillusioned Diestl comes into sight. He is recognized as a German soldier and is shot dead by Whiteacre.

Comment: Based on Irwin Shaw's best-selling novel, *The Young Lions* is an episodic film that is engaging for most of its 170 minutes. The film moves from one major character to another, changing back and forth as the plot unfolds, until the three stories converge at the end. There is adequate wartime action, but the main emphasis is on the individuals' inner conflicts. It is an ambitious film, and has a number of subplots, romantic and otherwise. It is difficult to keep track of everything. One point that is easy to overlook: Christian Diestl knew Margaret Freemantle before the war; thus, when Whiteacre kills Diestl, he unknowingly kills a man who has been a friend of the woman he plans to marry.

Van Cleef's Role: Van Cleef plays Sgt. Rickett, one of Noah's superiors. Rickett is first seen enforcing a punishment on Noah, but this provides little evidence about Rickett's character, as the order for the punishment comes from one of Rickett's superiors. Later, Rickett is seen enjoying the fights which pit Noah against much larger opponents. Rickett is also seen fraternizing with those soldiers after Noah has been brutally beaten. It is then apparent that Rickett is a man who is just using his rank and position to gain popularity. Later, Rickett is seen, a bit humbler, in combat with Noah and the rest of the company.

3.
Television Work

"If I do end up doing television, it would be because the script is damn good and there is room for good characterization in the thing for as long as the program will go." Lee Van Cleef made this statement in his 1979 interview with William R. Horner. Five years later, he starred in *The Master*, his only TV series. Although it had a brief and unsuccessful run, *The Master* remained available to viewers (in various formats) for more than ten years after its cancellation, allowing a large audience to decide whether Van Cleef actually did hold out for a worthwhile TV venture.

Created by Michael Sloan, *The Master* was an hour-long, weekly show that aired Friday nights on NBC from January 20 to August 31, 1984. It began its run in the 9–10 P.M. time slot and made the jump to the 8–9 slot in March.

The Master stars Van Cleef as John Peter McCallister, who abandons his Ninja sect and his home in Japan when he learns that he has a daughter named Teri living in the United States. Fearing that McCallister will betray Ninja secrets, the sect sends Okasa (Sho Kosugi), McCallister's former pupil, to locate and kill the man who was once his master.

Once in America, McCallister follows a lead to Ellerston, Illinois, but arrives too late to find Teri; she has already left. McCallister finds companionship when he teams with young drifter Max Keller (Timothy Van Patten), who agrees to aid him in his quest in exchange for Ninjitsu training. McCallister once again takes on the "Master" moniker as the two search for Teri, elude Okasa and fight against the injustices they encounter on their trip.

As the story progresses, more insight into the pasts of both Max and the Master is given. Max's mother and older brother died in a plane crash, and Max and his father, Patrick T. Keller (Doug McClure), have been estranged ever since. The mysterious past of the Master is cleared up somewhat when his U.S. military service in World War II and the Korean War is disclosed. During his military service, he became fascinated with the martial arts and remained in the Far East.

Generally the search for Teri dictated the duo's whereabouts, but occasionally Max and the Master have other agendas. McCallister helps a war pal in the episode "Kunoichi" and visits an old friend in "The Java Tiger." "State of the Union" finds the two in the town of Clearwater, where Max competes in a motorcycle race. The episode "Failure to Communicate" involves a visit to Max's father.

During its run, *The Master* was compared to *Kung Fu*, an earlier martial-arts TV series. But whereas the internationally popular *Kung Fu* lasted three years, *The Master* had a short life; only 13 episodes were shot before the series' cancellation. *Kung Fu* proved that martial arts fare could succeed on TV. *The Master* was obviously missing the ingredients necessary for this success.

The series' title character leaves a lot to be desired. Like Caine, the hero of *Kung Fu*, McCallister is somewhat out-of-touch with his American surroundings. But unlike *Kung Fu*'s hero, who is formidable despite his displacement, McCallister tries to assimilate into the culture; it seems the *Master* writers wanted a "hip" ninja. Consequently, McCallister is dated and unimpressive, using expressions like "Move it or lose it" (in "State of the Union") and clapping his hands to the beat of a dance song (in "Out-of-Time-Step").

Lee Van Cleef was not a great casting choice for the Master role, because at almost 60 years of age he was unable to do the physically demanding martial arts fight scenes. This made it necessary for trained Oriental stunt doubles (often easy to recognize) to perform fight scenes as the Master.

However, Van Cleef had narrow, Oriental-looking eyes which made the double less detectable when the Master fought in the hooded black bodysuit that exposed only his eyes. But the Master could not always be fighting in this outfit.

While the eye similarities did work in Van Cleef's favor, they were

Publicity photo for *The Master* shows Van Cleef in the garb that his character, ninja master John Peter McCallister, wears for his arrival in America.

not wholly convincing (they also had no relevance to the storyline, as the Master was described as "the only Occidental American ever to become a Ninja"). Thus, perhaps a more spry, capable lead would have been a better choice for John Peter "The Master" McCallister.

These might seem to be rather negative sentiments about a man who sincerely played the part in the best manner he possibly could. However, it should be noted that being able to discern a stuntman is the biggest defect of *The Master*. Not only does it detract the viewer during the fight scenes, it also hurts Van Cleef's credibility and raises the show's camp factor.

In Van Cleef's defense, he was a competent actor, unlike many of the martial artists-turned-actors, and delivered some moments of real brilliance as an actor. He also had a passing association with martial arts films, having previously appeared in *The Stranger and the Gunfighter* and *The Octagon*.

While Timothy Van Patten's portrayal is satisfactory, the character of Max Keller is certainly not *The Master*'s redeeming element. His function in the series, besides an occasional fight scene, consists of little more than dispensing wisecracks and gawking at McCallister. His unending amazement at his master's abilities is cloying, especially after the story continued past the first several episodes.

Another problem is the absence of sharp, witty dialogue. While the banter between Max and the Master is occasionally amusing, it is, on the whole, unimpressive. Usually, the humor comes when Van Cleef's Master speaks in a disgusted tone, as only he can.

The only angle *The Master* had that was unique during its 1984 run was its martial arts fighting. But instead of emphasizing that, it often gets bogged down in a plot which should have only existed as a backdrop for the fighting. Other shows that aired that year, such as the more popular *The A-Team*, had similar plots, which made *The Master*'s storylines—about things such as greedy land developers and fortune hunters—seem trite and tiresome. The stories also relied too often on the hostage-taken-for-ransom scenario.

The Master has a certain amount of martial arts legitimacy, due chiefly to the involvement of martial arts film star Sho Kosugi (who was also the Ninja choreographer and technical advisor). The Chi—which according to Eastern thought is the center of being—is mentioned in several episodes and thus incorporates an element of Eastern philosophy into the series.

Also impressive is the number of noteworthy actors who turned up in *The Master*. Both Janine Turner and Crystal Bernard made appearances before achieving their full-blown TV stardom. Demi Moore, who appeared in the series' first episode, later became a highly successful film star. Other noted actors seen in guest spots were David McCallum (known best for his role in TV's *The Man from U.N.C.L.E.*), George Lazenby (who played James Bond in one of the popular Bond features) and Bill McKinney (famous as the rapist in the 1972 survival film *Deliverance*).

By appearing in *The Master*, some veteran actors had a screen reunion with Lee Van Cleef. Van Cleef had previously appeared in films and TV with *Master* guests Jack Kelly (*Commandos*, "Man Down, Woman Screaming" episode of *City Detective*), Art Hindle (*The Octagon*), Claude Akins (*The Lonely Man, Joe Dakota*), J.D. Cannon ("Piney" episode of *Rawhide*) and Jonathon Chan (*The Octagon*). Perhaps the most special reunion came when Jock Mahoney appeared in the series' last episode, "A Place to Call Home." Mahoney's appearance illustrated how much the tables had turned since 1951, when Van Cleef did his first television work for Mahoney's series *The Range Rider*. (Mahoney was billed as "Jock O'Mahoney," an alternate version of his name, for his *Master* appearance.)

Several running gags, while not exactly side-splitting, give *The Master* some personality. The show's first episode begins with Max being thrown through a barroom window as his narration begins, "Hi, I'm Max Keller. This is how I usually leave a bar." Thus, as *The Master* gets underway, so does its first running gag. During the course of the series, Max's bar-window exits provide the finale for numerous barfights. The gag is used to its best effect when the Master witnesses a middle-aged man being thrown through a window and immediately recognizes him as Patrick T. Keller, Max's father.

The other regular gag also adds more personality to the series, but is a bit shameless. It involves in-joke references to Van Cleef's reputation as a Western movie actor. In "High Rollers," the final showdown takes place on a Western movie set, where McCallister remarks about how natural he feels in the setting. In "The Good, the Bad, and the Priceless," McCallister declines a job offer that involves dressing in Western attire, reasoning, "I'd never get dressed up that way." In "Failure to Communicate," a blind woman remarks that McCallister's aura reminds her of Clint Eastwood. McCallister smiles, replying, "Close." The episode

Van Cleef assumes a fighting stance in an alley for a scene from *The Master*.

"Rogues" has Hollywood-type Saul Robbins mistake the Master for a Spaghetti Western actor. As is evident from these examples, the *Master* writers overstepped reasonable bounds of the Lee Van Cleef-homage idea.

The Master's cancellation in the summer of 1984 did not keep the show from potential viewers. A few years later, the episodes were paired and released on home video as seven volumes of *Master Ninja*. The show's most impressive fight, from the first episode "Max," is included on *The Deadliest Art: The Best of the Martial Arts Films*, a 1992 home video compilation of martial arts fare. *The Master* reached a TV audience yet again (this time in its *Master Ninja* form) through *Mystery Science Theater 3000*, a cable television series that ridicules bad films.

Although it is unfortunate that Van Cleef never got better material, he was for a brief time the star of a weekly TV series, and this was only fitting for an actor who had done nearly everything else possible in a television career.

The Master

Aired: 1-20-84 to 8-31-84, NBC

Cast: Lee Van Cleef (John Peter "The Master" McCallister), Timothy Van Patten (Max Keller), Sho Kosugi (Okasa)
Creator: Michael Sloan
Producer: Joe Boston
Theme Music: Bill Conti
Narrator: Timothy Van Patten

"Max"

Aired: 1-20-84
Supporting Cast: Demi Moore (Holly Trumball), Claude Akins (Jason Trumball), Bill McKinney (Sheriff Kyle), John Lehne (Haviland), Clu Gulager (Christianson), Mike Abelar (Mechanic), Gerry Black (Truck Driver), John DiFusco (Man in Bar), Peter Looney (Jim Powell), W.T. Zacha (Bartender)
Director: Robert Clouse
Synopsis: Ninja master John Peter McCallister leaves Japan and his

ninja sect when he learns that he has a daughter named Teri living in Ellerston, Illinois. Teri's trail leads McCallister to an Ellerston airfield, and although she isn't there, McCallister sticks around to help airfield owner Jason Trumball (Claude Akins) protect his property from greedy land developer Christianson (Clu Gulager). Max Keller, a young drifter, also helps Trumball, and after the airfield is saved from Christianson, Max and the ninja search for Teri together, with the agreement that McCallister will become Max's "master" and give him ninja training. Meanwhile, a ninja named Okasa, who has been sent by the sect to kill McCallister, follows the runaway ninja and his new pupil.

Comment: The first and best episode of *The Master*, "Max" contains some great fight scenes, stylish sets (McCallister's home in Japan) and a noteworthy supporting cast.

"Out-of-Time-Step"

Aired: 1-27-84

Supporting Cast: Lori Lethin (Jill Patterson), Shanna Reed (Kelly Patterson), Brian Tochi (Jonathan Chan), Soon-Teck Oh (Lika), Charles Collins (Charlie Patterson), Colleen Shelly (Westerly), Dick Durock (Jerry), Jeff Imada (Bodyguard), Bill Saito (Bodyguard), Andrea Grey (Lady on Phone), Jay Turnbull (Patron in Bar), Suzi Horne (Teri)

Director: Ray Austin

Synopsis: Max and the Master's search leads them to a dance club owned by Charlie Patterson (Charles Collins). The Master is mistaken for the club's sentinel by Lika (Soon-Teck Oh) and Jonathan Chan (Brian Tochi), gangsters who are trying to force Charlie Patterson to pay for protection. Since the gangsters can't eliminate McCallister, they take as a hostage Kelly Patterson (Shanna Reed), the club owner's daughter. Charlie Patterson's other daughter, a paraplegic named Jill (Lori Lethin), helps Max and the Master rescue Kelly and wipe out the gangsters.

Comment: With its story resembling that of the martial arts film classic *Return of the Dragon*, "Out-of-Time-Step" manages to be exciting, with some good action performed by hard-to-detect stunt doubles. Soon-Teck Oh's Lika, one of McCallister's few ninja adversaries, is the series' best villain.

"State of the Union"

Aired: 2-3-84

Supporting Cast: Cotter Smith (Chad Webster), Crystal Bernard (Carrie Brown), Ritch Brinkley (Ralph Carter), Mickey Jones (Hog), David Roberts (Harold), Ellen Crawford (Annie), Sandy Edgerton (Waitress), Rick Najera (Ricky), Julie Ow (Asian Girl), Steffen Zacharias (Man), Debbie Christoffersen (Girl), Henry Wills (Man on Dock)

Director: Alan Myerson

Synopsis: Max and the Master side with a small-town cannery worker Carrie Brown (Crystal Bernard) struggling to start a workers' union against the wishes of the cannery's corrupt owners. During her fight, Carrie discovers that her missing older brother, who was also a union advocate, was killed by the cannery owners.

Comment: "State of the Union" is an especially poor episode. There are many plot inconsistencies and far-fetched action scenes (at one point, the Master defeats a Jeep full of thugs while riding on the back of Max's motorcycle).

"Hostages"

Aired: 2-17-84

Supporting Cast: George Lazenby (Mallory), David McCallum (Castile), Jennifer Runyon (Alicia), Randi Brooks (Serena), Monte Markham (Control), Robert Dowdell (Senator Clayton), Robert Hoy (Masterson), Wolf Muser (Palin), Stephen Andrews (Forbes), Haskell V. Anderson, Kiva Lawrence, George Schardt (Hostages), Hal Burton, Hany Ghorra, Fiona Guiness, Mike Muscat, Dick Warlock, Dino Scofield (Terrorists)

Director: Ray Austin

Synopsis: Max and the Master are present at a U.S. senator's garden party when the senator's daughter and guests are abducted by terrorists and held as hostages in a fortress. Accused of the crime, McCallister teams up with a super-spy named Mallory (George Lazenby) for a rescue mission and clears his name by freeing the hostages.

Comment: "Hostages" doesn't use the fortress locale to its best potential; much time could have been devoted to the Master and Mallory fighting enemies on staircases, hiding in rooms, running down corridors, etc. However, "Hostages" features one of the series' few attempts at continuity with the succeeding episode. At this episode's conclusion, Max suggests that he and the Master should travel to Las Vegas, and when the next episode ("High Rollers") begins, Max and the Master have arrived.

"High Rollers"

Aired: 3-2-84

Supporting Cast: Edward Edwards (John Craig), Art Hindle (Randy Blake), Angela Lee (Suzie), Charles Boswell (Weston), Michael M. Vendrell (Matteson), Michael Lemon (James Farland), Sandra Kronemeyer (Shana), Terri Treas (Tracy)

Director: Peter Crane

Synopsis: John Craig (Edward Edwards), a former security guard at the Grand Palace Casino in Las Vegas, conspires with Vietnam War pal Randy Blake (Art Hindle) in a scheme to rob the casino. Dancer Tracy (Teri Treas) is forced to help with the robbery when Craig and his bunch kidnap her daughter Suzie (Angela Lee) and hold her hostage on an old Western movie set. Max and the Master, caught up in all the trouble since their arrival in Las Vegas, rescue Suzie and foil the robbers' getaway.

Comment: A routine episode, "High Rollers" is noteworthy for putting Van Cleef back on a Western town set, where the Master not only does his usual chop-socking but also shoots a revolver. Actor Charles Boswell, who appears as one of the crooks, bears a striking resemblance to a young Lee Van Cleef.

"Fat Tuesday"

Aired: 3-9-84

Supporting Cast: Robert Pine (Beaumont), Mabel King (Willie), Susan Kase, Mike Genovese, Floyd Levine

Director: Sidney Hayers

Synopsis: An investigative reporter (Susan Kase) fears for her life after she accuses a prominent New Orleans citizen of gunrunning. Max and the Master protect the reporter and put a stop to the gunrunning.

Comment: In "Fat Tuesday," gunrunning is the antagonist's crime, as it is in the "Java Tiger" episode. As the title indicates, "Fat Tuesday" is set against the Mardi Gras celebration.

"Juggernaut"

Aired: 3-16-84
Supporting Cast: Diana Muldaur (Maggie Sinclair), William Smith (Alan Kane), Tara Buckman (Cat), Stuart Whitman (Hellman)
Director: Gordon Hessler
Synopsis: A group of farmers, including a mother and daughter (Diana Muldaur, Tara Buckman), are unable to get their produce to the market when a trucking firm creates a roadblock. With help from Max and the Master, the farmers form a convoy and push on through.
Comment: Before appearing in "Juggernaut," actor Stuart Whitman was the villain in the 1971 Van Cleef Western *Captain Apache*. "Juggernaut" introduces Tara Buckman's character Cat, who reappears in "The Good, the Bad, and the Priceless." Cat is *The Master*'s only recurring character (besides, of course, the three regulars).

"The Good, the Bad, and the Priceless"

Aired: 3-23-84
Supporting Cast: Tara Buckman (Cat), Janine Turner (Gina Lawrence), George Maharis (Simon Garett), Johnny Seven (Rosetti), Colby Chester, Oliver Clark
Director: Michael Caffee
Synopsis: Max and the Master track Teri to a New York modeling agency where she worked before disappearing. They instead find — and are fooled by — undercover law enforcement agent Gina (Janine Turner), who is posing as Teri in order to get information on crooked fashion designer Simon Garett (George Maharis). Both Garett and the Master seem convinced that Gina is actually Teri, and when Garett has Gina abducted, the Master is forced to steal the Crown Jewels in exchange for her safe release. In the end, Gina is saved, Garett goes to jail and the Master reveals that he knew Gina's true identity all along.
Comment: This episode is an opportunity to see the Master express emotions not previously demonstrated, when he meets the woman he believes (at first) is Teri. However, the cop-out ending, which has the

Master admitting that he suspected, then knew, that Gina was not actually who she claimed to be, is a chance wasted to see McCallister hurt emotionally. In this episode, Max believes that he is no longer useful as a traveling companion to his master, whom he thinks is reunited with his daughter. This raises an interesting possibility: Had *The Master* been a longer running series, there could have been a change in sidekicks.

"Kunoichi"

Aired: 4-6-84

Supporting Cast: Jack Kelly (Brian Elkwood), Kelly Harmon (Allison Branson), Rick Hill (Ron Gordon), William Capbell

Director: Gordon Hessler

Synopsis: Max and the Master head to Washington, D.C., thinking that Brian Elkwood (Jack Kelly), McCallister's Korean War pal, requested their assistance. Once they arrive in the capital, Max and the Master find that Elkwood — who is working as the President's right-hand man — never sent for help. Eventually they discover that Okasa and a mysterious female ninja were manipulating the Elkwood-McCallister friendship in hopes of killing Elkwood and framing the Master for murder. When Max and the Master put a stop to their plan, they unmask the female ninja and find that she is Elkwood's secretary Allison Branson (Kelly Harmon), who was trying to ruin a high-risk security operation by killing her boss.

Comment: "Kunoichi" (the word translates to "lady ninja," as Okasa explains in the episode) is a better-than-most episode, with a relatively large dose of action, a clever escape scene and a minimal amount of schmaltz. The first exchange between Van Cleef and Kelly — who previously worked together in film and television — was beautifully done and ranks as the highlight of acting in *The Master*.

"The Java Tiger"

Aired: 4-13-84

Supporting Cast: Dick O'Neil (Leo Fairchild), Kabir Bedi (Kruger), Cynthia Cypert (Shelly Fairchild), Anthony De Longis (Draper), Muni Zano (Tanehama), Linda Standaart (Hawaiian Girl), Gina Bolton (Waitress)

Director: Bruce Kessler

Synopsis: Max and the Master go to Hawaii to help assumed-dead private investigator Leo Fairchild (Dick O'Neil) and his daughter Shelly (Cynthia Cypert) search for the Java Tiger, a valuable gold statuette. But before they can get their hands on the item, they fend off Kruger (Kabir Bedi), a gunrunner and smuggler, and brave a booby-trapped cave.

Comment: An unimpressive cave sequence and an obviously phony volcano mar this episode. O'Neil's performance as the inept investigator Fairchild is pleasant.

"Rogues"

Aired: 4-20-84

Supporting Cast: Kaz Garas (Lt. Loring), Cindy Harrell (Talia Donovan), Paul Tulley (Jerry Donovan), Tony Swartz (Saul Robbins), Keith McConnell (Campion), Lynne Randall (Gretchen), Marcelyn Ann Williams (Marcellan), Frank Pesce (Officer Thomas), George Rugge (Officer Orum), Greg Gault (Officer Diehl), Yvonne Williams (Rima)

Director: Gordon Hessler

Synopsis: Talia Donovan (Cindy Harrell) enlists Max and the Master to search for her missing brother Jerry (Paul Tulley), a police officer on the Rodeo Hills force. They discover that Jerry knows too much about certain law-breaking cops led by Lt. Loring (Kaz Garas), and is in hiding from them. Max and the Master make the police force safe for Jerry's return as they put Lt. Loring's rogue cops to rest.

Comment: More than any other *Master* episode, "Rogues" makes good use of the locale of its climactic fight; the episode sees Max and the Master deal a finishing blow to the rogue cops in exciting fashion, with the two sides fighting up and down stairs and on an elevator. Not a great episode, "Rogues" does however contain a few notable scenes. In one sequence, Max and the Master discuss how their adventures had become much more than just a search for Teri, and even hint at regrets that it has gotten so dangerous. In a fight scene, a glimpse is shown of how exciting the McCallister character could have been. In it, Loring forewarns McCallister before he attacks, saying, "I don't want to hurt you." Smiling, the Master responds coolly, "Yes you do."

"Failure to Communicate"

Aired: 5-4-84

Supporting Cast: Doug McClure (Patrick T. Keller), Rebecca Holden (Laura Crane), Sho Kosugi (Okasa), J.D. Cannon (Gordon Hunter), Edd Byrnes (Lt. Ryan), Mark Goddard (Paul Stilwell), Marc Alaimo (Straker), Ashley Ferrare (Kathy Hunter), Aaron Dozier (Officer Lane)

Director: Sidney Hayers

Synopsis: Max and the Master visit Max's drunkard father Patrick T. Keller (Doug McClure), who has been tricked into helping some baddies with the abduction of a girl named Kathy Hunter (Ashley Ferrare). Since Kathy is the daughter of millionaire Gordon Hunter (J.D. Cannon), her ransom is set at $1,000,000. The criminals think that Patrick Keller's secretary Laura (Rebecca Holden) knows too much about their scheme, and she too is kidnapped. But while Laura is being abducted, Max and the Master rescue Kathy. The crooks still want money, though, and they demand $1,000,000 from Gordon Hunter for the safe release of Laura, whom the tycoon barely knows. Hunter is saved from this moral dilemma when Max, the Master and a sober Patrick Keller rescue Laura.

Comment: "Failure to Communicate" is the only episode in which the plot (Gordon Hunter's moral dilemma) has more potential for excitement than the martial arts action. But the episode does not center around Hunter's dilemma; Laura is kidnapped too late in the episode. The resolution — Max and the Master beating up the bad guys — is a cop-out.

"A Place to Call Home"

Aired: 5-11-84

Supporting Cast: Jock O'Mahoney [Mahoney] (Mark Richards), Doug Toby (Mike), Susan Woollen (Kim Anderson), Hunter Von Leer (Greg Richards), Murray McLeod (Price), Larry B. Williams (Clerk), Tish Smiley (Sara), Alison Boston (Alison), Kane Kosugi, James Gammon, Gary Pagett

Director: Gordon Hessler

Synopsis: Max and the Master lend a hand to Kim Anderson (Susan Woolen), who manages a home for juvenile misfits. The people at the home are persecuted by residents of the nearby town and by greedy land developer Mark Richards (Jock Mahoney), who wants to mine the uranium located under Kim's land.

Comment: "A Place to Call Home," as is evident from its title, is a schmaltzy episode with Max playing "big brother" to Mike, one of the more sullen kids. It's fun, though, to see Bobby, another kid from the home, display his martial arts prowess. Susan Woollen, who wrote "A Place to Call Home" and other *Master* episodes, makes a guest appearance in the episode.

Other Television Work

The Master accounted for only a small percentage of Lee Van Cleef's television career. Van Cleef worked extensively in television and rounded out his small-screen career with several telefilms, a comedy special and even commercials for snack foods, mufflers, and beer.

At times, television work was very important to Van Cleef, and he remembered these jobs with fondness. Van Cleef told William R. Horner in an interview for *Bad at the Bijou,* "I think that prior to the European move, the things I think about, more often than anything else ... are the television jobs. There were a lot of good ones...." Indeed, Van Cleef was involved with some very good television productions, and some of the actor's finest moments can be found in his television work.

On the following pages the reader will find a complete alphabetical listing of Lee Van Cleef's television credits. Particularly significant appearances are covered in some detail, including the show's original airdate, whether it was filmed in color or black and white, the running time and its network/syndication status. If the production is a Western, that fact is noted.

The Adventures of Kit Carson
"Incident at Wagontire"

195?, black-and-white, 30 minutes, syndicated (Western)

Cast: Bill Williams (Christopher "Kit" Carson), Don Diamond (El Toro), Lee Van Cleef (Gambler), Linda Stirling, Harry Harvey, Sr., Richard Garland, Joe Haworth, Steve Raines, Jay X. Brand

Director: John English

Synopsis: In the Western town of Wagontire, frontiersman Kit Carson (Bill Williams) uncovers fraud in the sheriff election, as he discovers that crooked candidate Judd Martin is illicitly supported by gamblers. Meanwhile, Carson's sidekick El Toro (Don Diamond) is jailed for the murder of Rand Barton, a stranger to Wagontire. El Toro is freed when Kit proves that Barton was a criminal outsider who tried to buy into the election fraud and was killed by the gamblers.

Comment: "Incident at Wagontire" is an improbable TV Western mystery aimed at children, with Kit solely exposing the gamblers' scheme. The episode's loose ends are tied up when Kit explains the mystery to the other characters at the episode's conclusion.

Van Cleef's Role: Van Cleef (who in a 1979 interview said that he enjoyed working with *Kit Carson* star Bill Williams) appears as the gambler who brawls with Carson in the episode's final fistfight (a stunt double does some of the fighting in Van Cleef's place). The brawl ends after El Toro pops out of a secret door in the floor and helps Kit handle Van Cleef. The set on which this fight occurs was also used in *Kit Carson*'s "The Missing Hacienda" episode (in which Van Cleef also appears), and the secret door is vital to "Hacienda"'s story.

The Adventures of Kit Carson
"The Law of Boot Hill"

195?, syndicated

The Adventures of Kit Carson
"The Lost Treasure of Panamint"

195?, syndicated

The Adventures of Kit Carson
"The Missing Hacienda"

195?, black-and-white, 30 minutes, syndicated (Western)

Cast: Bill Williams (Christopher "Kit" Carson), Don Diamond (El Toro), Lee Van Cleef (Sheriff Ned Jackson), Linda Stirling, Richard Garland, Harry Harvey, Sr., Glen Kilburn, James Diehl, Virginia Carroll, Pete Dunn

Director: John English

Synopsis: Surveyor Eli Thatcher is recording the property lines of rich cattle ranchers when he is badly wounded. El Toro (Don Diamond), the sidekick of Kit Carson (Bill Williams), takes the wounded surveyor to a nearby hacienda, and before Toro leaves, he is assured that Eli will receive medical attention. Toro returns to the hacienda with Kit and Sheriff Ned Jackson (Lee Van Cleef) to check on Eli, but the surveyor is not there, and the house's inhabitants deny having accepted him. Also, Toro notices that the interior of the hacienda looks different. Sheriff Jackson suggests that they are in the wrong house, but instead of finding the right house, he takes Kit and Toro along to arrest Red Hudson, the leader of a group of homesteaders. Kit realizes that the sheriff is in cahoots with the rich land owners, and that Eli is being held captive behind a secret door inside the hacienda. After a massive gunfight, Eli is freed, Red Hudson's name is cleared and the nearby town is in need of a new sheriff.

Comment: "The Missing Hacienda" is juvenile, extremely farfetched but fun. In one implausible scene, Kit sees smoke rising from the hacienda's chimney. Kit suspects the villains are burning some of Eli's important documents, and he climbs on the roof. Kit pours a bucket of water down the chimney just as the bad guys are throwing the documents on the fire. With the fire extinguished, one of the baddies grabs the documents and runs out the back door. Kit jumps off the roof, tackles him and saves Eli's papers.

Van Cleef's Role: Van Cleef has an unusually large supporting role in this episode. As Sheriff Ned Jackson, he accompanies Kit and Toro while they search for Eli, and the sheriff pretends to help. Sheriff Ned also spends time with Eli's captors, with whom he is in secret collaboration. Jackson appears in almost every scene and is on screen more frequently than Kit, the series' hero.

Adventures of Rin Tin Tin
"Rin Tin Tin and the Raging River"

11-5-54, ABC

The Alaskans
"Peril at Caribou Crossing"

As Roc, 2-28-60, ABC

The Andy Griffith Show
"Banjo-Playing Deputy"

5-3-65, black-and-white, 30 minutes, CBS

Cast: Andy Griffith (Andy Taylor), Ron Howard (Opie Taylor), Frances Bavier (Aunt Bea), Jerry Van Dyke (Jerry Miller), Lee Van Cleef (Skip), Herbie Faye

Director: Coby Ruskin

Synopsis: A carnival arrives near Mayberry, and the carnival banjo player, Jerry Miller (Jerry Van Dyke), is fired. Mayberry Sheriff Andy Taylor (Andy Griffith) gives Jerry a job as his deputy, but Mayberry's new lawman proves to be quite inept. Despite the bumbling of Jerry, two carnival pickpockets are caught and arrested.

Comment: "Banjo-Playing Deputy" was the last *Andy Griffith* filmed in black-and-white. Guest star Jerry Van Dyke is the brother of actor Dick Van Dyke.

Van Cleef's Role: Van Cleef plays Skip, one of the two pickpocketing, purse-snatching carnivalgoers who are caught at the end of the episode. Van Cleef appeared in other television comedy series such as *The Real McCoys* and *My Mother, the Car*.

Annie Oakley
"Annie Breaks an Alibi"

Black Saddle
"The Cabin"

As Frank, 4-1-60, ABC

Black Saddle
"A Case of Diphtheria"
> 1960, NBC

Bonanza
"The Blood Line"
> As Appling, 12-31-60, NBC

Branded
"Call to Glory"
> As Charlie Yates, 2-27-66, 3-6-66 and 3-13-66, NBC

Branded
"The Richest Man in Boot Hill"
> 10-31-65, NBC

Brave Eagle
"Shield of Honor"
> 1-11-65, CBS

Casey Jones
"A Badge for Casey"
> As Mort Clio, 1957

Cavalcade of America
"Duel at the O.K. Corral"
> 3-9-54, ABC

The Cheyenne Show/Bronco
"One Evening in Abilene"

As Chenn, 3-19-62, ABC

The Cheyenne Show/Bronco
"Trouble Street"

As Deputy Braden, 10-2-61, ABC

The Cheyenne Show/Bronco
"Yankee Tornado"

As Shanghai Williams, 3-13-61, ABC

The Cheyenne Show/Cheyenne
"A Man Called Ragan"

4-23-62, ABC

Cimmaron City
"The Town Is a Prisoner"

As Tom, 3-28-59

City Detective
"Man Down, Woman Screaming"

1954, black-and-white, 30 minutes, syndicated

Cast: Rod Cameron (Lt. Bart Grant), Jack Kelly (Tom Arthur), Lee Van Cleef (Kurt Hardin), Beverly Garland (Jeanie), Frank Ferguson, Tom Daly

Director: Herschel Daugherty

Synopsis: While preparing to leave the United States for a job in Bolivia, Tom Arthur (Jack Kelly) encounters two fleeing criminals, Kurt Hardin (Lee Van Cleef) and Jeanie (Beverly Garland). In an effort to protect their identities, Jeanie and Kurt abduct Tom, and although they do not discount the idea of murder, the two criminals decide to keep Tom alive while they try to peddle his passport and airplane ticket. But Tom had left clues behind in his apartment, and New York City police detective Bart Grant (Rod Cameron) picks up his trail. After Grant locates the criminals and their captive, he roughs up Kurt, handcuffs Jeanie and frees Tom Arthur.

Comment: Based on a Louis L'Amour story, "Man Down, Woman Screaming" features realistic dialogue between Tom and his captors, and all the guest actors give fine performances. However, Rod Cameron, the series' star, dishes out unsatisfactory acting. The clues that Tom leaves for Detective Grant involve an alarm clock radio, apparently a novelty at the time this episode was made.

Van Cleef's Role: Disappointingly, Van Cleef's Kurt Hardin, in his first two scenes, was either inconsistently scripted or played. In his first scene, the character promises to be one of Van Cleef's best villains; he is smiley, slick and charmingly sinister. His next scene opens with Kurt brutally beating Tom. Jeanie arrives and asks Kurt why he is beating their prisoner, and Kurt answers in a moronic voice, "He called me stupid." Most notable about this episode is that it is an early teaming of Lee Van Cleef with Beverly Garland and Jack Kelly. Van Cleef also worked again with Garland in a 1954 film, *The Desperado*, and the two appeared as husband and wife twice in 1956, in *It Conquered the World* and in the "Measure of Faith" episode of *Ford Theatre*. Van Cleef and Kelly appear together again in the 1968 film *Commandos*, and Kelly makes an appearance on the "Kunoichi" episode of Van Cleef's TV series *The Master*.

Colt .45
"Dead Reckoning"

As Davery, 1-24-58, ABC

Colt .45
"The Trespasser"

As Red Feather, 6-21-60, ABC

Crossroads
"Sky Pilot of the Cumberlands"

    11-2-56, ABC

The Dakotas
"Thunder in Pleasant Valley"

    As Slade Tucker, 2-4-63, ABC

Death Valley Days
"The Hat That Won the West"

    As Brogger, 11-9-62, syndicated

The Deputy
"Palace of Chance"

    As the Cherokee Kid, 5-21-60, NBC

Destry
"Destry Had a Little Lamb"

    As Ace Slater, 2-21-64, ABC

The Dick Powell Show
"Colossus"

    As Salty, 3-12-63, NBC

Ford Theatre
"Measure of Faith"

    10-24-56, black-and-white, 30 minutes, NBC
    Cast: Lew Ayres (Father John Gerald), Beverly Garland (Maria), Lee Van Cleef (Stanley Perrin), Nestor Paiva (Eduardo), Charles Evans

(Bishop Healey), William Boyett (Captain Norris), Don C. Harvey (Martin)

Director: James Neilson

Synopsis: After spending four years in a Communist Chinese prison camp, Catholic priest John Gerald (Lew Ayres) is released and makes his way to a U.S. Army camp in Hong Kong. Father Gerald gives the army information about the prison's sadistic interrogator, Stanley Perrin (Lee Van Cleef), whose cruel interrogation methods resulted in the loss of Gerald's left leg. Father Gerald returns to the United States and becomes the pastor of St. Anthony's church, which needs many repairs. When large sums of money are anonymously donated, Gerald tracks the money back to Stanley Perrin, who has moved near Gerald's church. Gerald visits his former interrogator and learns that Perrin has married and repented. Perrin and his wife (Beverly Garland) both threaten to commit suicide if Father Gerald alerts the authorities of Perrin's whereabouts. The priest knows that it is his duty to report Perrin, and he does so. But before the arresting officers arrive at Perrin's apartment, Gerald visits him and his wife and succeeds in preventing the suicides.

Comment: "Measure of Faith" is fast-moving; there is a lot of story packed in this half-hour drama showcase.

Van Cleef's Role: Van Cleef's role involved no action but was a difficult one. Without the use of flashbacks, his character had to represent the menace of his former brutal life. At the same time, he had to be convincing as a truly reformed person who had broken completely with his past life. By expression and manner of delivery, Van Cleef gives a credible performance in this difficult role.

Four Star Playhouse
"Trail's End"

    1-29-53, CBS

Frontier Doctor
"The Great Stagecoach Robbery"

    1956, syndicated

The Gene Autry Show
"Outlaw Warning"

>10-2-54

The Gene Autry Show
"Rio Renegades"

>9-29-53

Gunsmoke
"My Father, My Son"

>As Ike Jeffords, 4-23-66, CBS

Gunsmoke
"Old Flame"

>As Rad Meadows, 5-28-60, CBS

Gunsmoke
"The Pariah"

>As John Hooker, 4-17-65, CBS

The Hard Way (telefilm)

>2-27-80, color, 87 minutes, ITV network
>*Cast:* Patrick McGoohan (John Connor), Lee Van Cleef (McNeal), Donal McCann (Ryan), Edna O'Brien (Kathleen), Ronan Wilmot (Joe Flynn), John Cowley (Graveyard Caretaker), Derek Lord (Casey), Joe Lynch (Devane), Kevin Flood (Duval), Michael Muldoon (Hogan), James A. Stephens, Richard McAdoo (Mercenaries), Peter Brayham (French Hit Man), Mesag Muruko (Father Cressy)
>*Producer/Director:* Michael Dryhurst
>*Synopsis:* John Connor (Patrick McGoohan), one of Europe's most

proficient assassins, wearies of his profession and decides to retire. Though there is a constant need for Connor's services, news of his retirement doesn't bother McNeal (Lee Van Cleef), Connor's employer, who knows exactly how to extort more work from the assassin. Connor begins a quiet life in rural Ireland and declines McNeal's initial job offers, but when McNeal threatens Connor's estranged wife, he is forced to return to the job. McNeal assigns Connor to kill a Paris-bound priest named Father Cressy (Mesag Muruko), but the assassin backs out at the last minute. After Connor sends his wife to a safe place, he holds a meeting with McNeal, whose business has been ruined because Connor did not carry out the assignment. The two men begin a gun battle in a large, empty house, and McNeal mortally wounds Connor. But before the assassin dies, he manages a few last shots, and both men die together on the floor. Later, Connor's wife visits the grave of the husband she never understood and says, "Such a waste of a man."

Comment: The Hard Way, a film made for British television, uses the all-too-familiar "one last job" storyline but succeeds as an interesting character study. The believable low-key characterizations and good performances fill the void created by the lack of exciting action. Patrick McGoohan, a TV veteran, creates in Connor a wonderfully taciturn and intriguing character. *The Hard Way*'s dreary rural landscapes, drab interiors and haunting violin score (by Tommy Potts) create the atmosphere for this tragic tale.

Van Cleef's Role: Van Cleef realistically portrays McNeal as a businessman, and the character is obviously not meant to be the film's true antagonist. That role is filled by the state of the world, which makes assassins necessary. It is Connor's fate to be drawn to this line of work. Sympathy is created for Van Cleef's character in scenes that occur after Connor abandons the Cressy matter. In one, McNeal is held accountable for Connor's desertion; in another, McNeal defends himself from an attacker in a cramped public bathroom (this is the film's only exciting action until the climactic gun battle). McNeal is not meant to be as appealing a character as Connor, and the story accomplishes this by having McNeal assign Connor to kill a priest. Also, Van Cleef is allowed to add a touch of villainy to the part in the end gunfight, during which McNeal taunts Connor. *The Hard Way* is perhaps the best television production in which Van Cleef appears.

Have Gun, Will Travel
"Face of a Shadow"

    As Golias, 4-20-63, CBS

Have Gun, Will Travel
"The Treasure"

    As Corbin, 12-29-62, CBS

Hawaiian Eye
"The Stanhope Brand"

    As Manuel, 2-22-61, ABC

Hotel de Paree
"Sundance and the Man in Room Seven"

    2-12-60, CBS

Joey Bishop Show
"Double Exposure"

    As Charlie McCreedy, 2-7-62, NBC

Laredo
"Quarter Past Eleven"

    As Big Mike Kelly, 3-24-66, NBC

The Last Stagecoach West (pilot?)

    As Steve Margolis, 1954?, syndicated

Laramie
".45 Calibre"

    As Wes Torrey, 11-15-60, NBC

3. Television Work

Laramie
"Killer's Odds"

As Dawson, 4-25-61, NBC

Laramie
"The Stranger"

As Caleb, 4-23-63, NBC

Laramie
"Vengeance"

As Moe Morgan, 1-8-63, NBC

Law of the Plainsman
"Clear Title"

As Killer, 12-17-59, NBC

Lawman
"The Conclave"

6-14-59, ABC

Lawman
"The Deputy"

As Hawks Brother, 10-5-58, ABC

Lawman
"Man on a Mountain"

As Clyde Wilson, 6-12-60, ABC

Lawman
"The Return of Owny O'Reilly"

As Jake Saunders, 10-16-60, ABC

The Lone Ranger
"The Brown Pony"

5-14-53, ABC

The Lone Ranger
"Desperado at Large"

As Jango, 10-2-52, ABC

The Lone Ranger
"Stage to Estacado"

7-23-53, ABC

Man Behind the Badge
"The Case of the Desperate Moment"

6-25-55, CBS

The Master (series)

As John Peter McCallister, NBC. See previous section for details of episodes.

Maverick
"Red Dog"

As Wolf McManus, 3-5-61

Medic
"Day 10"
>11-1-54

The Millionaire
>As Howard Branch, 1-8-62

Mr. Lucky
>6-11-60, CBS

Mr. Lucky
"Dangerous Lady"
>As Kruger, 12-21-63, CBS

My Mother, the Car
"Burned at the Stake"
>As Nick Fitch, 10-12-65, NBC

Nowhere to Hide (telefilm)
>6-5-77, color, 90 minutes, CBS or NBC
>*Alternate Title: Fatal Chase* (home video)
>*Cast:* Lee Van Cleef (Ike Scanlon), Tony Musante (Joey Faber), Charles Robinson (Ted Willoughby), Lelia Goldoni (Linda Faber), Noel Fournier (Frankie Faber), Edward Anhalt (Alberto Amarici), Russell Johnson (Philip Montague), David Proval (Rick), Clay Tanner (Lee), John McLaughlin (Stan), Robert Hevelone (Giff), Richard Narita (Lou), Stafford Morgan (Ken), Blackie Dammett (John), Bud Davis (Rudy), Vince Di Paolo (Frederico), John Alderman (Vittorio), John Stefano (Pilot #1), Bill Yeager (Co-Pilot), Jack Starrett (Gus), Brian Cutler (Gaynes), Isaac Ruiz (Hernandez), Ric Dano (Torn), Gene Massey (Coxswain), Araceli Rey (Mrs. Amarrei), Huguette Pateraude (Deputy Rowan), John Randolph (Narrator)

Director: Jack Starrett

Synopsis: U.S. Marshal Ike Scanlon (Lee Van Cleef) is assigned to protect mob hit man Joey Faber (Tony Musante), who is scheduled to testify against his former boss, Alberto Amarici (Edward Anhalt). After the hit man is taken to a secluded island hiding place by Scanlon and other marshals, he has a change of heart and leaves Scanlon's protection, hoping to rectify his relationship with Amarici. But Faber finds that his return is not welcomed by his former boss; he narrowly escapes an attack by Amarici's thugs and returns to Scanlon and the island. Although Amarici makes another attempt, Faber reaches the courtroom in safety and Amarici is convicted.

Comment: Nowhere to Hide was both a telefilm and the pilot for a proposed, unsold series named *Scanlon*. It does not generate a bit of excitement. A sense of Faber's danger is never created and the ending is astoundingly anti-climactic. Charles Robinson and Russell Johnson, whose characters were intended to be series regulars, have little to do in the story, but the character played by Johnson (the Professor on the TV series *Gilligan's Island*) offers incidental interest. He plays a character named Montague, and in all sources the writer has consulted, his first name is listed as "Charles." However, close inspection of the show reveals that the name placard on the character's desk clearly reads "Philip Montague." *Nowhere to Hide*'s writer/producer Edward Anhalt appears in this telefilm, as does director Jack Starrett. *Nowhere to Hide* is based on a true story from the life of U.S. Marshal John Partington.

Van Cleef's Role: Capped with a toupee and outfitted in a Botany 500 wardrobe, Van Cleef plays U.S. Marshal Scanlon. Scanlon doesn't come off as being particularly tough or street-smart, and this possibly is due to the fact that Van Cleef's violent, often "R-rated" image in recent movies needed to be toned down for broadcast television. This telefilm was the first TV work the actor had done in over a decade.

The Range Rider
"Greed Rides the Range"

1952, black-and-white, 30 minutes, syndicated (Western)

Cast: Jack [Jock] Mahoney (Range Rider), Dick Jones (Dick West), Lee Van Cleef (Rocky Hatch), Gail Davis (Ann), Stanley Andrews, Kenneth MacDonald, Fred Krone, Kenne Duncan, Keith Richards, Riley Hill

Director: George Archainbaud

Synopsis: When a crook named Rocky Hatch (Lee Van Cleef) discovers gold on others' mining claims, he uses a team of bullying gunmen to scare away the miners, who live in a small community named Carterville. Range Rider (Jock Mahoney) and his sidekick Dick West (Dick Jones) arrive in Carterville and aid the last two remaining citizens, Ann (Gail Davis) and her father. Unbeknownst to even Ann, Hatch is secretly forcing Ann's father to do his dirty mine work. Range Rider and Dick West free Ann's father from servitude and imprison Hatch.

Comment: The Range Rider was not unlike other Western TV series intended for juvenile audiences, but it is enhanced by the realistic stunts performed by the series' star, stuntman-turned-actor Jock Mahoney (billed here as Jack Mahoney). This episode was made in 1951 and released in 1952.

Van Cleef's Role: This episode was reportedly one of Van Cleef's first two television jobs. The other is the "Outlaw's Double" episode of *The Range Rider*, also made in 1951. The two episodes contain almost identical casts and the same director, and they were probably made simultaneously or back-to-back. In a 1979 interview Van Cleef recalled doing "in the old days" more than one half-hour TV show a week, "jumpin' from one script to another. All within one day I would have changed wardrobe maybe 14 or 15 times and bounced back and forth from one script to another...." These two *Range Rider* episodes are possibly an example of this. In "Greed Rides the Range," Van Cleef is lead heavy Rocky Hatch, and the actor performs his own stunts.

The Range Rider "Outlaw's Double"

1952, black-and-white, 30 minutes, syndicated (Western)

Cast: Jack [Jock] Mahoney (Range Rider), Dick Jones (Dick West), Lee Van Cleef (Utah Joe), Gail Davis, Stanley Andrews, Kenneth MacDonald, Keith Richards, Kenne Duncan, Bob Woodward, Fred Krone

Director: George Archainbaud

Synopsis: Notorious bank robber Utah Joe (Lee Van Cleef) is spotted and chased by lawmen. Hoping to elude his pursuers, Joe steals the clothes of Range Rider (Jock Mahoney), who is swimming in a nearby lake. Utah Joe begins impersonating Range Rider, and when he learns that Range Rider has an assignment to guard the gold of the Evergreen

Smelting Company, he uses his new identity to try a heist. The robbery attempt is unsuccessful, but Joe kills a man while trying. Range Rider has to clear his name and expose Joe's scheme before he begins work at Evergreen.

Comment: Like other *Range Rider* episodes, "Outlaw's Double" features series star Jock Mahoney doing his own stunts.

Van Cleef's Role: Not outdone by stunt-performing star Jock Mahoney, Van Cleef also does his own stuntwork in this episode.

Rawhide
"The Enormous Fist"

As Fred Grant, 10-2-64, CBS

Rawhide
"Piney"

As Deck Summers, 10-9-64, CBS

The Real McCoys
"Grandpa Fights the Air Force"

11-26-59

Richard Diamond
"Rodeo"

As Ed Murdock, 5-27-63

Ride to Glory (made-for-TV movie)

1966, color, 120 minutes, NBC (Western)
Alternate Titles: "Call to Glory" (episodic), *Call to Glory* (theatrical, outside U.S.), *Blade Rider* (home video)
Cast: Chuck Connors (Jason McCord), Robert Lansing (Gen. George A. Custer), Kathie Browne (Jennie Galvin), H.M. Wynant (Lionel MacAllister), Lee Van Cleef (Charlie Yates), David Brian (Gregory

Hazin), Michael Pate (Crazy Horse), Felix Locher (Sitting Bull), Richard Tatro (Lt. Briggs), Gary New (Young Hawk), Greg Morris (Johnny Macon), Michael Keep (Chief Wateeka), Davis Roberts (Hawkins), Burt Reynolds (Red Hand), Noah Beery (Major Lynch), William Bryant

Directors: Harry Harris, Vincent McEveety, Alan Reisner

Synopsis: In 1875, the army's most notorious dishonorable discharge, Jason McCord (Chuck Connors), persuades a runaway Apache Indian named Red Hand (Burt Reynolds) to return to his reservation. Red Hand agrees, only to be shot dead by an Indian-hating major. McCord's next run-in with the Apaches occurs when he and Army Cpl. Johnny Macon (Greg Morris) are captured by Chief Wateeka (Michael Keep), and the two are forced to fight each other for freedom. McCord rides away a free man thanks to Macon's suicidal sacrifice. His next stop: President Grant's personal train coach. Grant sends McCord to Fort Lincoln to check on the political ambitions of Gen. George Custer (Robert Lansing), McCord's pal from their West Point days. Grant's suspicions are confirmed when McCord discovers that Custer is being manipulated into beginning a political campaign and into inciting an Indian war. McCord exposes the three men responsible for the scheme before bidding farewell to Fort Lincoln and its residents.

Comment: Ride to Glory is a 1966 television feature that was made by editing together three episodes of the TV series *Branded* (all three episodes are entitled "Call to Glory"). It was released theatrically outside of the United States in 1966, also as *Call to Glory*. As is evident from the plot synopsis, the three disjoined incidents are only loosely related by their American Indian themes. During the first two, McCord, in contact with both Indians and cavalrymen, is annoyingly pedantic as a self-appointed Indian/cavalry liaison. The incident with Custer, however, is much more palatable; it focuses on McCord's friendship with the general, and how the friendship withstands differing values.

Van Cleef's Role: Van Cleef is effectively nefarious as Charlie Yates, one of Custer's Indian-hating scouts. Yates is first seen battering an innocent Indian. Later, he is hired to put the meddlesome McCord out of the way. His first attempt to kill McCord is unsuccessful; on his second attempt, Yates knocks McCord unconscious and prepares to kill him. But before Charlie Yates can complete the deed, he is shot dead by the Indian who had suffered earlier from Yates' abuse.

The Rifleman
"The Clarence Bibs Story"

4-4-61, black-and-white, 30 minutes, ABC (Western)

Cast: Chuck Connors (Lucas McCain), Johnny Crawford (Mark McCain), Buddy Hackett (Clarence Bibs), Denver Pyle (George Tanner), Lee Van Cleef (Wicks), Joan Taylor (Millie Scott), X. Brands (Longden), John Milford (Reade)

Director: David Friedkin

Synopsis: A famed gunfighter named Longden (X. Brands) rides into the Western town of North Fork and, in an accidental shooting, is killed by North Fork's slow-witted mop boy Clarence Bibs (Buddy Hackett). Bibs is easily convinced when two mischief-makers declare him a master gunfighter. When news of Longden's death spreads, his gunfighting partner George Tanner (Denver Pyle) arrives to investigate the shooting. Tanner is told to leave town by Clarence, whose confidence is fueled by the mischief-makers. A reasonable man, Tanner realizes that Longden's death was an accident, and with help from Lucas McCain (Chuck Connors), who is filling in for North Fork's absent marshal, the whole matter is settled. Clarence must return to his mop job, but he has made a new friend in Lucas.

Comment: Despite its improbable plot, "The Clarence Bibs Story" is highly enjoyable. The performances are solid, with the realistically drawn McCain and George Tanner characters balancing out Clarence, played by comedian Buddy Hackett. *The Rifleman* is a series known for containing lessons and morals, and "The Clarence Bibs Story" is not without a dose of morality.

Van Cleef's Role: Van Cleef's character is Wicks, one of the two mischief-makers who convinces Clarence he is a master gunman. Wicks and the other mischief-maker, Reade (John Milford), are very mean-spirited, and in their search for an entertaining gunfight, they do not care if Clarence is put into a life-threatening situation. After Lucas McCain foils their attempt to pit Clarence against gunslinger George Tanner, Wicks and Reade, still hungry for amusement, want to engage in gunplay with the mop boy. Lucas fools the two, convincing them that Clarence's killing of Longden wasn't accidental but actually trick-shooting. The cowardly Wicks and Reade withdraw from their gunfight with Clarence.

The Rifleman
"The Deadly Wait"

    As Dan Mowry, 3-24-59, ABC

The Rifleman
"Death Never Rides Alone"

    As Johnny Drake, 10-29-62, ABC

The Rifleman
"The Prodigal"

    4-26-60, ABC

Ripcord
"The Money Mine"

    1961, syndicated

Riverboat
"Strange Request"

    As Luke Cragg, 12-13-59

The Schlitz Playhouse of the Stars
"The Black Mate"

    As Larkin, 6-18-54, CBS

The Schlitz Playhouse of the Stars
"The Blue Hotel"

    As Cowboy, 4-12-57, CBS

The Schlitz Playhouse of the Stars
"Four Things He'd Do"

2-5-54, CBS

77 Sunset Strip
"The Attic"

9-16-60, ABC

Sheriff of Cochise
"Fire on Chiricahua Mountains"

As Hackett, 11-2-56

The Slowest Gun in the West (special)

5-7-60 or 7-29-63, 60 minutes, CBS (Western)

Cast: Phil Silvers (Fletcher Bissell III, "The Silver Dollar Kid"), Jack Benny (Chicken Farnsworth), Bruce Cabot (Nick Nolan), Ted De Corsia (Black Bart), Jack Elam (Ike Dalton), Jean Willes (Kathy McQueen), Parley Baer (Collingswood), Tom Fadden (Jed Slocum), Gina Gillespie (Girl), Jeanne Bates (Wife), Paul Lukas (Jack Dalton), Robert J. Wilke (Butcher Blake), John Dierkes (Wild Bill), Lee Van Cleef (Sam Bass), Kathie Browne (Lulu Belle), Marion Ross (Elsie May), Jack Albertson (Carl Dexter)

Director: Herschel Daugherty

Synopsis: The citizens of Primrose, Arizona, elect as sheriff a cowardly newcomer named Fletcher Bissell III (Phil Silvers), whom they know will be unharmed, because the nearby notorious outlaws can't shoot at such a weakling without ruining their reputations. But the outlaws hire Chicken Farnsworth (Jack Benny), who is as cowardly as Bissell, and hope that their gunman will kill the sheriff.

Van Cleef's Role: Van Cleef's character Sam Bass was in reality an outlaw of the old West, as were some of the other characters in this TV comedy special. The real-life Sam Bass was a train, bank, and stagecoach robber who died at the age of 27. Van Cleef was in his late 30s when he portrayed the notorious outlaw.

Soldiers of Fortune
"Guns for El Khadar"

    1955, syndicated

Space Patrol
"Threat of the Thurmanoids"

    1952

Stagecoach West
"Never Walk Alone"

    As Lin Hyatt, 4-18-61, ABC

Stories of the Century
"Frank and Jesse James"

    As Jesse James, 1954, syndicated

Studio '57
"Deadline"

    2-26-56, syndicated

Tales of Wells Fargo
"Alder Gulch"

    As Cherokee Bob, 4-8-57, NBC

Tombstone Territory
"The Gun Hostage"

    As Sam Carver, 5-1-59, ABC

Trackdown
"The Town"

As Ben Fraser, 12-13-57, CBS

The Travels of Jamie McPheeters
"The Day of the Misfits"

As Raoul Volta, 12-15-63

TV Reader's Digest
"How Charlie Faust Won a Pennant for the Giants"

4-11-55, ABC

Twilight Zone
"The Grave"

As Steinhart, 10-27-61, CBS

The Untouchables
"The Unhired Assassin"

As Frank Diamond, 2-25-60 and 3-3-60, ABC; later edited together into feature length TV movie, *The Gun of Zangara*

Wagon Train
"The Jesse Cowan Story"

1-8-58, NBC

Wanted: Dead or Alive
"The Empty Cell"

As Jumbo Kane, 10-17-59

Wire Service
"The Night of August 7th"

    11-1-56, ABC

Yancy Derringer
"Outlaw at Liberty"

    As Ike Melton, 5-7-59, CBS

Zorro
"Welcome to Monterey"

    10-9-58, ABC

Appendix: Chronological Listing of Films

The films in which Van Cleef appears are listed here in the order in which they were initially released. This listing is based on the best information available to the writer.

1952 High Noon
       Untamed Frontier
       Kansas City Confidential
1953 Bandits of Corsica
       The Beast from 20,000 Fathoms
       Vice Squad
       Jack Slade
       The Lawless Breed
       White Lightning
       Arena
       The Nebraskan
       Tumbleweed
       Private Eyes
1954 Rails into Laramie
       Princess of the Nile
       Gypsy Colt
       The Desperado
       Arrow in the Dust
       Yellow Tomahawk
       Dawn at Socorro
1955 Treasure of Ruby Hills
       The Big Combo
       Ten Wanted Men
       I Cover the Underworld
       Road to Denver
       A Man Alone
       The Vanishing American
1956 The Conqueror
       Pardners
       It Conquered the World
       Tribute to a Bad Man
       Red Sundown
1957 Accused of Murder
       The Quiet Gun

Appendix

	The Badge of Marshal Brennan	1969	Sabata
	China Gate	1970	Barquero
	Gunfight at the O.K. Corral		El Condor
	The Lonely Man	1971	Captain Apache
	The Last Stagecoach West		Bad Man's River
	Joe Dakota		Return of Sabata (possibly 1972)
	Gun Battle at Monterey		
	Raiders of Old California	1972	The Magnificent Seven Ride
	The Tin Star		The Grand Duel
1958	Day of the Bad Man	1973	Mean Frank and Crazy Tony
	The Bravados	1974	The Stranger and the Gunfighter
	The Young Lions		
	Machete	1975	Take a Hard Ride
1959	Guns, Girls and Gangsters	1977	God's Gun
	Ride Lonesome		Kid Vengeance
1961	Posse from Hell		The Perfect Killer
1962	The Man Who Shot Liberty Vallance		Nowhere to Hide (telefilm)
	How the West Was Won	1978	The Squeeze
1965	For a Few Dollars More	1980	The Octagon
1966	The Good, the Bad, and the Ugly		The Hard Way (telefilm)
	The Big Gundown	1981	Escape from New York
	Ride to Glory (for TV)/Call to Glory (from TV)	1984	Codename: Wildgeese
			The Killing Machine
1967	Day of Anger	1985	Jungle Raiders
	Death Rides a Horse	1986	Armed Response
1968	Beyond the Law	1988	The Commander
	Commandos	1989	Speed Zone
		1990	Thieves of Fortune

Bibliography

"Baddies Behind Bars." *TV Guide*, pp. 12–13, August 31, 1957.

Barabas, Suzanne, and Gabor Barabas. *Gunsmoke: A Complete History and Analysis of the Legendary Broadcast Series*. Jefferson, N.C.: McFarland, 1990.

Bawden, Liz-Anne, ed. *The Oxford Companion to Film*. New York: Oxford University Press, 1976.

Beck, Ken, and Jim Clark. *The Andy Griffith Show Book*. New York: St. Martin's, 1985.

Betts, Tom. *Starring Lee Van Cleef*. Unpublished manuscript.

"The Big Gundown" advertisement. *New York Times*, August 23, 1968, page 33.

Brooks, Tim, and Earle Marsh. *The Complete Directory to Prime Time Network TV Shows, 1946–Present*. New York: Ballantine, 1988.

Buscombe, Edward, ed. *The BFI Companion to the Western*. New York: Atheneum, 1988.

Clark, John. "Peebles and Bam Bam!" *Premiere*, April 1993.

Corman, Roger, with Jim Jerome. *How I Made a Hundred Movies in Hollywood and Never Lost a Dime*. New York: Random House, 1990.

Cowie, Peter, ed. *World Filmography*. New York: Barnes, 1977.

Crowther, Bosley. Review of the film "For a Few Dollars More." *New York Times*, July 4, 1967, p. 33.

Cumbow, Robert C. *Once Upon a Time: The Films of Sergio Leone*. Metuchen, N.J.: Scarecrow, 1985.

Frayling, Christopher. *Spaghetti Westerns: Cowboys and Europeans from Karl May to Sergio Leone*. London and Boston: Routledge and Kegan Paul, 1981.
Gianakos, Larry James. *Television Drama Programming: A Comprehensive Chronicle*. Metuchen, N.J.: Scarecrow, 1978, 1980, 1987.
Goldberg, Lee. *Unsold Television Pilots, 1955–1988*. Jefferson, N.C.: McFarland, 1990.
Halliwell, Leslie. *The Filmgoer's Companion*. 4th ed. New York: Hill and Wang, 1974.
Hardy, Phil. *The Western*. New York: Morrow, 1983.
Hayes, David, and Brent Walker. *The Films of the Bowery Boys*. Secaucus, N.J.: Citadel, 1982.
Helt, Richard C., and Marie E. Helt. *West German Cinema Since 1945*. Metuchen, N.J.: Scarecrow, 1987.
Horner, William R. *Bad at the Bijou*. Jefferson, N.C.: McFarland, 1982.
Jones, Ken D., Arthur F. McClure, and Alfred E. Twomey. *Character People*. New York: Barnes, 1976.
Kaplan, Mike, ed. *Variety International Showbusiness Reference*. New York: Garland, 1981.
Katz, Ephraim. *The Film Encyclopedia*. New York: Crowell, 1979.
Kiesalt, Charles John. *The Official John Wayne Reference*. Secaucus, N.J.: Citadel, 1985.
Kiral, Cenk. "A Fistful of Leone Trip." *Radikal*. August 16, 1997.
Klisz, Anjanelle M. *The Video Source Book*. 16th ed. Detroit: Gale Research, 1995.
Lee Van Cleef obituary. *New York Times*, December 18, 1989, page D13.
Lee Van Cleef obituary. *Variety* 337, no. 11 (December 20, 1989), p. 4.
Leonard, William Torbert. *Theatre: Stage to Screen to Television*. Vol. 11. Metuchen, N.J.: Scarecrow, 1981.
Lloyd, Ann, and Graham Fuller. *The Illustrated Who's Who of the Cinema*. New York: Macmillan, 1983.
McClure, Arthur F., and Ken D. Jones. *Heroes, Heavies and Sagebrush*. New York: Barnes, 1972.
Marill, Alvin H. *Movies Made for Television, the Telefeature and the Miniseries, 1964–1984*. New York: New York Zoetrope/Baseline, 1984.
Marquis Who's Who. *Who's Who in America*. 40th–45th ed. New Providence, N.J.: Marquis Who's Who, 1978–1989.
Martin, Mick, and Marsha Porter. *Video Movie Guide 1994*. New York: Ballantine, 1993.

Monaco, James, et al. *The Encyclopedia of Film*. New York: Perigee, 1991.
Nash, Jay Robert, and Stanley Ralph Ross. *The Motion Picture Guide*. Vols. 1–9. Chicago: Cinebooks, 1985–87.
_____, and _____. *The Motion Picture Guide*. 1987, 1990 Annuals. Chicago: Cinebooks, 1987, 1990.
O'Donnell, Owen, ed. *Contemporary Theater, Film & Television*. Vol. 8. Detroit: Gale Research, 1990.
Parish, James Robert. *The Tough Guys*. New York: Arlington House, 1976.
_____. *The Great Cop Pictures*. Metuchen, N.J.: Scarecrow, 1990.
_____, and Michael R. Pitts. *The Great Western Pictures*. Metuchen, N.J.: Scarecrow, 1977.
_____, and _____. *The Great Gangster Pictures II*. Metuchen, N.J.: Scarecrow, 1987.
_____, and Vincent Terrace. *The Complete Actors' Television Credits*. Vol. 1. 2nd ed. Metuchen, N.J.: Scarecrow Press, 1989.
Parmentier, Ernest, ed. *Filmfacts*. Vols. 14 (1971) and 15 (1972).
Pitts, Michael R. *Western Movies: A TV and Video Guide to 4200 Genre Films*. Jefferson, N.C.: McFarland, 1986.
Quinlan, David. *Quinlan's Illustrated Registry of Film Stars*. New York: Holt, 1981.
Rachow, Louis, and Katherine Hartley. *Guide to the Performing Arts, 1968*. Metuchen, N.J.: Scarecrow, 1972.
Selby, Spencer. *Dark City: The Film Noir*. Jefferson, N.C.: McFarland, 1984.
Stewart, John. *Italian Film: A Who's Who*. Jefferson, N.C.: McFarland, 1994.
Terrace, Vincent. *Encyclopedia of Television Series, Pilots, and Specials*. New York: New York Zoetrope/Baseline, 1985, 1986.
_____. *Fifty Years of Television: A Guide to Series and Pilots, 1937–1988*. New York: Cornwall, 1991.
Thomas, Nicholas, ed. *International Dictionary of Films and Filmmakers. Vol. 3: Actors and Actresses*. 2nd ed. Detroit: St. James, 1992.
Weaver, John T. *Forty Years of Screen Credits, 1929–1969*. Metuchen, N.J.: Scarecrow, 1970.
Weisser, Thomas. *Spaghetti Westerns: The Good, the Bad and the Violent*. Jefferson, N.C.: McFarland, 1992.
Weldon, Michael, et al. *The Psychotronic Encyclopedia of Film*. New York: Ballantine, 1983.

Willis, John. *Screen World. Vol. 33: Films of 1981.* New York: Crown, 1982.

Yoggy, Gary A. *Riding the Video Range: The Rise and Fall of the Western on Television.* Jefferson, N.C.: McFarland, 1995.

Index

Numbers in **boldface** refer to pages with photographs.

A-Team 148
Aames, Willie 99–100
Accused of Murder 9, 35
Adios, Sabata 19
The Adventures of Kit Carson 138, 159–161
Adventures of Rin Tin Tin 161
Akins, Claude 91–92, 102, 149, 151–152
The Alaskans 162
Albertini, Giampiero 58
The Andy Griffith Show 162
Angel Eyes (character) 26, 76–77, **78**
Annie Oakley 162
Arena 8, 35–36
Armandariz, Pedro, Jr. **105**
Armed Response 24, 29, 36–38
Arrow in the Dust 8, 38
Askew, Luke **105**

Backlash 34
Bad at the Bijou 5, 28, 159
Bad Day at Black Rock 92
Bad Girls 29
Bad Man's River 21, 38–39

Badge of Marshal Brennan 9, 40, 120
Baker, Carroll 21, 51–52
Baldwin, Peter **135**
The Bandits of Corsica 8, 40–41
Barquero 20, 21, 27, 41–42, 106, 119
Barry, Gene 53
Bartlett, Richard 91
Bavarian Beer commercial 24
The Beast from 20,000 Fathoms 8, 42–43, 58
Bernard, Crystal 149, 153
Bernds, Edward 118, 141
Beyond the Law 19, 30, 44, **45**, 46, 62, 80
The Big Combo 9, 46–47, 88
The Big Gundown **16**, 17, 19, 20, 30, 47, 48, **49**, 50, 80, 131
Bite the Dust 34
Black Saddle 162–163
Boetticher, Budd 122
Bonanza 163
Bond, Ward 82, 106–107
Boone, Richard 74–75, 131–132
Borgnine, Ernest 24, 55–56, 69
Bowery Boys 118
Bradbury, Ray 43

191

Brand, Neville 94, **95**, 96, 102–103, **103**, 134
Branded 17, 163, 177
Brando, Marlon 10, 142–143
The Bravados 10, 50–51
Brave Eagle 163
Bridges, Lloyd 7, 83–84
Bronson, Charles 13, 18, 21
Brown, Jim 68, 96, 98, 130
Brynner, Yul 19, 21, 106
Burr, Raymond 40–41, 106–107

Cagney, James 136–137
Cahn, Edward L. 82
Calhoun, Rory 25, 60–61, 142
Call to Glory 17
Captain Apache 21, 27, 41, 51–53, 142
Carey, Harry, Jr. 25
Carpenter, John 23, 71
Carr, Thomas 67
Carradine, David 24, 36–37
Carson, Johnny 24
Casey Jones 163
Cavalcade of America 163
Chameleon 34
Cheetos commercial 24
The Cheyenne Show 164
China Gate 9, **11**, 53, 54, 55
Cimmaron City 164
City Detective 136, 149, 164–165
Claxton, William 119
Clift, Montgomery 10, 142–143
Clinton Music Hall Players 5
Codename: Wildgeese 24, 55–56, 57, 130
Cole, Nat "King" 53, 55
Coleman, Herbert 116
Collins, Alan 24, 55, 93, 125
Collins, Joan 50–51
Collins, Lewis 55–56, 57
Colt .45 165
The Commander 24, 27, 56–58
Commandos 19, 58–59, 149, 165
The Conqueror 9, 10, 59–60
Cook, Elisha, Jr. 35, 68, 102, **103**
Cooper, Gary 1, 7, 8, 83–84
Corman, Roger 9, 88
Cotten, Joseph 7, 138–139

Creed of Violence 34
Crime Boss 34
Crispino, Armando 58
Crist, Judith 22
Crossroads 166

The Dakotas 166
Davis, Jim 40, 100, 119, 140
Dawn at Socorro 8, 9, 60–61, 64, 102
Dawson, Anthony M. 21, 22, 24, 25, 55, 57, 66, 93, 127, 128, 130
Day of Anger 17, 61–63
Day of the Badman 10, 63–64
The Deadliest Art: The Best of the Martial Arts Films 151
Death Rides a Horse 17, 30, 64, **65**, 65–66, 80
Death Valley Days 166
The Deputy 166
The Desperado 8, 67–68, 102, 165
Destry 166
The Dick Powell Show 166
Dickinson, Angie 53, 54
Django (character) 19
Douglas, Gordon 41
Douglas, Kirk 9, 22, 81
Duke, Doris 5

Eastwood, Clint 12, 15, 17, 18, 21, 71–72, 73, 76–77, 149
El Condor 20, 21, 68–69, 98
Elam, Jack 18, 81, 84, 94, 96
Escape from L.A. 71
Escape from New York 23, 27, 69, **70**, 70–72, 93
Everett, Wilbur 4

A Fistful of Dollars (Per un pugno di dollari) 12, 13, 15, 17, 34, 73
Fleisher, Richard 36
Fonda, Henry 13, 85, 134
For a Few Dollars More **14**, 15, 19, 20, 25, 26, 27, 30, 66, 71, 72, **73**, 73–74, 103
Ford, John 85, 108
Ford Theatre 90, 165, 166–167

Forest Lawn Cemetery 25
Foster, Preston 6, 94, **95**
The Four Horsemen 34
Four Star Playhouse 167
Franklin, Sidney A., Jr. 80
Frayling, Christopher 13, 15
Fregonese, Hugo 139
From Dunkirk to London 34
Frontier Doctor 167
Fuller, Samuel 53

Gannaway, Albert C. 40, 120
Garland, Beverly 67–68, 88, 90, 164–165, 166–167
Garrett, Leif 74, 76, 96, 98
Gaucho 34
Gemma, Giuliano 17, 61–63
The Gene Autry Show 168
God's Gun 22, 67, 74–76
The Good, the Bad, and the Ugly 2, 15, 20, 26, 27, 30, 73, 76–77, **78**
The Grand Duel 21, 27, 30, 78–80
Gray, Coleen 38
Greene, Jaclynne **87**
Guillerman, John 68
Gun Battle at Monterey 9, 38, 80–81
Gunfight at the O.K. Corral 9, 81–82, 91, 102
Guns, Girls, and Gangsters 10, 22, 82
Guns of the Magnificent Seven 106
Gunsmoke 168
Gypsy Colt 8, 82–83

Hagen, Ross 36–37
Hahn, Jess 39, 78, 110
The Hard Way 22, 168–169
Harryhausen, Ray 43
Hathaway, Henry 85
Have Gun, Will Travel 170
Hawaiian Eye 170
Hayden, Sterling 38, 80–81
Heaven Can Wait 5
Hevelone, Barbara 22, 25
Hibbs, Jesse 120
High Noon 1, 7, 8, 57, 83–85, 131, 134
Hindle, Art 112–113, 126, 149, 154
Hittleman, Carl K. 80

Holliman, Earl 46, 81
Horner, William R. 5, 145, 159
Hotel de Paree 170
How the West Was Won 12, 85–87
Howard, Rance 7, 25
Howard, Ron 7

I Cover the Underworld 9, **87**, 87–88
Incredible, USS 4
Indio Black 19
Ireland, John 81
It Conquered the World 9, 88, **89**, 90, 165

Jack Slade 8, 90–91
Joe Dakota 9, 26, 91–92, 149
Joey Bishop Show 170
Jones, Harmon 117
Jungle Raiders 24, 93–94, 130
Juran, Nathan 138

Kahle, Patsy Ruth 4, 5
Kane, Joe 100
Kane, Joseph 35, 123, **140**
Kansas City Confidential (*The Secret Four*) 6, 7, 8, 29, 94, **95**, 95–96, 120
Karlson, Phil 94
Karson, Eric 112
Keller, Harry 63
Kelly, Jack 58, 149, 164–165
Kennedy, George 106
The Kentuckian 34
Kid Vengeance 22, 27, 76, 96, **97**, 98
The Killing Machine 23, 99–100
King, Henry 50
Kinski, Klaus 24, 55–56, 72
Kiss of Death 112
Kosugi, Sho 145, 148, 151
Kramer, Frank (Gianfranco Parolini) 19, 20, 21, 74–76, 79, 121–122, 125
Kramer, Stanley 6
Kung Fu 146

L.V.C. Music 25
L'Amour, Louis 136, 165

Lancaster, Burt 9, 81
Laramie 170–171
Laredo 170
Lassie Come Home 83
The Last Stagecoach West 9, 100, 170
Laven, Arnold 140
Law, John Phillip 17, 64–66
Law of the Plainsman 171
The Lawless Breed 8, 64, 91, 101–102
Lawman 171
Lazenby, George 149, 153
Leone, Sergio 12, 13, 14, 15, 16, 17, 72–73, 76–77
Levin, Henry 102
Lewis, Jerry 114
Lewis, Joseph 46
Logan, Joshua 5
Lollobrigida, Gina 21, 39
Loma, J. Anthony 99
Lone Pine 10
The Lone Ranger 172
The Lonely Man 9, 102–103, **103**, 149
Lourie, Eugene 43
Lucking, William **105**
Lupo, Michele 110

Machete 10, 104
MacMurray, Fred 10, 63–64
The Magnificent Seven 21, **105**, 106
The Magnificent Seven Ride 21, 104, **105**, 105–106
Mahoney, Jock 7, 91, 149, 158, 174–176
Mako 36–37
A Man Alone 8, 106–108
Man Behind the Badge 172
The Man from Far Away 34
The Man Who Shot Liberty Valance 12, 108–109
Man Without a Star 34
Manduke, Joe 96
Mann, Anthony 134
Marshall, George 85
Martin, Dean 10, 113–114, 142–143
Martin, Gene [Eugenio] 39
Marton, Andrew 83
Marvin, Lee 12, 13, 108–109
Mason, James 21, 39

The Master 23–24, 100, 145–146, **147**, 148–149, **150**, 151–159, 165, 172
Maverick 172
Mazza, Marc 78
McCallum, David 149, 153
McCarthy, Michael 133
McClory, Sean **87**
McClure, Doug 146, 158
McDonald, Frank 136
McGoohan, Patrick 168
McGowan, George 104
McKinney, Bill 149, 151
Mean Frank and Crazy Tony 22, 27, 62, 110–111
Medic 173
Mercenary for Any War 34
Midas commercial 24
Milian, Tomas 47, 48, 50
Milland, Ray 106–107
Miller, Dick 36–37, 88
Miller, Joan 12, 14, 22
The Millionaire 173
Mr. Lucky 173
Mister Roberts 6, 7
Mitchell, Gordon 44–45
Moore, Demi 149, 151
Morricone, Ennio 13, 16, 17, 73, 77
Mortimer, Colonel Douglas **14**, 27, 72, 73, 73, 74, 103
Mulock, Al 18, 76
Murphy, Audie 116, 137–138
The My Mother Car 162, 173
Mystery Science Theater 3000 151

Naked Street 34
Nasscimbene, Mario 59
Nazarro, Ray 40
The Nebraskan 8, 111–112
Neumann, Kurt 104
Norris, Chuck 23, 112–113
Nowhere to Hide 22, 173–174

Oates, Warren 41–42
The Octagon 23, 27, 72, 93, 112–113, 148, 149
Once Upon a Time in the West 17
Operation 'Nam 34

Ortolani, Riz 17, 62
Our Town 5

Palance, Jack 13, 74–75, 102
Parolini, Gianfranco *see* Kramer, Frank
Pardners 9, 29, 113–114
Payne, John **6**, 7, 94, **95**, 96, 120, 123
Peck, Gregory 10, 50–51
The Perfect Killer 22, 27, 115–116, 128
Perkins, Anthony 102–103, 134, **135**
Petroni, Giulio 65
Pistilli, Luigi 64–65, 72, 76
Pleasence, Donald 56–57, 69, 71
Posse 29
Posse from Hell 12, 116–117
Powell, Dick 59
Puppo, Romano 44, 57, 64
Princess of the Nile 8, 117
Private Eyes 8, 118
A Professional Gun 34

The Quick and the Dead 29
The Quiet Gun 9, 119

Raiders of Old California 9, 40, 119–120
Raiders of the Lost Ark 93
Rails into Laramie 8, 120
Range Rider 2, 7, 149, 174–176
Rawhide 17, 149, 176
Ray, Fred Olen 24, 36–37
The Real McCoys 162, 176
Red Sun 21
Red Sundown 9, 34, 61
Ressel, Franco **18**, 124–125
Return of Sabata 21, 76, 121–122
Return of the Seven 106
Richard Diamond 176
Ride Lonesome 10, 122–123
Ride to Glory 176–177
The Rifleman 178–179
Ringo (character) 19
Ripcord 179
Riverboat 179
Rivero, Jorge 23, 99

Road to Denver 8, 120, 123
Robbins, Marty 40, 119–120
Robinson, Edward G. 140–141
Romitelli, Santa Marie 75
Run Man, Run 16
Russell, Kurt 23, 69, **70**, 71

Sabata 18, 19, 76, 103, 122, **124**, 124–125
Sabata (character) **18**, 19–20, 21, 103, 121–122, **124**, 125
Sabato, Antonio 44, **45**
Sanchez, Pedro (Ignazio Spalla) **124**
Santi, Giancarlo 79
Sartana 19
Scalawag 34
Scanlon prospective series 22, 174
Schlitz Playhouse of the Stars 179–180
Schuster, Harold 90
Scott, Randolph 10, 122–123, 131–132
Screen Stars magazine 8
Sears, Fred F. 111
Selander, Lesley 38, 142
77 Sunset Strip 180
Sheriff of Cochise 180
Sherman, George 60
The Shootist 25
The Showdown 34
Singer, Alexander 52
Sirko, Marlon 22, 115
Sloan, Michael 145, 151
Slowest Gun in the West 180
Soldiers of Fortune 181
Sollima, Sergio 16, 48, 50
Somerville, N.J. 3, 5, 8, 12
Somerville Gazette 8
Space Patrol 181
Spaghetti Westerns book 15
Spalla, Ignazio *see* Sanchez, Pedro
Speed Zone 24–25, 125–126, 133
Spielberg, Steven 24
Springsteen, R.G. 88
The Squeeze 22, 27, 127–128, 130
Stagecoach West 181
Stander, Lionel 44, 127
Stegani, Giorgio 44
Stewart, James 85–87, 108
Stories of the Century 91, 100, 181

Index

The Stranger and the Gunfighter 21, 22, 27, 128–130, 148
Strode, Woody 18
Studio '57 181
Sturges, John 81
Sundown 34
Suntory advertisement 24

Take a Hard Ride 22, 98, 130–131
Tales of Wells Fargo 181
Taurog, Norman 114
Ten Wanted Men 8, 131–132
Thieves of Fortune 24–25, 132–134
Thorpe, Richard 85
The Tin Star 9, 103, 134–135, **135**
Tombstone 29
Tombstone Territory 181
Tonight Show 24
Trackdown 182
Tracy, Spencer 86, 137
The Travels of Jamie McPheeters 182
Treasure of Ruby Hills 8, 136
Tribute to a Bad Man 9, 29, 136–137
Trieste File 34
Tucker, Forrest 41, 119, 140
Tumbleweed 8, 137–138
Turner, Janine 149, 156
TV Guide 22, 23, 50
TV Reader's Digest 182
Twilight Zone 182
Tyler, Harry 87

Una desperado 22
Untamed Frontier 7, 138–139
The Untouchables 182
Unforgiven 29

Van Cleef, Alan (son) 5
Van Cleef, Clarence LeRoy (father) 3
Van Cleef, David (son) 10
Van Cleef, Deborah (daughter) 5
Van Cleef, Denise (daughter) 12
Van Cleef, Lee: **6, 11, 14, 16, 18, 47, 54, 65, 70, 73, 78, 87, 89, 95, 97, 103, 105, 124, 135, 147, 150**; auto accident 10; death 25; early jobs 3–5; funeral 25; heart disease 23, 25; marriages 4, 8, 12, 22; naval service 4–5, 27; physical appearance 26–27; school 4; on violence in his films 28–29
Van Cleef, Marion Levinia Van Fleet (mother) 3
Van Doren, Mamie 82
Van Patten, Dick 100
Van Patten, Timothy 100, 145, 148
The Vanishing American 8, 140
Vice Squad 8, 140–141
Volonte, Gian Maria 72

Wagon Train 182
Wallach, Eli 15, 18, 20, 76, 85
Walsh, Raoul 101
Wanted Dead or Alive 182
Wayne, John 9, 25, 59–60, 107, 108
White Lightning 8, 141–142
Whitman, Stuart 21, 51–52
The Wild West 22, 34
Wilde, Cornel 46
Williams, Adam **103**
Wire Service 183
Wise, Robert 136

Yancy Derringer 183
The Yellow Tomahawk 8, 142
The Young Lions 10, 142–144
Yucca Flats, Nevada 9, 60

Zorro 183